STUDY GUIDE

James W. Corey
University of Miami

P⊙litics
AMERICA

Second Edition

THOMAS R. DYE

PRENTICE HALL, Upper Saddle River, NJ 07458

© 1997 by PRENTICE-HALL, INC.
Simon & Schuster / A Viacom Company
Upper Saddle River, New Jersey 07458

10 9 8 7 6 5 4 3 2

ISBN 0-13-258369-0
Printed in the United States of America

CONTENTS

INTRODUCTION TO THE STUDENT STUDY GUIDE

This study guide has two purposes:
- A. Help students learn the material found in the textbook <u>Politics in America.</u>
- B. Enable students to better prepare for examinations based on this material.

There are several ways to study a textbook. Some students like to outline chapters which helps to organize the material. Others use Hi-lites to emphasize important words or ideas. Some use pencils and pens for the same. Some prefer to make marginal notes. It is clear that there are many different paths to the same goal-learning the material.

Still there are other ideas which can help. Start at the end of the chapter. Often the author provides a summary of the chapter (as in the case of this textbook). Other authors will sometimes list particular words or phrases which are important to understand. Our textbook author provides this word list throughout each chapter.

Studies have shown that more human learning and retention takes place when we start to read and when we finish reading a chapter or article. What we read in the middle is more weakly retained. Obviously, saving several chapters to read the night before the examination is not very effective. You should discipline yourself to read the assigned chapter before each class period. Allow yourself a specific allocated time-90 minutes for example. Read the summary, look for key words and phrases, then start reading the chapter from the beginning. Read for about 10-15 minutes. Take a short break. Read for another 10-15 minutes and then another short break. When you finish, take a few minutes to summarize in your mind what you have read. Then take the sample test which is included in each chapter in this study guide. The correct answers are in the rear of the book, but don't cheat. Answer the questions from the information you have read and absorbed-then and only then-check your answers. If you missed more than a few, try to determine why. What are you missing the most-true/false or multiple choice?

To assist you in the organization of the chapter material we have prepared a <u>partial</u> chapter outline. <u>There will be places in the outline which are blank.</u> Your challenge is to complete these blank sections in the outline and answer any additional questions that are posed in the outline. You will have to use the textbook to do these tasks which should help you to understand the material better.

To summarize: Our recommended study strategy is to:
- A. Read the chapter summary notes at the end of the chapter
- B. Complete the partial chapter outline
- C. Hi-lite important words as indicated by the author and where these are used in the text
- D. Read the chapter in detail in short spurts. Hi-lite as needed.
- E. Take the sample quiz at the end of the chapter.
- F. Review missed questions and sections in the chapter that covered the

questions.

Two final notes: First, reading the textbook and using this study guide <u>do not, repeat do not</u>, substitute for regularly attending classes. Often additional or more current material is presented in class lectures and if you do not understand a concept or idea, it may be clarified in class. If you do not understand something ask a question in class (if you can). Or see your professor during their office hours. Or where available, send an E-Mail question. Second, the textbook author, your instructor and myself all have a common goal-that you succeed in learning more about our national government.

Your success is our goal. Good luck!

CHAPTER OUTLINE

I. POLITICS-who gets what, when and how.
II. POLITICAL SCIENCE
    A.   WHO-participants
    B.   WHAT
    C.   HOW
    Study Figure 1-1 which provides detailed information on the who, how and what of politics.
    D.   What distinguishes government from other organizations?
        1.   Decisions that affect the whole of society
        2.   Uses _____ legitimately.
    E.   Government legitimacy works because:
        3.   Habit of citizen compliance
        4.   Respect for law and order. Question: Do the Freedmen and militia groups threaten government legitimacy?
        5.   Citizens trust government. Has American trust in government eroded over time? Is citizen trust of government currently high or low? See feature: What do you Think-Can You Trust the Government?
III. PURPOSES OF GOVERNMENT-Most are found in the Preamble to the U.S. Constitution.
    A.   Collect Taxes-the average American pays $.40 of every dollar earned to the combined levels of national, state and local government.
    B.   Legislation and Regulation. Congress passes about _____ laws and states pass a combined total of _____ laws while the national bureaucracy issues _____ rules and regulations annually.
    C.   Establish justice and ensure domestic tranquility.
        1.   Thomas Hobbes-life without government short and violent. Hobbes noted that men formed a social contract to:

            _____

        2.   Civil disobedience-disputes legitimacy of a law. Is this needed in a democracy? See Feature: Conflicting view.
    D.   Provide for common defense. Generally refers to external attacks by hostile powers.
    E.   Promote General Welfare.
        1.   Public v. Private goods. Why are some goods public? What are some examples?
        2.   Regulate the economy. A country's wealth is measured by its Gross Domestic Product (GDP) which is defined as:

            _____.

        3.   What is the U.S. GDP? How much government spending is part of the total GDP?

4. Regulate externalities which are _____.
   What are some examples?
5. Income transfers which are also called Redistribution.
   What are some examples cited by the author? See Up Close Features (B) and (C) on what services are provided by various levels of government.

F. Secure the Blessing of Liberty.
   1. Law and order
   2. Ensure equal treatment under the law.
   3. Protect freedoms and rights.

IV. DEMOCRACY
   A. Originated with the early Greeks.
   B. Has variety of meanings-even used by non-democratic countries.
   C. Essential elements include:
      1. Individual dignity-Natural law-John Locke
      2.
      3.
      4.
   D. Paradox of democracy
      1. Majority rule, but minority rights.
      2. Madison in Federalist Paper #10 argued against pure democracy and for a representative democracy also called a republican government. What is the difference?
      3. Limited government: U.S. government uses separation of power of the executive, legislative and judicial and the concept of checks and balances between the branches to restrain the majority and also the concept of federalism (national/state governments) to limit the national government.
      4. Judicial review of laws and government actions not part of the U.S. Constitution but later became operational and further restrains both the national and state governments.
      5. Constitutions are the chief means to limit or restrain government.

V. FORMS OF GOVERNMENT
   A. Authoritarian v. Totalitarian-Is there any essential difference between the two?
   B. Direct v. Representative Democracy. Local government uses direct democracy in town meetings and most state governments use popular referendums, initiatives and recall elections as forms of direct democracy.
   C. Representative democracy requires:
      1. Representatives selected by the votes of all the people.
      2.
      3.
      4.

VI. WHO REALLY GOVERNS

2

A. Elitism. Few govern, the many are governed.
B. Elites have power, the masses do not.
C. Elites can be responsive to the public or ignore it; they may be self-seeking or public spirited; they may be responsive or unresponsive; and the elite structure may be open or closed.
D. Elites are characterized by:
    1. Wealth
    2. Well educated
    3.
    4.
    5.
    6. Anglo-Saxon Protestant
E. Pluralism emphasizes competing group interaction for political power. Individuals participate as members of a group. Power is widely dispersed.
WHICH PARADIGM-ELITISM OR PLURALISM-BEST DESCRIBES THE ACTUAL GOVERNMENT OF OUR AMERICAN DEMOCRACY?

CHAPTER ONE SAMPLE QUESTIONS

TRUE-FALSE QUESTIONS:

1. Only government can legitimately use force.

2. American trust in government is at an all-time low since 1964.

3. The longest and most brutal violence in American history was between whites and native Americans.

4. The first political philosopher to conceptualize the social contract was John Locke.

5. Civil disobedience implies a willingness to accept a penalty for breaking the law.

6. National defense would be an example of a public good.

7. Second hand smoke could be considered an externality.

8. Payments to the poor for welfare equal over thirty percent of government transfer payments to individuals.

9. Even totalitarian regimes often include the word democracy in the official name of their country.

10. John Locke advanced the right of revolution.

MULTIPLE-CHOICE QUESTIONS:

11. Which of the following is not a governmental participant in politics:
    A. White House staff
    B. Voters
    C. Judges
    D. Members of Congress

12. The combined tax take of all levels of government from the average American is what percent of earned income:
    A. 25%   B. 30%   C. 35%   D. 40%

13. The U.S. Gross Domestic Product is about:
    A. $1.5T   B. $2.5T   C. $7T   D. $10T

14. The principle activity of the federal government in terms of spending is:
    A. National defense
    B. Social Security and Medicare   C. Welfare
    D. Education

15. The principle activity of the state and local governments in terms of spending is:
    A. Highways   B. Healthcare
    C. Welfare   D. Education

16. All but one of following are essential elements of democracy:
    A. Communal dignity
    B. Equal protection of the law.
    C. Equal opportunity to participate in public decisions.
    D. Majority rule decision making.

17. All but one of the following were used by the framers of the U.S. Constitution to limit the power of the political majority:
    A. Republican government   B. Separation of powers
    C. Checks and balances   D. Judicial review.

18. Which of the following is the principal means used to limit government.
    A. Laws   B. Regulations
    C. Constitutions   D. Statutes

19. A representative democracy has all but one of the following attributes:
    A. Representatives selected by a vote of all the people.
    B. Closed elections.
    C. Freedom of expression for both candidates and voters
    D. Periodic elections.

20. Which of the following popularized the term "power elite"?
    A. Harold Lasswell   B. C. Wright Mills
    C. Thomas R. Dye   D. Harmon Ziegler

CHAPTER ONE SAMPLE QUESTION ANSWERS

1. **True**. Criminals sometimes use force, but this is not recognized as legitimate. Only an established government can use force legitimately.
2. **True.** See graph on page 5.
3. **True.** See Conflicting View, page 6, second paragraph.
4. **False**. Thomas Hobbes was the first.
5. **True.** See Conflicting View on page 8, second column.
6. **True.** No private investor has the capital to invest in national defense.
7. **True.** Second hand smoke affects non-participants and may be an appropriate area for the government to regulate.
8. **False.** Individual payments to the poor are 20%. See page 11.
9. **True.** See example on page 12.
10. **True.** See People in Politics, page 14.
11. **B.** Voters are non-government participants; all the rest are government participants.
12. **D.** The government takes $.40 of every dollar earned.
13. **C.** See Up Close, page 10.
14. **B.** See graph on page 11.
15. **D.** See graph on page 11.
16. **A.** Individual dignity not communal dignity.
17. **D.** Judicial review was not part of the Constitution but pronounced by the U.S. Supreme Court as a judicial power.
18. **C.** Only a constitution can restrain government; all the others can be changed at will by the government.
19. **B.** Open elections are essential; closed elections would be more typical of a totalitarian regime when only the regime's candidates would be on the ballot.
20. **B.** See page 21.

CHAPTER TWO-POLITICAL CULTURE

I- POLITICAL CULTURE. Widely shared ideas based on values and beliefs that help to determine who should govern, how and for what end. Values are more deeply rooted; a belief is more subject to change. Currently, there is much discussion about the need to return to stronger moral values in our society-in families and communities. Some values that have been mentioned include: honesty and respect for others.

    A.   Political culture is a generalization; there are many variations which are sometimes described as political subcultures.

    B.   Political culture can often have contradictions, eg. equality v. slavery and segregation. Still, the value of equality can often be a catalyst for change.

    C.   Political culture may be applied selectively. Freedom of speech v. Radical speakers. See Up Close-Freedom Yes, but for Whom?

II- LIBERAL TRADITION IN AMERICA

    A.   Liberalism stresses individual liberty, worth and dignity.

    B.   Classical liberalism began in the 18th Century as an attack of the feudal hierarchy in place in Europe which consisted of:

        1.   Monarchy

        2.

        3.

        Noted writers include:

            a.   Voltaire   French

            b.   John Locke

            c.   Jean-Jacques Rousseau

            d.   Adam Smith   English

            e.   Thomas Jefferson

    C. Belief in liberalism caused America's founders to:

        1. Declare independence from England

        2.

        3.

    D. The writings and ideas of John Locke were particularly influential:

        1. Natural law gave inalienable rights-life, liberty and property.

        2. Social contract made to establish government.

        3. Government activity should be minimal as well as restrictions on individuals.

    E. Capitalism as an economic idea is closely related to classical political liberalism.

        Both stress individual rationality. Capitalism emphasizes the concept of private property and its use by individuals.

III- DILEMMAS OF EQUALITY

    A.   Equality is an honored value in the American Political Culture. It competes with liberty as the most important value.

    B.   The founders believed in legal equality-political equality was not achieved until this century when women and minorities gained political rights such as voting.

    C.   Equal opportunity=equal chance to succeed. Immigrants came to this country for its opportunities. Equal opportunity is a widely shared value.

D. <u>Equal results</u>=share of income and goods. Under this concept inequalities in income are intolerable. This concept is <u>not</u> a widely shared value. See Figure 2-1.

E. Fairness-most Americans believe in fairness, but disagree on what is fair. Most support concept of a public safety net which should support the poor, but most do not support a cap on earnings. There is some concern about the growing gap between CEO and worker incomes.

IV- INEQUALITY OF INCOME & WEALTH

A. Dividing the U.S. population into fifths (quintiles), we see that since 1929, the lower fifth of our population receives a small share of U.S. wealth, while the upper fifth receives almost half of U.S. income. This group has lost some relative ground since 1929. However, since 1970, the income gap of the poorest and richest quintiles has increased.

B. Recent income inequality is caused by:
  1.　　Decline in manufacturing jobs and increase of jobs in the service sector.
  2.
  3.
  4.

V- SOCIAL MOBILITY. The possibly of social mobility (better job, more income. etc) reduces class conflict and diminishes class consciousness.

A. Social mobility seems to be slowing.

B. Related to the concept of equal opportunity

C. There is a change in the composition of both the highest and lowest quintiles of income.

VI- NATION OF IMMIGRANTS

A. About _____% of the U.S. population is foreign-born.

B. The U.S. accepts more immigrants than all the other nations of the world combined.

C. Most immigrants come for economic opportunity

D. Immigration policy is a responsibility of the national government.

E. Various acts have been passed by Congress to deal with immigration:
  1. 1882-restricted "undesirables" and most Asians.
  2. 1921-_____.
  3. 1965-abolished national quotas-preferences for family and job skills.
  4. 1986-(Simpson-Mazzolina Act)_____

  _____

F. Each year, there are approximately _____legal immigrants and _____visas are issued for travel, study or business.

G. Illegal immigrants.
  1. Porous U.S. borders.
  2. Immigration and Naturalization Service (INS) estimates _____ illegals/year; unofficial estimates _____/year.

3. INS estimates 4 million illegal immigrants; unofficial estimates are
_____.

4. Persons have no right to enter the U.S., but once here they are entitled to due process of the law and equal protection of the law.

H. Cultural Conflict

1. Past immigrants were quickly assimilated into American society.

2. Current policy seems to be promotion of multi-culturalism and not assimilation by emphasizing bi-lingual education, voting and minority voting districts.

3. Economists differ whether immigrants create jobs and new businesses or create a surplus of labor and lower wages. Also in dispute is that while immigrants have to pay taxes, there is a question whether they use more government services than is covered by the taxes they pay.

4. Current efforts are underway to deny illegal immigrants welfare benefits and even legal immigrants some benefits. As a consequence, there has been a great rush for legal immigrants to become U.S. citizens. These reform efforts are opposed by some immigrant groups, such as Hispanics and industry groups that benefit from cheap immigrant labor.

VII. IDEOLOGIES: LIBERALISM AND CONSERVATISM

A. Ideology=consistent and integrated system of ideas, values, and beliefs.

B. Almost a third of Americans avoid an ideological tag.

C. Today, people identifying as conservatives outnumber those identifying as liberals.

D. Modern conservatism=Rugged individualism plus respect for traditional values.

1. Free Market

2.

3.

4. Belief in tradition, law and order.

Modern conservatives claim to be true believers in the classical liberal tradition.

E. Modern conservatives recognize frail human nature and consequently emphasize the role of traditional values.

F. Modern liberals see government as necessary to provide economic security and protect civil rights. Government power is seen as a positive force. They seek comprehensive change rather than incremental change, eg. President Clinton's ill-fated health care proposal. Government intervention is seen as necessary to solve society's problems in education, welfare, housing, etc.

G. Some liberals have changed labels-liberals who saw government programs designed to solve societal programs as ineffective and wasteful, now advocate free market and traditional institutions, such as family or church to solve these problems. They now call themselves neo-conservatives. Liberals who still see government programs as necessary, but now advocate economic growth to be of a higher priority call themselves neo-liberals.

VIII IDEOLOGICAL BATTLEGROUNDS: FOUR PERSPECTIVES

To complicate matters more, two additional ideologies in addition to liberalism and conservatism emerge: <u>Populism</u>-liberal in economic affairs, but conservative on social issues. <u>Libertarians</u> prefer minimal government-both in regards to the economy and society.

IX   DISSENT IN THE UNITED STATES. Currently, both the right and left extreme radicals reject the democratic model.

A. Those at the far right of the political spectrum are fascists who believe in the supremacy of the state (under their control) and white race.

B. On the far left are Marxists who wrote about the exploitation of the working class. Lenin was the genius who took the theory of Marxism and put it into practice in the former Soviet Union. Lenin stressed the necessity of a small cadre of professional revolutionaries as the vanguard of the working class and also developed the theory of imperialism wherein developed countries exploited underdeveloped countries. Marxism-Leninism became the philosophical basis of Communism which included government ownership of all the means of production and distribution. The concept of private property was abolished. All property belonged to the state. The Party controlled the government.

C. Socialism is on the left spectrum, but not as far as Communism. Socialists believe in government ownership of <u>main</u> industries, but not all private property. They also support the democratic political process.

D. The collapse of Communism increased the movement to free markets and political democracy. This process has been labeled the "End of History" Do you think this label is premature?

E. Academic radicalism is found in the "politically correct" movements on academic campuses. The evils of capitalism are attacked as well as Western civilization-institutions, language, and culture which are labeled as racist, sexist, etc. Opposition to these views is not well tolerated by these radicals who label opponents as patriarchial pigs, among other epithets.

CHAPTER TWO SAMPLE QUESTIONS

TRUE-FALSE QUESTIONS.

1. Classical liberalism grew out of the eighteenth-century Enlightenment.

2. Since 1954, there has been a growing number of the general population that oppose restrictions on freedoms, even of unpopular groups, such as communists and atheists.

3. Political equality is synonymous with legal equality.

4. Compared to other industrialized nations, Americans are less in favor of the government reducing income differences.

5. Income inequality increased in the United States because of reduced federal social welfare payments in the 1980s.

6. Inequality of wealth is even greater than inequality of incomes in the United States.

7. The United States accepts more immigrants than all the other nations of the world combined.

8. Most immigrants come to the U.S. to escape political repression.

9. Since 1965, the number of Americans that think that should be increased has been shrinking.

10. Conservatism is a belief in the value of free markets and limited government.

MULTIPLE-CHOICE QUESTIONS.

11. All but one of the following are associated with the 18th Century Enlightenment:
    a. John Locke   b. John Smith
    c. Thomas Jefferson   d. Jean-Jacque Rousseau

12. Those advocating that educational test scores for all children should be about equal would be identified as favoring:
    a. Equality of opportunity   b. Equality of Results
    c. Reverse discrimination   d. Prejudice.

13. Affirmative action would be most identified with those favoring:
    a. Equality of opportunity   b. Equality of Results
    c. Reverse discrimination   d. Prejudice.

14. Which of the following is <u>not</u> used to measure family wealth:
    a. bank accounts
    b. cars
    c. mortgages
    d. petty cash

15. Which of the following is the strongest determinant of family wealth?
    a. age   b. education   c. gender   d. race/ethnicity

16. The INS estimates about how many illegal immigrants live in the U.S.?
    a. 400,000   b. 10 million   c. 4 million d. 3 million

17. A neo-conservatist would be associated with all but one of the following:
    a. Belief that government social programs were ineffective
    b. Government direction of economic industrial growth
    c. Concern about social problems   d. Family values

18. Which of the following would <u>not</u> be favored by liberals?
    a. government regulation of business
    b. protection of civil rights
    c. More prisons
    d. decriminalize marijuana.

19. Which of the following would be associated with minimal government interference in both the economic and social spheres?
    a. Liberals   b. Conservatives   c. Populists   d. Libertarians

20. Academic radicalism is most associated with:
    a. affirmative action   b. conservatism   c. political correctness
    d. populism

CHAPTER TWO SAMPLE QUESTION ANSWERS

TRUE-FALSE

1. **TRUE**. It is also associated with the Age of Reason. See page 29.

2. **FALSE** See Upclose "Freedom Yes, but for whom to say what?" Four graphs show that since 1954, growing numbers of Americans have become more tolerant. See pages 30-31.

3. **FALSE**. The Constitution speaks of equality under the law. This is quite different than political equality such as voting or citizenship which was not made part of the Constitution until after the Civil War (15th Amendment). See page 32.

4. **TRUE**. Page 35 shows that in most European countries, citizens favor government actions to reduce income differences.

5. **FALSE**. Government spending for welfare did not decline per se, but only the rate of growth in welfare spending.

6. **TRUE**. The top 1% of U.S. citizens own 40% of the nation's wealth. For example, Bill Gates of Microsoft is considered to be the richest private individual in the world at this time. See page 37.

7. **TRUE**. Surprising, but true. America is still the beacon that attracts people from all over the world as the land of opportunity. See page 39.

8. **FALSE**. Most come for economic opportunity. See page 39.

9. **TRUE**. See Page 33. In 1994, over 65% of Americans thought that immigration should be decreased.

10. **TRUE**. See page 45.

MULTIPLE CHOICE

11. **B**. Adam Smith was a classical economist. John Smith was associated with the Massachusetts colony. See Page 29.

12. **B**. Equality of results assumes everyone finishes at the same line. See page 33.

13. **B**. Affirmative action was originally conceived to help with equality of opportunity, but now has been justified to ensure equal results.

14. **D**. Petty cash is not considered, but outstanding mortgages are used to reduce a family's wealth. See page 37.

15. **A**. Age cuts across all other factors as the key determinant of family wealth. See page 38.

16. **C**. While the INS estimates 4 million, other put the total much higher to 10 million. See page 42.

17. **B**. This is the principal separation between a neo-liberal and neo-conservative. Neo-conservatives do not rely on the government to help solve social problems. See page 48.

18. **C**. More prisons. Liberals favor early intervention aimed at solving social conditions that create career criminals. See page 50.

19. **D**. See page 52.

20. **C**. The agenda of academic radicalism is labeled "political correctness". It has an Orwellian toleration of dissent.

CHAPTER THREE-THE CONSTITUTION

I.   CONSTITUTIONAL GOVERNMENT. A written constitution provides the framework of a government of laws, and not of individuals.

    A.   Personal freedoms are protected and beyond the reach of governments or popular majorities.

    B.   Government power is often limited by a constitution. Powers are granted and some are restricted.

    C.   Constitutions usually provide a policy decision mechanism.

    D.   The procedure for changing a constitution is usually provided and normally requires a supermajority of 2/3 or 3/4 for approval of changes.

    E.   Constitutions are the supreme law of the land. They are superior to ordinary laws passed by a legislative body.

    F.   The sanctity of a constitution is based on respect-that of the government and people.

II.   CONSTITUTIONAL TRADITIONS

    A.   Magna Carta (1215). First written document which forced King John to recognize feudal rights and set a precedence of limiting monarchial power.

    B.   Mayflower Compact (1620). In essence, the first written "social contract." The governed established a government by popular consent.

    C.   Colonial Charters (1630-1732). Royal decrees which officially established governments either as proprietary colonies (Maryland, Pennsylvania and Delaware), or royal colonies. Two colonies were granted self-rule (Connecticut and Rhode Island). King James II tried to revoke the Connecticut charter which the colonialists hid in a oak tree. Later kings acquiesced to the charter.

    D.   The Declaration of Independence (1776). The First Continental Congress met in 1774 with delegates from 12 of 13 colonies. They prepared a petition of grievances to send to the King. Instead of a reasoned reply to this petition, the British sent troops in 1775 from Boston to outlying areas of Concord and Lexington to seize arms held by the colonialists. They were met with resistance of the Minutemen in irregular warfare-hit and run, harassing attacks and the British retreated to Boston. The Revolutionary War for independence had begun. The Second Continental Congress met in 1775 and designated George Washington to take command of the colonial troops. Although there was still some hope for reconciliation, this hope died by the summer of 1776 and on July 2nd, the Congress decided to declare independence from Great Britain. Thomas Jefferson was selected to write the Declaration which was formally approved on July 4, 1776. Jefferson used several of Locke's ideas regarding the rights of individuals and consensual government. The war dragged on for many years and was finally terminated in 1781 when British forces under General Cornwallis made the tactical error of taking a position on a peninsula. This error might not have been so disastrous had not the British Navy temporarily lost control of the seas to French and Spanish naval forces. Therefore, Cornwallis could not be resupplied from the sea and could not break out of the peninsula.

E. Articles of Confederation (1781-1789). During the period 1776-1781, the emerging nation was governed by the Second Continental Congress. This Congress proposed the Articles of Confederation in 1777, but the last state Maryland did not ratify them until 1781 (Unanimous consent was required). The articles provided for a single house with each state having one vote. Congress appointed judges and military officers. It did not have to power to collect taxes, but could borrow and print money. This was a confederation government of independent states. It was not a national government of the people.

III. TROUBLES CONFRONTING A NEW NATION. The new U.S. government had made several notable advancements.

    A. These included:

        1. Independence from the world's most powerful nation.

        2.

        3. Established a viable peace.

        4.

        5. Created an effective army and navy.

        6.

        7. Laid foundations for national unity.

    B. But the political structure was unsatisfactory to many influential groups-bankers and investors who held U.S. bonds, plantation owners, real estate developers, merchants and shippers. Why would these groups be dissatisfied?

    C. Financial difficulties. With no power to tax, the new government had no way to pay back the money they had borrowed to finance the war. U.S. bonds lost 90% of their face value.

    D. Commercial obstacles. Each state could erect their own tariffs for imported goods from either outside the country or a neighboring state. The national government had no power to regulate interstate commerce. Under this situation, it was impossible even to develop a national market. High tariffs led to a thriving industry of smuggling. This situation had a modern sequel. High cigarette taxes in New York city led some entrepreneurs to purchase cheap cigarettes in North Carolina and smuggle them into New York.

    E. Currency problems. Both the national government and state governments printed currency. States had "legal tender" laws which required creditors to accept the state currency for payment of debts in the state. Some states printed too much money which lost value. If the creditor refused this devalued money, the debt was canceled. Naturally, banks and creditors felt threatened by this "cheap money."

    F. Civil disorder. Debtors resisted efforts of creditors to collect debts and resisted efforts of tax collectors and sheriffs. The most serious incident occurred in western Massachusetts with Shay's Rebellion. While relatively a minor incident, it did arouse anxiety of the nation's leaders and commercial interests who began to call for a strong central government to "ensure domestic tranquility."

F.   The Road to the Constitution. Both Virginia and Maryland claimed the Potomac River and the Chesapeake Bay. In the Spring of 1785, a conference was held to try to resolve this problem. Since George Washington's home was on the Potomac and he owned 30,000 acres upstream, he had a personal interest in the resolution of this problem and lent his home and prestige for the meeting. One result of the meeting was a call for another general economic conference to convene in Annapolis, Maryland in 1786. Instead of concentrating on commerce and navigation, this conference called for a general constitutional convention to remedy the defects in the Articles of Confederation. In 1787, the Congress called for a convention to meet in Philadelphia for the sole and express purpose of revising these Articles. This is not what happened.

IV.   THE NATION'S FOUNDERS. The 57 delegates to the Philadelphia convention quickly discarded the idea of revising the Articles. The Virginia delegation led by James Madison drafted a new constitutional document which became the basis of further discussion. The convention convened on May 25th, 1787 and quickly elected George Washington as President of the convention, made a decision to scrap the Articles and write a new constitution establishing a new (and much stronger) national government. The delegates were very prestigious-well educated, men of means. Many were lawyers. Most had some type of previous governing experience-11 had served as military officers in the Revolutionary War, 42 had been members of the Congress and 40 had held high state offices, including three who were Governors. Most had a cosmopolitan or nationalistic outlook.

V.   CONSENSUS IN PHILADELPHIA. Consensus was achieved on most issues.

    A.   <u>Liberty and property.</u> Locke's writing about natural law and each person with inalienable rights-life, liberty and property which the founders believed conflicted with the institution of slavery.

    B.   <u>Social contract.</u> People establish a government and agree to obey its laws and pay taxes for the protection of their natural rights. This is what gives a government legitimacy. If a government violates individual liberties, they break the social contract, lose legitimacy and can be overthrown by the people.

    C.   <u>Representative government.</u> Instead of a monarchy, the founders decided to form a republican government governed by representatives of the people. Still, the Constitution provided for only one part of the government to be directly elected by the people-the House of Representatives. It is for this reason that the House still calls itself "The People's House."

    D.   <u>Limited Government.</u> The founders believe that unlimited power was dangerous and that the constitution should limit the power of the government. A system of checks and balances was established to divide power among the branches of government.

    E.   <u>Nationalism.</u> Most founders believed in the necessity of a strong, national government.

VI.   CONFLICT IN PHILADELPHIA.

    A.   <u>Representation.</u> Several plans were presented.

1. The <u>Virginia plan</u> called for a two chamber legislature-a lower house elected by the people of each state and an upper house chosen by the lower house. The Congress would have the power to nullify any state law thought to violate the Constitution thus assuring national supremacy. The legislature would chose the executive and judicial officers of the government (somewhat like a parliamentary system). A "council of revision" could veto Congressional acts. This plan was greatly debated, but not adopted.

2. The <u>New Jersey plan</u> favored state supremacy. As under the Article of Confederation, each state would have just one vote. It proposed separate executive and judicial branches and provided for powers of taxation and regulation of commerce for the new Congress. It also included the now famous National Supremacy clause-the Constitution and federal laws would be supreme over state constitutions and laws.

3. <u>Connecticut Compromise.</u> Also called "The Great Compromise." It called for a two chamber legislature-just as we have now. A lower House elected by the people of each state and seats allotted according to the population of each state; and an upper chamber, the Senate in which every state, regardless of size, would have two members. This compromise was essentially between the small states who were afraid of power of the larger states; and the larger states which thought they deserved more power. It was a win-win compromise. See Table 3-1 for a side-by-side comparison of these three plans.

B. <u>Slavery.</u> A contentious issue even though slavery was legal in 12 of the 13 states. The South believed that slaves should be included in the population count of their states for representation purposes in the lower House. Nonslave holders argued that only free men should be counted. The infamous 3/5 Compromise emerged wherein a slave would count as 3/5ths of a person for population and direct tax purposes. No direct taxes were every enacted until the demise of slavery, so the South won more than they lost. The South was also successful in writing a clause in the Constitution that supported the return of runaway slaves. Another compromise involved the prohibition of the importation of more slaves-under the Constitution, Congress was forbidden to halt further importations until the year 1808.

C. <u>Voter Qualifications.</u> There was much discussion whether voters should be men of property (note the discussion concerned only men). The Constitution left voter qualification to the states (This was later changed by amendments to the Constitution).

VII. RESOLVING THE ECONOMIC ISSUES. This was one of the main concerns of the Constitutional Convention.

A. <u>Levying Taxes and Duties.</u> The national government was given its own taxing authority. Article VI of the Constitution obligated the new national government to pay the debts of the old "national" government. The government collected most of its revenue from tariffs-a fee imposed on imports. This was favored by American manufacturers since it made foreign goods more expensive. No tariffs were permitted for exports which favored the South which relied more heavily on exports. Direct taxes on individuals was prohibited. The power to tax and spend was given exclusively to the legislature.

B. Regulating Commerce. This gives the national government power to regulate foreign commerce and among the states. The Constitution specifically forbid the states to levy tariffs on goods shipped across state lines. In effect, these provisions created the world's first Common Market.

C. Protecting Money. Only the Congress was given the power to coin money and regulate its value. States no longer could print money.

VIII. PROTECTING NATIONAL SECURITY. During the Revolutionary War, there was no regular Army. Troops came from state militias.

A. Under the new Constitution, Congress was given the authorization to declare war and support a regular army and navy.

B. Commander-in-Chief. The new office of President was made the Commander-in-Chief of the Armed Forces. Question: Who was the only Commander-in-Chief ever to lead the armed forces directly into conflict?

C. Foreign Affairs. The national government assumed this responsibility. This power is shared by the executive and legislature. The President can appoint ambassadors, but these must be confirmed by the Senate. The President can negotiate treaties, but these must be ratified by the Senate. The power of the purse also gives Congress a hand in foreign affairs.

IX. THE STRUCTURE OF THE GOVERNMENT.

A. The new structure of government established by the Constitution implemented the Founder's beliefs in:
1. Nationalism.
2.
3. Republicanism.
4.
5. Protection of liberty and property.

B. National Supremacy. The Constitution, laws and treaties take precedence and are the supreme law of the land which judges are to uphold and state laws shall not supersede.

C. Federalism. A novel concept where power is divided between two distinct, autonomous authorities-the national government and state governments. Each have their sphere of independence and authority:
1. Legal authority over their citizens.
2.
3.
    States select national office holders-Representatives and Senators.
4. States provide electors for the Electoral College which really elects the President (not the popular vote for President every four years).

18

5.   States must ratify all proposed amendments to the U.S. Constitution.

D.   Republicanism. Delegated or representational power from the people to gifted individuals to govern. (This was the original concept-some might quarrel with this idea today.) See Table 3-2 for the four-decision making bodies in the government.

E.   Democracy. The people do not make decisions at the national level, but rather these decisions are made by representatives of the people. At the state level, there are certain decisions which are made by the people themselves. While this national arrangement may appear to be "undemocratic" in modern terms, even a representative government was radical when the Constitution was enacted in 1787.

X.   SEPARATION OF POWERS AND CHECKS AND BALANCES

A.   Separation of Power=creation of three branches of the government-legislative, executive and judicial. Each has distinct powers which can act as a check on the others.

B.   Legislation originates in the Congress. Once approved, it must be signed or vetoed by the President. For example, President Clinton has vetoed several bills sent from the Republican controlled Congress. However, Congress can override a Presidential veto if both the House and Senate pass the bill again by a 2/3 margin. Presidents may suggest legislation in State of the Union addresses, and Executive Departments may even draft proposed legislation. But the actual bill must be proposed by a member of the legislature.

C.   The President appoints Ambassadors and other high officials, but the Senate must concur in the appointments. The President and State Department can negotiate treaties, but the Senate must ratify these treaties. The President must execute the laws, but Congress provides the funds. Congress must authorize the creation of executive departments and agencies. And Congress has the power of impeachment of executive officers, including the President.

D.   The President appoints all federal judges, including the U.S. Supreme Court, but the Senate must approve all nominations. The Congress determines the number of judges in all courts. Congress can also impeach judges. It would look like the judiciary is without much power except for the doctrine of judicial review-the courts can review all laws and actions of the federal government to determine if they are constitutional, i.e. valid. Review Figure 3-1 for a more detailed look at checks and balances.

XI.   JUDICIAL REVIEW-This doctrine was not part of the original Constitution, but rather was announced by the Supreme Court in the case of Mulberry v. Madison (1803).

XII.   CONFLICT OVER RATIFICATION. The founding fathers were clever in devising a ratification procedure that gave the new Constitution a fighting chance. Two devices were used.

A.   Ratification Vote. Instead of a unanimous approval of the states (which was part of the Article of Confederation for important items such as amendments), the founding fathers called for the approval of only 9 states to ratify the document.

B.   <u>Ratification Procedure</u>-Instead of state legislatures, the founding father specified that special ratifying conventions would be used.

C.   <u>Ratification Campaign</u>-The founding fathers urged speedy approval and waged a very professional (for those days) media campaign to convince the people to support the new Constitution. Three supporters, James Madison, Alexander Hamilton and John Jay wrote a series of article under the pen name <u>Publicus</u> that were published in major newspapers. In these articles, they provided a detail defense of the new document. These articles were later collected and published as a complete set simply called <u>The Federalist Papers.</u> Even today, they serve as a source of understanding of the thinking and rationale that guided the drafters of the Constitution. Two of these articles are included in the textbook appendix. The supporters of the Constitution called themselves Federalists-their opponents were known as Anti-Federalists. The later opposed the Constitution because it would create an "aristocratic tyranny", would trample state governments, lacked a Bill of Rights. See People in Politics-Madison and Conflicting View of the Anti-Federalists.

XIII. <u>BILL OF RIGHTS</u>.

A.   There were a few liberties specified in the original Constitution: prohibition of <u>ex post facto</u> laws, limited definition of treason, writ of <u>habeas corpus</u> and trial by jury.

B.   The Federalists did not think any further definition was required because the people's liberties were protected by state constitutions and the new national government was one of specified or enumerated powers. They could not interfere in liberty, because this was not an enumerated power. However, this did not satisfy the skeptics and to secure ratification in such states as New York, Massachusetts and Virginia, the Federalists promised to support the addition of a Bill of Rights to the Constitution.

C.   James Madison drafted the amendments based on over 200 suggestions from the states. Congress approved 12 amendments, but the states ratified only 10 and these became the Bill of Rights-the first ten amendments to the Constitution. <u>In 1992</u>, the states ratified one of the other 12 dealing with Congressional pay-this is the 27th Amendment to the Constitution. See Table 3-3 for a discussion of the Bill of Rights.

D.   The Bill of Rights applied only to actions of the Federal government. It was not until passage of the 14th Amendment after the Civil War that the Bill of Rights was eventually made applicable to state and local governments as well.

XIV. <u>CONSTITUTIONAL CHANGE</u>.

A. <u>Formal change</u>. Amendments are used to formally change the Constitution. Over 10,000 amendments have been suggested but few make it any further. There is a two step process.

      1.   <u>Proposal</u>. An amendment may be proposed by a 2/3 vote in each branch of Congress. An amendment may also be proposed by a constitutional convention called by Congress at the request of 2/3 of the states.

2. Ratification. A proposed amendment needs a 3/4 approval of state legislatures or ratifying conventions. Congress specifies which method will be used.

3. All successful amendments except one were passed by Congress and ratified by state legislatures. The 21st Amendment appealing Prohibition directed to ratifying conventions by Congress who was fearful the legislatures dominated by prohibitionists would defeat the proposed amendment.

4. Table 3-4 provides a list of current amendments to the Constitution.

B. Informal Change

1. Judicial Interpretation. Using the doctrine of judicial review, the Supreme Court has given meaning to the "necessary and proper" clause , "equal protection of the law" which was used in segregation and voting cases, and found the right to privacy in the Constitution which was used to establish the right to an abortion.

2. Presidential and Congressional. Presidents have expanded presidential power by acting. President Jefferson purchased the Louisiana Territory from France in 1803, but the Constitution is silent on this presidential action. Presidents from Washington to Clinton have used the armed forces in over 200 hostile actions; although this is not a specified power of the president.

3. Custom and Practice. The Constitution is silent on political parties, yet these can play a key role in the checks and balance of the government.

CHAPTER THREE SAMPLE QUESTIONS

TRUE-FALSE QUESTIONS

1. Constitutionalism is a government of laws based on the principle that government power should be limited.

2. Under the Articles of Confederation, the Continental Congress had the power to tax the states, but not the people.

3. Under the Articles of Confederation, each state printed its own money.

4. The Founders who wrote the Constitution were very unsure of their ability to do so.

5. Under the original Constitution, the people elected Representatives and Senators to the Congress.

6. Written into the Constitution was a provision that required the return of escaped slaves.

7. If there is a conflict between a treaty and the Constitution, the former prevails.

8. Impeachment applies only to the Executive and Judicial branches.

9. The power of judicial review is contained in the original Constitution.

10. The most effective complaint of the Anti-Federalists was the lack of a Bill of Rights in the Constitution.

MULTIPLE-CHOICE QUESTIONS

11. Which of the following is considered as the first written "social contract?"
    a. Magna Carta   b. Mayflower Compact   c. Colonial charters
    d. Declaration of Independence

12. The Declaration of Independence was signed in the year:
    a. 1774   b. 1775   c. 1776   d. 1781

13. Under the Articles of Confederation, the Congress had all but one of the following powers:
    a. taxation   b. print money   c. make war and peace   d. borrow money

14. Which event was the key stepping-stone for the Constitutional Convention:
    a. Shay's Rebellion   b. Alexandria meeting   c. Annapolis Convention
    d. Revolutionary War

15. The founders shared a consensus on all but one of the following ideas early in the Constitutional Convention:
    a. Liberty and property
    b. Representation in the Congress
    c. Social Contract
    d. Limited government

16. During the Constitutional Convention, there was conflict over all but one of the following:
    a. Representation   b. Slavery   c. Voter qualifications   d. Nationalism

17. Congress was given power to do all but one of the following:
    a. declare war   b. levy taxes   c. print money   d. tax exports

18. The first ten amendments to the U.S. Constitution are called:
    a. Bill of Rights   b. informal changes   c. judicial review
    d. Custom and Tradition

19. Changes to the Constitution can be proposed by:
    a. the House of Representatives   b. The Senate   c. The President
    d. Constitutional Convention

20. Informal changes to the Constitution include all but one of the following:
    a. Presidential interpretation   b. Congressional interpretation
    c. Judicial interpretation   d. amendments

CHAPTER THREE SAMPLE QUESTION ANSWERS

TRUE-FALSE QUESTIONS

1. **TRUE**. This is the essence of Constitutionalism. See page 62.
2. **FALSE**. The Continental Congress did not have the power of taxation; they could only make requests. See Page 64.
3. **TRUE**. See page 65.
4. **FALSE**. They were extremely confident of their abilities. See page 67.
5. **FALSE**. Only one part of the government was directly elected by the people-the House of Representatives. See pages 70-71.
6. **TRUE**. See pages 71-72.
7. **FALSE**. The Constitution is the Supreme law of the land. See page 78.
8. **TRUE**. Congress has the power to discipline its own members. Expulsion at the extreme end of their powers. See page 79 and Figure 3-1.
9. **FALSE**. It was a self-announced power of the Supreme Court in the case of Marberry v. Madison. See page 81.
10. **TRUE**. See page 85.

MULTIPLE-CHOICE QUESTIONS

11. **B**. See page 62.
12. **C**. 1776 is the correct answer. If you did not get this correct, shame on you. See page 63.
13. **A**. The Congress had to petition the states for money. They only provided an estimated 10% of the money so requested. Congress did not have to power to !evy any taxes on the states or individuals.
14. **C**. The Annapolis Convention petitioned Congress to call a constitutional convention. See page 66.
15. **B**. Representation in the legislature proved to be one of the main obstacles to consensus. See page 70.
16. **D**. Nationalism was one of the points of consensus. See page 70.
17. **D**. Congress is forbidden by the Constitution to tax exports. This provision was adopted to appease the Southern states who were heavily involved in exports. See page 74.
18. **A**. Hopefully everyone gets this question right! It's pretty basic. See page 85.
19. **D**. Maybe a tricky question. Neither the House or Senate can propose an amendment on their own. Both houses must concur by a 2/3 vote. So the correct answer is a constitution convention which is the second way amendments can be proposed. See page 86.
20. **D**. Amendments are formal changes to the constitution.

<h1>CHAPTER 4-FEDERALISM</h1>

I.   INDESTRUCTIBLE UNION, INDESTRUCTIBLE STATES. The Civil War tested the proposition whether the nation was a voluntary association of states, or a permanent, indissolvable union. The answer was delivered in the nation's bloodiest carnage where over 500,000 lost their lives. After the Civil War, in Texas v. White, the Supreme Court noted that the Constitution looked at an industrictible union formed by indestructible states.

    A.   <u>Federalism.</u> One of the checks and balances envisioned by the founding fathers was the division of power between the national government and state governments. This division is called federalism. Both are autonomous-that is have a separate existence and powers.

    B.   <u>Unitary system of Government.</u> A system of government where the national government is supreme and any powers exercised by lower governments are granted by the national government. Most governments in the world, including Great Britain and France follow this model.

    C.   <u>Confederation.</u> In this arrangement, the states had most of the power and the national government depended on the states. This was the situation under the Articles of Confederation. See Figure 4-1 for a pictorial display of these governments.

    D.   <u>Federal government.</u> In spite of the current overwhelming influence of the federal government, there are over 86,000 governmental units in the United States. They provide many services-education, sewage, garbage removal, fire and police protection, etc. State governments are really unitary models. i.e. local governments receive their power from their state government. Some of these powers are specified in state constitutions and others are transferred in a more blanket Home Rule" which allows the local government to pass any law provided it does not conflict with national or state laws. Under this concept, some 60,000 of the 86,000 government units levy taxes to support their activities.

    E.   <u>Intergovernmental Relations</u>. The interaction between the national, state and local government levels.

II.   WHY FEDERALISM? THE ARGUMENT FOR A "COMPOUND REPUBLIC". The Founding Fathers sought to protect minorities from the "tyranny of the majority" and saw federalism as one way this could be accomplished. There are seven arguments used to support federalism:

    A.   <u>Protection of Liberty.</u> The Founding fathers saw federalism as part of a double security system: The division of power between a national and state governments (federalism) and the separation of powers between the three branches of the national government. Competition between these entities was seen as a means of protecting liberty.

    B.

    C.

D.   Improving Efficiency. Local and state governments can provide many services more efficiently that a national government-police, garbage removal, etc.

E.

F.

G.   Manage Conflict. Conflicting issues can be resolved regionally or locally rather than escalated up to the national level.

H.   Disadvantages of Federalism:
    1.   Can obstruct action on national issues-Civil Rights is a good example.
    2.   Permits state and local leaders to frustrate national policy. Obstruction of waste sites, airports, road, etc. are examples
    3.   Uneven distribution of government benefits-education, welfare, taxes are good examples.
    4.   Obstructs uniformity in policy.

III.   THE ORIGINAL DESIGN OF FEDERALISM. The original scheme of government envisioned the national government as one with limited, specified powers; national and state governments exercising some concurrent powers; all other powers reserved to the states; with some powers being specifically denied within the Constitution; and the states playing some role in the composition of the national government.

A.   Delegated Powers. Article I, Section 8 lists 17 specific powers granted to the national government. These collectively are referred to as delegated or enumerated powers. The last clause in this Section enables Congress to make laws which are necessary and proper to carry out the 17 delegated powers. This clause is known as the "Necessary and Proper Clause" which has been the major source of all the implied powers of Congress. This is also called the "elastic" clause since it is so flexible.

B.   National Supremacy. Clearly provides for the supremacy of federal law over state or local laws.

C.

D.

E.   Powers denied to the Nation and the States. The Bill of Rights clearly limits both the national and state governments from abridging individual liberties.

F.

IV.   THE EVOLUTION OF AMERICAN FEDERALISM. Although not much has changed in the formal documentation of power, over the 200 years of our country, it is unarguable that power has flowed up, that is, from the state and local government level to the national level. There have been various periods in the development of federalism:

A. State-Centered Federalism, 1787-1868. The states reigned supreme in this period. The national government was just beginning to define itself. The Civil War played a key role in this development.

B. Dual Federalism 1868-1913. The national government limited its role to its delegated powers and the states handled domestic issues. This period has been described as "layered cake."

C. Cooperative Federalism 1913-1964. The distinction between national and state responsibilities began to erode and was caused by many factors: Industrial Revolution and a national economy; the Federal income tax started in 1913 which shifted financial resources to the federal government; two world wars; and the Great Depression. FDR's New Deal funded massive public works projects which were welcomed by state leaders. During this period, the federal government intervened in labor, agriculture, business practices, public assistance, employment services, child welfare, public housing, urban renewal, highway construction, and vocational education. Most of these programs were carried out at the local or state level but funded with federal money. This merging of responsibilities has been described as "marbled cake." This period featured cooperation between the national and state/local governments.

D. Centralized Federalism, 1964-1980. With the introductions of LBJ's Great Society, national goals became predominant. Congress went way beyond its enumerated powers relying on the "elastic clause" to legislate on almost any program. The U.S. Supreme Court did not consider the reserved states powers of the 10th Amendment to be any barrier to this increased federal activity. Sometimes this period is referred to as "Pineapple upside-down cake" where the frosting is on top.

E. New Federalism 1980-1985. The attempt to reverse power from the national government back to the states. While there was some shift of responsibilities, but federal money did not always go with the flow resulting in the state having to assume responsibilities and pay with their own resources. This situation is described as "unfunded mandates."

F. Representational Federalism, 1985--- The 1985 Supreme Court Garcia decision virtually eliminated the concept of state powers conflicting with the national government. The Supreme Court threw cold water on the reserved powers of the 10th Amendment and essentially told the states that they elect political representatives and it is their job to protect state's rights. Thus, the concept of "representational federalism." This decision essentially eliminated the constitutional division of powers between the federal and state governments.

V. KEY DEVELOPMENTS IN AMERICAN FEDERALISM.

A. McCulloch v. Maryland and the Necessary and Proper Clause. The crux of this issue was creation of a national bank. Where in the enumerated powers of

27

Congress is a national bank. This was the Jeffersonian argument. Hamilton argued that the enumerated powers included the printing of money and that a bank was a depository of money and the creation of the bank could be implied by the Necessary and Proper Clause. The issue came to a head when the State of Maryland attempted to impose a tax on the operations of the national bank in that state. In reaching a decision in the McCulloch v. Maryland case, the Supreme Court first had to consider: Was creation of the bank constitutional? Chief Justice Marshall gave a broad interpretation to the clause: If the end is legitimate and within the scope of the Constitution and the appropriate means are adopted toward that end and which are consistent with the letter or spirit of the Constitution, then it is constitutional. Thus, the Court found the national bank to be constitutional. The second issue was whether a state could tax the operations of the national government? Not if the National Supremacy clause had any meaning-state governments cannot interfere with federal laws.

B.   Secession and the Civil War. Did a state have the right to oppose national law to the extreme of secession? The was the argument of John Calhoun. But this argument was settled by the North's victory in the Civil War. In addition, three amendments were added to the Constitution as a further limitation on states:

1.   The 13th Amendment which abolished slavery
2.   The 14th Amendment which established due process for the deprivation of life, liberty and property; and equal protection of the law.
3.   The 15th Amendment which prohibited the states from denying the vote to black males.

C.   National Guarantees of Civil Rights. Starting in 1925, the Supreme Court began to require states to protect civil liberties in the Bill of Rights by a process called "selective incorporation." That is, the Court on a case by case basis found the civil liberties of the Bill of Rights applicable to the national government also applicable to state/local governments. The Brown v. Board of Education was a watershed in that the Supreme Court for the first time used the 14th Amendment to call for a full assertion of national authority in the field of civil rights. Mainly Southern states resisted the efforts of the federal government to integrate schools. In extreme cases, state authorities tried to interpose themselves by ordering state military forces to bloc integration. These efforts were rejected by the Supreme Court and national government which ordered regular Army units or Federal Marshalls to enforce the Court's decision.

D.   Expansion of Interstate Commerce. Prior to the New Deal, the Supreme Court had interpreted the regulation of interstate commerce clause very narrowly; however in the 1930s interpreted it to mean any activity which substantially affects the national economy.

E.   Federal Income Tax and Federal Grants. With the funds provided by a federal income tax, the federal government began a program of establishing programs subject to federal direction that provided money grants to states for highway construction, vocational education, etc. In accepting the money, the states had to comply with the federal requirements.

VI. MONEY AND POWER FLOW TO WASHINGTON. Through its power to spend for the general welfare, there is almost no activity or program beyond the reach of the federal government-education, welfare, transportation, police protection, housing, hospitals, libraries, urban development, etc.

A. Grant-in-Aid. Single most important source of federal influence over state and local activities. This is defined as a transfer for funds from one higher level of government to a lower level on some type of matching basis for some specific purpose and subject to prescribed conditions of the grantor. Participation in the grant-in-aid program is voluntary. More than 20% of state funds come from federal grants. Figure 4-3 shows in what areas these funds are used. There are three principal types of federal grants:

1.

2.

3. General Revenue Sharing. Began during Nixon Administration. Originally given to states and local governments with minimum strings. Money could be used where needed. Amount of money determined by complex formula-population, tax effort and population income level. States dropped from program in 1981. Entire program died in 1986-budget crunch of national government and opposition to program by states.

VII. COERCIVE FEDERALISM: PREEMPTIONS AND MANDATES. In place of offering money with strings attached, Congress has undertaken to intervene in areas traditionally reserved to the states and forced states to comply with its programs and regulations. The National Supremacy clause allows the federal government to preempt a state law. This preemption can be total or only partial:

A. Total Preemption. The federal government assumes all responsibility in the area-copyrights, bankruptcy, railroads, and airlines.

B. Partial Preemption. State law on a subject is valid as long as it does not conflict with a federal law. If the Occupational Safety and Health Administration (OSHA) has not promulgated an industrial or work standard and a state government has their own standard, then the state standard would apply. But if OSHA promulgates a standard in the same area, it supercedes the state standard.

C. Standard partial Preemption. Permits state standards to supercede federal standards, if the state standard is more stringent. Most applicable in environmental regulation area.

D.   Federal Mandates. Direct order to a state or local government to perform a service or comply with a federal law. These mandates cover a wide area:

1.   Age Discrimination Act, 1986-forbids mandatory retirement ages for public or private employees.

2.   Asbestos Hazard Emergency Act, 1986. Schools must inspect and remove asbestos from buildings.

3.   Safe Drinking Water Act, 1986. Established national standards for drinking water and waste treatment.

4.   Clean Air Act, 1990. Bans municipal incinerators and requires emission inspections in some areas.

5.   Americans with Disabilities Act, 1990. State and local government buildings must accommodate handicapped.

6.   National Voter Registration Act. 1993. Motor voter bill that required states to register voters at driver license offices, welfare offices, etc.

E.   "Unfunded Mandates". Federal mandates often cause state and local government to spend money to comply with the mandate. If the federal mandate does not include money for the states/local governments, this is, in effect, an "unfunded mandate." An article in the Winter 1996 issue of State and Local Government Review indicated that the cost to state/local governments of unfunded mandates between the years 1983-1994 amounted to almost $11B in 1992 dollars.

VIII.   A DEVOLUTION REVOLUTION? The 1994 election of a Republican House to join the Republican Senate and a majority of States Governors who are Republicans brought a renewed call of decentralization from Washington back to the states. This is called "devolution." Some of its elements may include:

A.   Consolidation of Categorical grants into Bloc grants.

B.   Welfare Reform. There will be some attempt to give states more leeway in child support programs and AFDC. Also some programs may be combined into bloc grants.

C.   End to Federal Entitlements? Welfare entitlements may be a thing of the past. Efforts are underway to restrict the number of years on welfare, deny payments for more children born while on welfare, deny welfare to teenage mothers, etc. Even in the area of Social Security (the great entitlement program), there is some talk to moderating entitlements and reducing payments for the wealthy.

D.   Continuing Strings? It is unlikely that Congress will ever cut all strings attached to funds it appropriates.

CHAPTER FOUR SAMPLE QUESTIONS

TRUE-FALSE QUESTIONS

1. Federalist type governments are the most common in the world today.

2. An example of a confederation would be the United States during the period 1781-1787.

3. The elastic clause refers to the Necessary and Proper clause in Article I, Section 8 of the Constitution.

4. The period referred to as "marble cake" was the era of Cooperative Federalism.

5. A key feature of New Federalism was the centralization of power in the national government.

6. Representational Federalism in effect obliterates the historic meaning of federalism.

7. People have more confidence in state government than in the national or local government.

8. General Revenue Sharing started during the administration of President Johnson.

9. The Supreme Court upheld the Gun-Free School Zones Act of 1990.

10. About twenty percent of state budget revenue comes from federal grants.

MULTIPLE-CHOICE QUESTIONS:

11. The Supreme Court case that declared the union and states to be indestructible was:
    a. Mulberry v. Madison (1803)
    b. Texas v. White (1869)
    c. McCulloch v. Maryland (1819)
    d. Wickard v. Filburn (1938)

12. The interaction between different levels of government is called:
    a. Home Rule   b. Confederation   c. Unitary
    d. Intergovernmental Relations

13. In America today, there are approximately how many governments?
    a. 50   b. 60,000   c. 86,000   d. 1

14. All but one of the following are favorable arguments for federalism:
    a. Protects liberty   b. Concentrates power   c. Increases participation
    d. Encourages policy innovation

15. All but one of the following are disadvantages of federalism:
    a. Improve efficiency   b. Can obstruct action on national policies.
    c. Obstructs uniformity   d. Local issues can override national priorities.

16. Which of the following was not part of the original Constitution?
    a. Enumerated powers   b. National supremacy
    c. Concurrent powers   d. Implied powers

17. The Congress passes legislation to provide funds for municipalities to construct sewage treatment plants. This would be an example of:
    a. Categorical grant   b. Bloc grant   c. General Revenue Sharing
    d. Preemption

18. Congress passes an Air Quality Control law that allows states to impose even more stringent standards. This would be an example of:
    a. Preemption   b. Total preemption   c. Partial preemption
    d. Standard partial preemption.

19. The demise of General Revenue Sharing was a result of:
    a. Budget deficits   b. Opposition of Democrats   c. Opposition of governors
    d. Opposition of local governments   e. Answers a & c.

20. All but one of the following are considered as part of the devolution revolution:
    a. More reliance on bloc grants   b. Welfare reform
    c. Less Federal strings   d. Unfunded mandates

CHAPTER FOUR SAMPLE QUESTION ANSWERS

TRUE-FALSE QUESTIONS

1. **FALSE**. Unitary system of governments are the most common. See page 98.
2. **TRUE**. Today there are few examples of confederation. Switzerland is one of the few.
3. **TRUE**. Because the Courts have used the clause to extend the power of the government in almost every area.
4. **TRUE**. See page 107.
5. **FALSE**. An effort was made to shift power from Washington back to the states.
6. **TRUE**. See discussion page 109.
7. **TRUE**. See Feature-What Do you Think-Which Government Does the Best Job?
8. **FALSE**. It started under President Nixon's New Federalism. See Page 119.
9. **FALSE**. In a rare victory for the states, the Supreme Court in a close 5-4 decision for the first time in 60 years recognized a limit to Congress's power over interstate commerce.
10. **TRUE**. See Page 118.

MULTIPLE-CHOICE QUESTIONS:

11. **B** See footnote 2 on page 126.
12. **D** The phrase almost gives the answer away--see Page 98.
13. **C** As amazing as it may seem, we have many layers of government. See page 98.
14. **B** Rather than concentrate power, federalism diffuses power. See page 102
15 **A** Promoting efficiency is an advantage of federalism. See pages 102 and 104
16. **D** Implied powers were a result of the McCullogh v. Maryland case. See page 111
17. **A** A grant for a specific project is categorical. See page 118.
18. **D** See Page 120.
19 **E** See page 119.
20 **D** See pages 121-124.

CHAPTER 5-OPINION AND PARTICIPATION

I. Public opinion is important in a democracy because the government depends on the consent of the governed. Whether government should represent the interests or the will of the people is what separates the trustee or delegate models of representation. The public's opinion is often weak, unstable, ill-informed or non-existent on specific policy issues. For example, the efforts to cut Medicare expenses. The Republican plan was to hold the growth of expenditures to 7%. Yet many elderly think the Republican plan was to cut their precious Medicare. The absence of well-formed public opinion provides greater leeway to politicians and also increase the influence of special interest groups who are well informed on issues. Still, politicians ignore public opinion polls at their peril. Since many voters are single issue voters, the candidates "right" position on the issue, could determine their vote. The determination of public opinion is a thriving industry called survey research-it is used not only by politicians, but also by the media, and businesses (here it is called market research, but it is essentially the same).

A. Respondent Knowledge Levels. Generally, very low. Many give answers with little knowledge. Few will admit to being ill-informed. WHAT IS YOUR POLITICAL KNOWLEDGE. CAN YOU NAME THE VICE-PRESIDENT? CAN YOU IDENTIFY YOUR TWO U.S. SENATORS? YOUR REPRESENTATIVE TO CONGRESS? YOUR STATE SENATOR AND REPRESENTATIVE? See Figure 5-1 to see how you compare with an average American.

B. Halo Effect. People give good answers in that no one wants to admit to bigotry or racial bias. Few will admit to not-voting. See Figure 5-2.

C. Inconsistencies. Poor survey questions that are leading questions often produce desired answers. For example: "No child should go hungry in the U.S. Do you favor or disfavor cutting welfare programs for children." How many people will favor hunger for children? Often just the wording can make a difference: "Do you favor aiding the poor?" generally elicits a favorable response. "Do you favor cutting welfare?" generally gets positive answer, yet the two are inconsistent.

D. Instability. Many people answer questions spontaneously with little thought.

E. Salience. Is the issue hot? Is it covered in the news? These are the issues that people think about. They change over time as shown in Figure 5-3.

F. Survey mechanics. Consult the Up Close Feature-Can we Believe in Polls. Random samples are used in most polls. Random means that everyone in the population has the same potential chance of being selected as a participant. Most polls are done by telephone-cheaper and quicker. Some bias because people with no phone cannot participate. National surveys generally seek about 1,100 participants. Each survey has a calculated sampling error-typically a +/- range. In addition, a probability is calculated-a confidence factor. The typical national survey uses a +/- 3% sampling error and 95% confidence factor. Let's say that our survey indicated that 65% favor legalized abortion. Since we have a +/- 3% range, the actual percentage could be between 62%-68%. Our confidence factor would say that if we could survey the entire U.S. population, 95% of the time, the favorable response would fall within the range of 62-68%.

II.   SOCIALIZATION: THE ORIGINS OF POLITICAL OPINIONS.
    A.   <u>Socialization</u> = learning of values, beliefs and opinions.
    B.   Socialization begins at an early age with identification of authority figures and role models, e.g. parents, policemen.
    C.   Socialization also occurs in the following:
        1.   <u>Family</u>. Early political identification mirrors that of family. When family has split party loyalty, child most often mirrors mother's political leanings or becomes independent. Policy identification is less certain-usually not discussed in families.
        2.

        3.

        4. Generational and Life-Cycle Effects.

        5. <u>Media Influence.</u> Most Americans get their news via and trust TV as their source. TV alerts listeners to issues-"sets agenda." Does not try to form opinion, but rather causes listeners to think about the issue. Amount of coverage often determines public perception of its importance.

III.   IDEOLOGY AND OPINION.
    A.   <u>Ideology</u> = Fairly, consistent and integrated set of principles. Often set in liberal-conservative framework. For further information, consult Table 5-3.
    B.   Most people do not have a consistent ideology, i.e., their opinion may change depending on the issue.

IV.   GENDER AND OPINIONS. Men and Women do not differ greatly on most policy issues, even on so-called women's issues. There are two areas of difference: Use of violence-men are more supportive of the death penalty and less in favor of gun control. The other difference is political party. More women identify as Democrats. See Figure

5-4 for Gender differences on issues.

V. RACE AND OPINION. There are major differences of opinion here. Most whites believe there is little discrimination against blacks in jobs, housing or education and that societal differences are caused by lack of motivation of blacks. Naturally, most blacks believe the opposite. There are some areas of agreement: Blacks are not genetically inferior to whites and education is the key to black success. Blacks generally favor a more activist government role. See Figure 5-5 for white-black opinion differences.

VI. POLICY AND OPINION. Political leaders are relatively unconstrained by public opinion in making policy decisions. Special interest groups are much more effective. Therefore, the influence of elites (those who participate in the political process) is strengthened by the weak or non-existent public opinion on most issues. Political participation is the essential link between opinion and policy.

    A. Individual Participation in Politics. Political scientists studying this problem have a simplified model-check-book or sweat participation. Only the well-to-do have the means for check-book participation. They contribute money or in-kind support-cars, offices, machines, planes, etc. Sweat participation means working in a campaign-stuffing envelopes, making calls. Figure 5-6 shows American participation in various political activities.

    B. Securing the right to vote. There were many steps necessary in securing the right to vote for all Americans.

        1. Elimination of Property Qualifications. The Constitution left the qualification of voters up to the states. Most states has some kind of property qualification for voting up until 1840.

        2.

        3. Continued Denial of Voting. Democrats in the South used the white primary to select candidates (tantamount to election and also denying blacks entry into political office). Declared unconstitutional in 1944 by the U.S. Supreme Court in Smith v. Allwright. Poll taxes, literacy tests and terrorism (KKK) were also used to intimidate and discourage black voting in the South.

        4. Civil rights Act, 1964, the Twenty-fourth Amendment (1964) and Voting Rights Act, 1965. Summarize what they did.

        5. Nineteenth Amendment

6.   Twenty-Sixth Amendment

7.   National Voter Registration Act, 1993 (Motor-Voter Act).

VII.   WHY VOTE? American voter turnout is measured: <u># of people who voted</u>
                                                            # of eligible voters

Most other country's turnout is measured: <u># of people who voted</u>
                                                          # of registered voters

WHAT DIFFERENCE DO YOU SEE BETWEEN THE TWO?
American voter turnout is shown in Figure 5-7 for Presidential election years and
"off-year" congressional election years. Comparison of American and foreign
voter turnout is at Compare to What Feature-Voter Turnout in western
Democracies (p. 157). In some countries, voting is mandatory. In most, the
government assumes responsibility to register voters.

A.   <u>Rational Voter.</u>   To be completely rational, a voter should make the following
calculation:

1.   <u>Cost of Voting</u>-(Registration, information gathering, voting) <u>minus</u>
<u>Benefit of Voting</u> (Your candidate wins) multiplied by the probability that
your vote will be decisive. The cost of voting is rather easy to calculate.
The Benefit of voting is not. A winning candidate may not support what
he/she promised. Most times your vote is not decisive. How many
elections are decided by one vote? Therefore, it is not rational to vote.

2.   <u>Intrinsic rewards of voting</u>- what are some????

B.   <u>Voter Registration.</u> Double burden for voters. But motor-voter locations may
ease this burden. Some states are experimenting with on-line registration. Voter
Registration appeared during Progressive Era to prevent fraudulent voting.

VIII.   POLITICS OF VOTING. Democrats generally favor less requirements, Republicans
more. Motor-voter bill was passed by Democratic Congress and signed by Democratic
President. However, early returns indicate that contrary to expectations, this law has

favored the Republican party more than the Democratic party.

A.   <u>Stimulus of Competition.</u> The more exciting the race, the greater the voter turnout.

B.   <u>Political Alienation</u>. Those who are cynical about government are less likely to vote.

C.   <u>Voter Intensity.</u> The more turned-on the voter, the more likely to vote.

D.   <u>Explaining voter turn-off.</u> The decline in voter turnout is explained by:
1.   Political alienation.
2.   Negative media coverage of politics and politicians
3.

4.

Presence of a relatively, strong well financed independent candidate Ross Perot led to greater voter participation in the 1992 election.

IX.   VOTERS AND NONVOTERS. There are several factors that distinguish those voting and not voting:

A.   <u>Education.</u> This appears to be the most important determination in voting. The more educated, the more likely to vote. Education heightens political awareness and interest in politics. It promotes political efficacy.

B.

C.

D.   <u>Race.</u> With income and education held constant, there is no difference between white and black voter turnout. Hispanics have a lower turnout.

X.   NONVOTING: WHAT DIFFERENCE DOES IT MAKE?

A.   Lack of participation question legitimacy of democracy.

B.   Non-voting is not the same as being denied the right to vote.

C.   Class bias of non-voters is cause for concern.

D.   There are very few significant policy difference between voters and non-voters.

XI.   PROTEST AS POLITICAL PARTICIPATION. The First Amendment guarantees the right to peaceful assembly and redress of grievances. Some forms of protest are less acceptable-See What Do you Think-What Forms of Protest are Acceptable?

A.   <u>Protests</u>. Call attention to an issue. Publicity is sought. Media coverage of protest is important. Goal is to arouse public support. Protests are used by "out" groups not "inside" groups.

B.   <u>Civil Disobedience.</u> Breaking of "unjust laws." Perpetrators are willing to accept punishment. Effort is to call public's attention to unjust laws. Civil Rights is a good case example.

C. Violence. The extreme form of protest. Can include riots, assassinations, etc. Destructive in nature.

D. <u>Effectiveness of protests.</u>
1. More effective when aimed at specific problems or laws.
2. More effective when targets officials who have power to make change.
3. More effective if goals are limited-getting a hearing.
4. Not too effective in changing laws or improving conditions that caused protest.

CHAPTER FIVE SAMPLE QUESTIONS

TRUE-FALSE QUESTIONS

1. Public opinion is generally weak and ill-informed.

2. A majority of Americans can name their two U.S. senators.

3. Most presidential election polls since 1972 have predicted the winner within a $\pm$ 3% error range.

4. There is strong evidence between the teaching in our public schools and the political attitudes of students.

5. College seniors are generally more liberal than college freshmen.

6. Jewish respondents tend to be more liberal on most issues compared to other religious groups.

7. Surveys taken since 1970, show that the political ideology of college students has become more conservative.

8. The print media has the most influence in shaping our political opinions.

9. There is a large gender gap between men and women on most issues.

10. Women are more likely to be Democratic than men.

MULTIPLE-CHOICE QUESTIONS

11. John Jones did not vote in the past election. Yet when asked in a recent poll whether he had voted, he replied in the affirmative. This is an example of:
    a. Knowledge levels
    b. The "Halo Effect"
    c. Inconsistencies
    d. Salience

12. In a survey, a range of ($\pm$ 3%) is known as:
    a. random survey
    b. Confidence factor
    c. Sampling Error
    d. Bias error

13. In 1995, according to Gallop surveys, people are most worried about:
    a. Illegal drug use
    b. Unemployment
    c. Budget deficits
    d. Crime/violence

14. In college, Maria was influenced by a liberal professor and self-identified as a liberal.
After graduating from law school and working several years in a prestigious law firm, she now is
more conservative. This change was most likely caused by:
   a. Family   b. Media
   c. Generational and Life-cycle   d. grade school experience

15. Comparing blacks and white, all but one of the statements are more descriptive of blacks:
   a. Support for a positive, active role of government
   b. Are more liberal
   c. Belief that education is the key to black success.
   d. Differences in living standards is due to discrimination.

16. Which best describes black and white opinion on the legalization of marijuana?
   a. Blacks favor more than whites
   b. Whites favor more than blacks
   c. There is virtually no difference between white and black opinion.
   d. The question has never been asked.

17. Which of the following forms of political participation enjoys the most support:
   a. Running for Office
   b. Writing or calling officials
   c. Discussing politics
   d. Voting

18. Which of the following amendments gave the right to vote to women:
   a. 15th   b. 19th   c. 24th   d. 26th

19. If one performed a cost/benefit analysis, what condition/conclusion would
be true about the act of voting?
   a. It is impossible to calculate the cost of voting.
   b. It is rational to vote.
   c. One vote makes a difference.
   d. It is difficult to calculate the benefits of voting.

20. Which of the following factors is most predictive regarding voters:
   a. Education level   b. Age   C. Race   d. High income

CHAPTER FIVE SAMPLE QUESTION ANSWERS

TRUE-FALSE QUESTIONS:

1. **True.** Public Opinion is very fickle. See page 128.
2. **False.** A majority of Americans know that they have two senators, but only 25% can name them. See Figure 5-1, page 129.
3. **True.** Only two polls in the 1980 election fell outside the range. See page 131.
4. **False.** Students seem to be more influenced in college than in K-12 schooling. See page 137.
5. **False.** The influence of liberal professors and more general acquisition of learning tend to make seniors more liberal. Refer to page 138.
6. **True.** See Table 5-2.
7. **True.** Refer to page 141. Liberal and middle of the road has gone up and down over the years. Only conservative has been in the same direction.
8. **False.** This is the age of TV and it gets the prize for being most influential. See page 143.
9. **False.** Most men and women see alike even on "women's issues." See page 145.
10. **True.** This difference started in 1980. See page 146.

MULTIPLE-CHOICE ANSWERS

11. **B** The "halo effect" is to give good citizen answers. This is a good example. See page 128.
12. **C** Sampling error based on the population size. A later number of respondents could lower the error, but cost is often prohibitive. See page 130.
13. **D** What most concerns the majority of citizens rarely remains consistent. See page 133.
14. **C** Age most often has a mellowing affect. See page 139.
15. **C** Majorities of both blacks and whites agree that education is the key. See page 146.
16. **C** On this issue, there is virtually no difference-80% are against the legalization. See page 147.
17. **D** Voting is by far the most practiced political participation. See Figure 5-6
18. **B** In 1920 all women finally received the right to vote by ratification of the 19th amendment. See page 151.
19. **D** A tough question. Answers a-c are false. Only answer D is true. See pages 152-153.
20. **A** The more education, the more likely to vote.

<u>CHAPTER 6-MASS MEDIA</u>

I. THE POWER OF THE MEDIA
    A. Our knowledge of politics and political leaders comes to us largely through the mass media. Few of us have the first hand opportunity to work in the inter circles of government nor are we usually intimate friends of political leaders.
    B. The Mass Media can normally be broken into two principle areas:
        1. <u>Electronic Media</u> which would include television, radio, the Internet, cable TV.
        2. <u>Print Media</u> which includes newspapers, news magazines, motion pictures, and books. See Up Close-Media is a Plural Noun for a fuller description of these media.
    C. Media power is concentrated in major TV networks-NBC, CBS, ABC, Fox, CNN. C-Span; leading newspapers-<u>The New York Times, Washington Post</u> and <u>The Wallstreet Journal</u>; and the weekly news magazines-<u>Time, U.S. News & World Report</u> and <u>Newsweek.</u> The columnists, anchors, editors, etc. of these media essentially control what we see and hear. **According to Figure 6-1, which TV network has the most audience. Which news magazine is most read? Which newspaper?**
    D. Of all the media, television is the most powerful. It is multi-dimensional. We see and we hear. There is virtually at least one TV set in every American home and studies show it is turned on for at least 7 hours per day.. For this reason, TV is the first true <u>mass</u> media. Television is watched and believed as accurate by more people than any other media.
    E. Media people claim they merely "mirror" reality and what they see in society. However, they decide what will be reported, how much time will be allotted, what footage will be used, etc. This gives them the power to shape the news, not merely report it. Professor Thomas Patterson of Syracuse University specializes in political communications and noted that in the 1960s, 80% of reporting was descriptive and only 20% interpretative. In the 1990s, the percentages have reversed. Eighty percent today is interpretative-that is a focus on <u>why</u> instead of <u>what</u>.
II. SOURCES OF MEDIA POWER. The media is protected by the First Amendment. The media is not neutral, but an active participant in challenging government officials, debating public issues and defining society's problems.
    A. <u>Newsmaking</u>. Deciding what is "news" and who is "newsworthy" is the most important source of media power. Politicians
    B. have hate-love relationship with media. They crave the public attention, but fear attack by the media. The media seeks out the sensational, the dirt, the corruption. The focus of the media on the White House travel office, the misuse of FBI files, drug use by White House personnel, Whitewater, etc. is illustrative. Politicians and their campaign advisors use the media when they can-the "sound bite" featuring the candidate in a favorable location, saying a few short sentences, may

43

make the evening news. This is free publicity!

C.   <u>Agenda Setting.</u> This is the power to decide what will be decided. It is the power to frame issues, present alternatives, and create political issues. By having absolute power to screen the news, the media has the power to set the public agenda. Starvation in Africa is nothing new and when ignored by the media, most are unaware. But let the media feature a few minutes of vivid footage of starving children and suddenly it becomes an issue.

D.   <u>Interpreting.</u> Media not only frames the news, but they also provide interpretation of the event. News is reported in "stories". The selection of visual footage is very important. People remember better what they see than hear. Some common themes are present in most news stories-good guys v. bad guys, little v. big guys and appearance v. reality. Media also selects expert sources-the airline expert commenting on a crash, the terrorist expert commenting on a bomb. etc.

E.   <u>Socializing.</u>

F.   <u>Persuading.</u>

III.   THE POLITICS OF THE MEDIA.

A.   Media politics are shaped by:
1.
2.
3.

B.   <u>Sensationalism.</u> News is selected for its emotional impact. There is a bias toward violence, conflict, scandal, corruption, sex, personal lives of politicians and celebrities. Scare stories also make "good" news-street crime, drug use, AIDs, nuclear power plant accidents, global warming, etc.

C.   <u>Negativism.</u>

D.   <u>Muckraking.</u>

E.   <u>Liberalism</u>. Most of the media elite have liberal leanings. A few conservative commentators are given space to present the appearance of impartiality. In talk radio, there is much more conservative influence. **Are Hollywood opinion leaders more liberal or conservative? More Democratic or Republican?**

IV.   MEDIATED ELECTIONS.

A.   <u>The Media and Candidate-Voter Linkage.</u> The media is the link between voters and candidate. In the past, strong party organizations in local communities could get out the vote. Today, this has been replaced largely by TV. Candidates, therefore, must have great communication skills, i.e. appearance, personality, warmth, friendliness, humor, etc. Image is more important than substance. TV is tougher than the print media. People see as well as hear the candidate. In the print media, people can only read words of the candidate.

B.   <u>The Media and Candidate Selection.</u>

C.   <u>The Media and the Horse Race.</u>

D.   <u>The Media as Campaign Watchdogs.</u> Professor Thomas Patterson's analysis of the 1992 presidential campaign was that candidate's communication was positive 85-90% of the time. Negative advertising was divided almost equally. However, election stories that focused on these negative ads were 90% of news coverage. Media focus on the negative contributes to public alienation of politics. Media attention on personal scandal focus their attention on every aspect of a candidate's life, personal, financial, past history, etc. Personal scandal captures more audience attention than policy issues.

45

E.   The Media and Political Bias. The media tries to balance their coverage of both the Republican and Democratic candidates. They are usually more critical of front runners than the underdog.

V.   FREEDOM VERSUS FAIRNESS. Early press was very partisan. Not until the beginning of this century did the media try to become independent. Even during the time of President Franklin Roosevelt, the reporters for the Hearst newspaper chain were forbidden to write anything favorable about the President. The Constitution protects freedom of the press; it does not guarantee fairness.

    A.   Prior Restraint. Best understood as government censorship of the press. The U.S. Supreme Court ruled in the Pentagon Papers case that the government may not prohibit even the publishing of stolen, Top Secret government documents. While the government may not censure, they may be able to muzzle the press, especially in combat areas. This was a hard lesson the military learned from the Vietnamese War. See Conflicting View: Muzzle the Media to Win the War.

    B.   Press versus Electronic Media.

    C.   Equal-Time Requirement. The Federal Communications Commission requires broadcast media to offer equal time and rates to political candidates wishing to use the media for advertisements. But this requirement does not apply to news programs, news specials or talk shows. Nor does it apply to Presidential addresses or press conferences. Sometimes the media offers free time for the opposition party to respond, although it is much more truncated in terms of time.

VI.   LIBEL AND SLANDER. False, harmful written communication is called libel. The same type of communication if spoken is called slander. These types of communication are not protected by the First Amendment.

    A.   Public Officials. As a result of the NY Times v. Sullivan case (1964) it is more difficult for public officials to prove slander or libel. They must not only prove the communication to be false and that it was known to be false, but that it was made with "malicious intent" which has been interpreted as reckless regard for the truth. This is very difficult to prove in court and as a consequence the media can say virtually anything about a public official. In fact, they have tried to broaden public official to include public figure. The Westmoreland case cited in the text is a good example of this problem.

    B.   Shielding Sources. Reporters often give a promise of confidentiality (Shield) to sources. The media feels their ability to gather information would be seriously compromised if they had to reveal the identity of sources to the police or in court proceedings. The U.S. Supreme Court has not given blanket protection to the media, but several states have passed shield laws that would apply in their states.

VII.   MEDIA EFFECTS: SHAPING POLITICAL LIFE.

A. Information and Agenda-Setting Effects. Media does not tell us what to think, but does tell us what to think about. However, information overload (too much info) may diminish effectiveness of the media. This is especially true for political news.

B. Effects on Values and Opinions.

C. Direct Effects on Public Opinion. Studies show that opinion changes were heavily influenced by media messages.
    1. Anchors, reporters and commentators had greatest impact.
    2. Independent experts had less impact.
    3. A popular president can change some public opinion. An unpopular one cannot.
    4. Interest groups have a slightly negative impact on public opinion.

D. Effects on Behavior.
    1. TV is likely to reinforce behavior rather than change it.
    2. Political ads are more useful getting supporters to the polls than in changing opponents into supporters.
    3. TV political advertising is more influential with marginal voters.

CHAPTER SIX SAMPLE QUESTIONS

TRUE-FALSE QUESTIONS:

1. About 2/3s of American homes have cable TV.

2. Of the nation's 10,000 radio stations, FM stations far outnumber AM stations.

3. Television is the most powerful medium in communication.

4. Government and media are natural adversaries.

5. Media professionals are neutral observers of American politics.

6. Newsmaking is the most important source of media power.

7. Politicians have a love-love relationship with the media.

8. Agenda setting is closely related to newsmaking.

9. Most direct persuasion comes to us through paid advertising.

10. Image is crucial to modern political campaigning on the TV media.

MULTIPLE-CHOICE QUESTIONS:

11. Which of the major TV news networks claims the greatest audience?
    a. CBS   b. ABC   c. NBC   d. CNN

12. Which weekly news magazine claims the most readership?
    a. Time   b. Newsweek   c. U.S. News & World Report
    d. National Geographic

13. Which of the following daily newspapers claims the most readership?
    a. New York Times   b. Washington Post   c. Wall Street Journal
    d. USA Today

14. Which media do people believe the most?
    a. TV   b. Radio   c. Newspapers   d. Magazines

15. Rather, Jennings and Brokaw are stars of:
    a. radio   b. Stage   c. Screen   d. TV

16. The media bias toward bad news is called:
    a. Agenda setting   b. Sensationalism   c. Liberalism d. Negativism

17. The watchdog activity of the press is also called:
    a. Agenda setting   b. Sensationalism   c. Muckraking   d. Negativism

18. Which of the following does not describe Hollywood Opinion Leaders:
    a. Liberal   a. Democratic   c. Support of gay rights   d. Religious person

19. A newspaper is about to publish an article which tells how to make a pipe bomb. Because of terrorist activities, the U.S. government thinks the publication could be injurious to national security. They ask a court to issue an injunction to stop publication of the article. This would be called:
    a. Prior Restraint   b. Slander   c. Libel   d. Equal-Time Requirement

20. Citizens of which nation have more confidence in their media:
    a. Germany   b. United States   c. Spain   d. France

21. The first paid political commercial ad appeared in the year:
    a. 1952   b. 1956   c. 1960   d. 1966

22. The first televised debate between presidential candidates involved:
    a. Eisenhower v. Stevenson   b. Kennedy v. Nixon
    c. Johnson v. Goldwater   d. Nixon v. McGovern

23. The first negative political ad was during which presidential campaign:
    a. 1952   b. 1956   c. 1960   d. 1964

24. The first incumbent president to appear in a Presidential debate was:
    a. Lyndon Johnson   b. Richard Nixon   c. Gerald Ford
    d. Jimmy Carter

25. Which was the first war to take place on live TV?
    a. Korean War   b. Vietnamese War   c. Persian Gulf War
    d. Israeli-Arab War

TRUE-FALSE ANSWERS:

1. **TRUE.** Sounds like a lot, but this is the number cited on page 170.
2. **FALSE.** The number of AM and FM stations is about equal. See page 170.
3. **TRUE.** We live in the TV age. See page 170.
4. **TRUE.** See Page 172.
5. **FALSE.** They are active participants not neutral observers. See page 172.
6. **TRUE.** Deciding what's on the news is power. See page 172.
7. **FALSE.** It is a love-hate relationship. See page 174.
8. **TRUE.** By setting the agenda-what to cover-this is what makes the news. See page 174.
9. **TRUE.** Whether persuading us to buy a product (commercial advertising) or vote for a candidate (Political advertising). See page 176.
10. **TRUE** Because the viewer can see as well as hear the candidate, image is very important. See page 179.

===

MULTIPLE-CHOICE ANSWERS:

11. **A** CBS news is number one. See Figure 6-1.
12. **A** Time magazine gets the honors. See Figure 6-1
13. **C** Wall Street Journal which is noted for its financial news, but also provides good political news and information on current events.
14. **A** TV by far. See Figure 6-2.
15. **D** As anchors of the network evening news they are heard by more people than any other individuals-Pope or President. See Page 173.
16. **D** Bad news is a focus on negativism. Reporting good news would be a positive approach to the news.
17. **C** In the old days, it was called "muckraking". Today the modern term is the "watchdog" function of the press.
18. **D** Can't find much religion in Hollywood. See page 181.
19. **A** Prior restraint is the government's attempt to censor news. See page 185.
20. **B** U.S. citizens have much more confidence in our media and also its influential power than citizens of other countries.
21. **A** Shortly after TV became commercial, the 1952 race of Eisenhower featured the first political ad-in black and white, of course.
22. **B** In 1960, Vice-President Richard Nixon debated his challenger John F. Kennedy.
23. **D** The famous "Daisy Girl" ad was the first negative ad and this was during the 1964 campaign.
24. **C** Gerald Ford, the only President not elected by the electoral college, was also the first incumbent president to debate in the 1976 campaign.
25. **C** The Persian Gulf War was the first in <u>live</u> TV.

CHAPTER SEVEN-POLITICAL PARTIES

I.   THE POWER OF ORGANIZATION. Politics depends on organization-organizing people to run for office and influencing public policy.

       A.   <u>Political Organizations</u>-serve an intermediaries between individuals and the government.

             1.   Political parties-concerned with winning public office.

             2.   Interest groups-concerned more with public policies.

II.   AMERICAN PARTIES: A HISTORICAL PERSPECTIVE. Parties were not in existence at the time of the Constitution. They were viewed as divisive factions.

       A.   <u>First Party System.</u> George Washington stood above parties. But they coalesced around two of his cabinet members-Alexander Hamilton-Secretary of the Treasury and Thomas Jefferson-Secretary of State. Jefferson opposed Hamilton's creation of a national bank and the use of federal funds to pay off war debts.

             1.   Hamilton, John Adams and others formed the <u>Federalist</u> party. This party was centered in New York and New England and tended to represent merchants, manufacturers and shippers.

             2.   Jefferson and his followers formed the <u>Democratic-Republican</u> party. This party represented agricultural interests, from the small farmer to the plantation owner.

             3.   In the election of 1796, Adams narrowly defeated Jefferson. The election of 1800 featured the same candidates. The Democrat-Republicans appealed to the populace by printing campaign literature and grass-roots organization. The Federalists who were more elitist did not. The result was the victory of the Democrat-Republicans. But a major problem came out of this election. Under the original Constitution, electors had two votes. The person receiving the most votes would be President and the second highest number of votes would be the Vice-President. If no one received a majority, the House of Representatives would elect the President. Aaron Burr was Jefferson's running mate. The Democrat-Republican electors dutifully cast their ballots for Jefferson and Burr, resulting in a tie with neither receiving a majority of the electoral votes. The election passed to the House of Representatives which the Democratic-Republicans controlled. Some of the Federalist representatives thought of trying to cast their vote for Burr (which he encouraged) but in the end Jefferson was elected as the third President of the United States. This 1800 election was remarkable because it was the first time in history the control of a government passed peacefully from one party to another as a result of an election outcome. It is still rare in the world today.

             4.   The election of 1800 was the death of the Federalist party. They never again elected a president or controlled Congress. They ceased to exist in 1820.

B.   Second Party System. Jacksonian Democrats and the Whigs.
   1.   In the elections of 1824, Andrew Jackson won more popular votes and more votes in the electoral college than any other candidate, but did not receive a majority of votes in either venue. Again, the election of the president passed to the House of Representatives where the Democratic-Republican party was fractionalized and they elected John Quincy Adams as president. Jackson and his supporters in 1825 in essence formed a new party by dropping the name Republican from the Democratic party label. Jackson also:
      a.   Democratized the party-it pressed states to choose presidential electors by popular vote rather by the state legislatures. It also urged states to drop property qualifications for voting. As a result, the number of voters grew substantially.
      b.   Nationalized the party-began to mobilize voters on behalf of its candidates.
   2.   Jackson's opponents formed the Whig party which included the remnants of the Federalist party. They also adopted the Democrats' tactics of a national campaign and popular organizing. By 1840, they were able to capture the White House with William Henry Harrison as their candidate.

C.   Third Party system. The birth of the Republican Party.
   1.   It was formed in 1854 to oppose the spread of slavery into the western territories. By 1860, the issue of slavery had split the Democratic party into Northern and Southern wings. The Whig party disintegrated and most supporters joined the new Republican party. The election of 1860 saw four main candidates. None won a majority of the popular vote, but Lincoln was elected president by the electoral college.
   2.   The aftermath of the Civil War found the Republican party representing the industrial north and the Democratic party the agricultural south. The Republican party was dominant during the period 1860-1912 winning every presidential election except two won by the Democratic candidate Grover Cleveland.

D.   Fourth Party System-Republican Dominance
   1.   The 1896 election was notable, because of William Jennings Bryant. A populist, he was nominated by the Democrats. He was a brilliant speaker and a religious fundamentalist. He sought to have the Democratic party represent the "have-nots", particularly the debt-ridden farmers of the South and West. The U.S. at the time was on the gold standard. i.e. the dollar was backed by gold. He proposed a silver standard which was in plentiful supply in the West. Changing to a silver standard probably would have led to inflation, lowering the value of the dollar. This would have enabled the indebted farmers to pay their debts with "cheaper" dollars. The Republican party appealed to the industrial north calling for high tariffs, protection for manufacturers, and a solid monetary (gold)

standard that would lead to prosperity for industrial workers. Thus, the Republican party cast its lot with industrial workers, small business owners, bankers, and large manufacturers. Black Americans also supported the party of Lincoln. The wealthy class worried about a possible victory of a populist raised a huge amount of money. Marcus Hanna was the campaign finance manager and raised $16 million. Republican William McKinley won in a landslide.

    2.   The Republican party dominated the presidential scene until 1912 when the party was split by Teddy Roosevelt who wanted to run again as president but was not chosen by the Republican party. He formed the Bull Moose party and as a third party candidate split the Republican vote enabling the Democratic candidate, former Princeton political science professor Woodrow Wilson to win as president. But in 1920, the Republican party came back to win again the presidency until 1932.

D.   <u>Fifth Party System-The New Deal Democrats</u>. The stock market crash of 1929 and the Great Depression that followed resulted in a complete loss of confidence in the business and political leadership in place and the people voted for Franklin D. Roosevelt as the Democratic candidate in 1932. In the 1928 election, the Democrats had nominated Governor Al Smith, a Catholic as their candidate. While he did not win, it did pull many northern, urban voters into the Democratic party.

    1.   In addition, the depression saw major realignments of voters to the Democratic banner:

        a.   Working class and union members.

        b.

        c.

        d.

        e.   Poor people.

        f.

    2.   The New Deal passed a great deal of social legislation-welfare and Social Security. This legislation provided support for workers, the aged, disabled, widows and children, and farmers. Republican Dwight Eisenhower was elected president 1952-1960; otherwise the Democratic party dominated this era. Eisenhower was actually courted by both parties as their candidate, but he chose the Republican standard.

E.   <u>Sixth Party System-New Republican Majority?????</u>

    1.   The Vietnamese War and turmoil of civil rights convoluted the Democratic party and the 1968 convention in Chicago saw police attacking unruly demonstrators and the party changing its rules to allow more minority and women representation in future conventions.

    2.   By the 1972 convention, the party convention represented the views of antiwar protestors, civil rights advocates, feminist organizations, and liberal activists. The Republicans painted the Democrats as ultraliberal,

quotas. These positions were far to the left of many in the Democratic party and the American electorate as a whole. Republican Richard Nixon won reelection in 1972.

3. The Watergate burglary and its aftermath resulted in Nixon's resignation (the first president to do so) and the entry of Gerald Ford as president. Ford's pardon of Nixon resulted in Democrat Jimmy Carter winning by a narrow margin in 1976.

4. Ronald Reagan came storming back for the Republicans in 1980 and his coalition was represented by:

a. Economic conservatives-worried about high taxes and excessive government regulation.

b.

c.

d.

e.

5. Reagan was popular and the "Great Communicator." In addition, the Republican gained control of the Senate and Southern Democrats in the House voted for some Republican proposals to cut taxes. Reagan was successful his first two years. But increased defense spending and failure to cut social spending saw an increase of the deficit. Middle class Americans began to identify with the Republican party and the Democratic party still was identified with its special interests-black Americans and other minorities, government employees, union leaders, liberal intellectuals, feminist organizations, and environmentalists. Republicans portrayed the Democrats as liberals when the mood of the country was swinging in a more conservative direction. Reagan won reelection in 1984 and Bush was elected as president in 1988.

6. Clinton and the "New Democrats". The increasing alienation of the Democratic party from mainstream voters, caused many Democratic governors and senators to form the Democratic Leadership Council led by the Governor of Arkansas-William Clinton. The council concluded that the party's traditional support for social justice and welfare overshadowed its commitment to economic prosperity. This view represented the neo-liberal view discussed in Chapter 2.

7. Clinton was the party's nominee in 1992 and attacked Bush for a faltering economy (the central theme of his campaign was: It's the economy, stupid!). He also downplayed the traditional liberal special interests in the party, but they supported his candidacy nonetheless (they could not support Bush). The Perot factor made it a three man race and Clinton won the most votes capturing 43%. But this meant he was a minority winner. Once in office, Clinton acted more as a traditional liberal than a moderate-his nominations for Surgeon General, Attorney General and Supreme Court came under fire, his gay policy for the Armed Forces and the health

Supreme Court came under fire, his gay policy for the Armed Forces and the health care policy developed under guidance of his wife-Hillary.

8. The Republican resurgence in 1994 confounded all the experts. Not only did the Republicans regain control of the Senate (lost in 1986), but they also captured the House for the first time in 40 years. They also captured a majority of state governorships. Not one single Republican incumbent lost a race for Senator, House or governor. How can this resurgence be explained? The national mood seems to resent "big" government and the Democratic party has been labeled as this (Clinton's healthcare bill), the party of tax and spend and more government regulation. The Republicans favor devolution (passing some federal programs back to the states), lower taxes, less spending, especially on social welfare and less regulations. The Republicans were able to hold on to their gains in the elections of 1996. In the Senate, they gained two seats and in the House, the Republicans lost 10 seats but still have a working majority.

III. POLITICAL PARTIES AND DEMOCRATIC GOVERNMENT. Political parties are essential to one of the main functions of a democracy-the contesting of elections to control the government. But political parties in the U.S. have weakened as other organizations and structures have replaced traditional party activities: special interest groups, the mass media, independent candidates and organizations, primary elections, social welfare programs and the career civil service.

A. Responsible Party Model: A special committee of the American Political Science Association in 1955 formulated a theoretical model of what a party should do in a democracy:

1. Adopt a platform outlining its principle and policy positions.
2.
3.
4.
5. Organize the legislature to ensure party control to carry out it policies.
6.

If responsible, disciplined parties offered clear policy proposal to voters who would cast their ballots based on this information, then the winning party would have a "popular mandate" to act. **WHY DON'T AMERICAN PARTIES FIT THE MODEL? HINT: PARTY DISCIPLINE.**

B. American political parties have never resembled the Responsible party Model (the closest resemblance are political parties in parliamentary democracies). American parties stress winning over principles. To win, requires voting coalitions and thus it is virtually impossible to have a unifying platform that would appeal to every member of the coalition. Thus, party platforms are mushy and try to appeal to a broad cross-section of society. Both parties try to position themselves in the middle of the voter spectrum because this is where most of the voters lie. Hence, there is little substantial policy difference between the two major parties. Still, the American public sees some differences. See What Do

AREA OF HEALTH CARE, NATIONAL DEFENSE, TAXES, ETC.?

C.   Republican's "Contract with America." During the 1994 congressional campaign, Republican House leader Newt Gingrich attempted to implement a responsible party model. The Contract with America contained 10 specific policy proposals, House candidates were recruited and endorsed the contract . Senate Republicans did not. The results of the contract are mixed. See Up Close-page 212.

D.   Erosion of Traditional Party Functions.

1.   In the areas of campaign organization and finance, parties play only a limited role. Candidates are often self-seeking, not selected by party elders. Campaigns are financed by contributions solicited by the candidate's organization, not the party.

2.   Today, campaigning is a professional operation-media, polling, campaign material. Party nominees are selected in primary election by the party's registered voters, not by party bosses. Normally, the party does not even endorse a candidate in the primary election. Once nominated, the candidate relies mostly on his organization, friends, etc.

3.   If elected, the party has no way to maintain party discipline-there are some sanctions available-committee assignments, pet project denial. But these are exercised rarely. For example, in the welfare reform bill vote in the House, 50% of Democrats voted for the bill and 50% voted against the bill which was endorsed by the Democratic president.

4.   Parties no longer have the capability to perform social services-like public jobs, pot hole filling, housing, etc. These are now done by government. Formerly, these were done by political machines, especially for newly arrived immigrants. In return, they asked for the vote of whom they aided. This system was called patronage.

IV.   PARTIES AS ORGANIZERS OF ELECTIONS. There are two types of elections: partisan where a candidate runs under a party label and non-partisan where candidates are not identified on the ballot under a particular party. State and national government offices are normally partisan elections. Some local government offices are non-partisan-county commissioners or school boards are some examples. Most partisan candidates identify with one of the major parties. Candidates running as independents do not normally fare well. See Up Close: Independent Politics: The Perot Factor.

A.   Party Conventions. Early in our history, candidates were chosen by party leaders. Later, starting in 1832, this was replaced by party conventions organized at all levels-from local wards to national conventions. These conventions nominated party candidates.

B.   Party Primaries. Today, the majority of states use party primary elections to chose their party's candidates. The primary election was a result of the progressive era's goal of minimizing the influence of party bosses. This change has succeeded in weakening the power of party leaders to chose party candidates. There are two types of primary elections:

1.   Closed primaries-only voters pre-registered as party members can vote in

1. Closed primaries-only voters pre-registered as party members can vote in this election.
2. Open primaries-on election day, voters can chose which party list of candidates they prefer. In other words, a registered Republican can choose to vote in the Democratic primary. In Alaska and Washington, voters can choose from either list of party candidates. The ability to "cross-over" opens a potential for "raiding" that is, seeking to get your party voters to vote for the other party's weakest candidate. This would ensure that your party candidate faces the weakest candidate of the opposition. However, there is not much evidence that this occurs in open primary states. .Runoff elections are used by some states if a candidate does not obtain a majority of the votes cast. Other states simply allow the candidate who receives the most votes to be the winner.
3. General Elections. Normally Democratic and Republicans contesting for office and any independent or write-in candidates appear on the general election ballot. Registered voters can vote here as they choose, either by voting a straight party ticket or splitting their vote among the various candidates. State laws make it difficult for independent or write-in candidates to get on the ballot.

V. WHERE'S THE PARTY? Political scientist V.O. Key identified three party levels:

A. Party-in-the-Electorate. These are essentially the party voters. Here party activity has declined as more voters register as independents and even party voters split their vote.

B. Party-in-the-Government. Essentially party elected or appointed officials. The lack of party discipline has weakened party activity in this area as well.

C. Party as Organization. This includes party leaders, workers, delegates, etc. In this area, party activity has strengthened, primarily because of technology-computers and communications.

D. National Party Structure. The party conventions held every four years possess the formal authority of the party. They not only choose the presidential and vice-president nominees, but approve party platforms, approve party rules, etc. But they essentially rubber stamp decisions made by party leaders. The National Democratic and Republican committees nominally act for the party between conventions. These committees are composed of members from all the states. However, the day to day work of the party is undertaken by the Party Chairperson and national committee staff. The chair is normally chosen by the party's nominee for president. Their principal mission is to raise campaign funds and assist the party's candidates.

E. State Party Organizations. Each party in the state has a state committee and state chairperson. Most have full-time staffs for public relations, research, fund raising and voter registration. They sometimes also seek out candidates for difficult races. i.e. challenging a well-entrenched incumbent.

F. Legislative Party Structures. Legislatures are organized by parties. The majority party meets in a party caucus to select leadership positions-Speaker, whips, etc. The minority party also caucuses to elect its leaders. Committee chairs and membership is determined by party affiliation.

  G. <u>County Committees</u>. In most of the 3,000 counties in the U.S., both major parties have a county committee which works with city and county candidates.

VI. NATIONAL PARTY CONVENTIONS. Meet every four years. Main event is ratification of party presidential nominee who really was previously selected in party primaries and caucuses. Last contested nomination was in 1952 when the Democratic party convention took three ballots to select Adlai Stevenson who lost to Eisenhower in the general election. The convention is really a media event. A lot of hoopla, carefully selected speakers to extol the party faithful, selection of the VP nominee, etc.

  A. <u>Convention Delegates</u>. Selected by states. About 80% are selected as a result of primaries. Generally, the number of delegates corresponds to the strength of the party in the state. Most delegates are party activists, ideologically motivated and strongly committed to the presidential candidate. <u>Democratic</u> delegates are more <u>liberal</u> than the average Democratic voter and <u>Republican</u> delegates are more <u>conservative</u> than the average Republican voter. Democratic delegates are likely to include more minorities, women and union members.

  B. <u>Party rules</u>. These are ratified at national convention and often concern delegate selection rules and voting procedures in state delegations. The Democratic party rules now allow for <u>superdelegates</u>-elected and party officials.

  C. <u>Party Platforms.</u>

  D. <u>Running Mate Selection</u>. The selection of the Vice-Presidential candidate is always made by the presidential candidate and dutifully ratified by the convention. Sometimes this is the only suspense in the convention-who will get the nod?

  E. <u>Campaign Kickoff.</u>

VII. THE PARTY VOTERS

  A. <u>Party Identification.</u> Traditionally more people have self-identified as Democrats, but this identification has been eroding recently because of an increase in independent identification and an increase in Republican identification. Today voter identification is almost equally split between Republican, Democratic and Independent. See Figure 7-7

  B. <u>Independents.</u> The fastest growing voter identification. As voters become disillusioned with the two major parties, they register as non-affiliated or independent.

C.   <u>Dealignment</u>. The process of loosening party ties. Shift from strong to weak party affiliation or independent.

D.   <u>Party Loyalty in Voting</u>. Party identification is the strongest influence on voter choice in an election. Still, split ticket voting does occur. This is particularly more true for Democratic voters who may vote Republican for President and Democratic for state/local officials. See Figure 7-7.

E.   Voter Realignment. A massive shift of voters to one party that results in party control of government for a lengthy period of time . Political scientists agree that realignments occurred in 1824, 1860, 1896, and 1932. This results in a cycle of about every 36 years. According to this schedule, the next should have happened in 1968. While Nixon was elected as a Republican, the Democrats still controlled the Congress and state governments. Thus, the case for realignment is murky.

F.   <u>Voter Support</u>.

     1.   The Democratic party receives disproportionate support (more support than average) from:

         a.   Catholics

         b.

         c.

         d.   Less educated

         e.   Lower income

         f.

         g.

         h.

     2.   The Republican party receives disproportionate support from:

         a.   Protestants

         b.

         c.

         d.

         e.

         f.   White Collar workers

         g.

         h.   Small town dwellers

     Republicans have made major inroads with one social group-Southern whites who have shifted their allegiance from the Democratic party primarily over the issue of civil rights.

VIII.   THIRD-PARTY PROSPECTS. Generally dim. While the public mood is fertile, voter support is weak. See Table 7-1. The efforts of the Reform party financed by Ross Perot bears watching in 1996. An argument for third parties-see A Conflicting View: Trash the Two-Party System.

IX.   WHY THE TWO-PARTY SYSTEM PERSISTS. No third party candidate has won the presidency and few have won Congressional seats. Why not?

A.   <u>Cultural Consensus</u>. The values of democracy, capitalism, free enterprise, individual liberty, religious freedom, and equality of opportunity are widely shared. There is little support for fascist or authoritarian parties. Because of the separation of church and state, there is no political party with a religious identification, such as in Europe. Likewise, socialist parties have existed but not attracted much support, primarily because the Democratic party was home for union members and workers. Most Americans are grouped at the political center. Radical or fringe groups do not attract much support. For a review of political parties in other parts of the world-see Compared to What: Political parties of the World.

B. <u>Winner-Take-All Electoral System</u>

C. <u>Legal Access to the Ballot</u>

X. THIRD PARTIES IN THE U.S. SYSTEM. In spite of our fascination with the major parties, there are some third or minor parties in American politics. These can be grouped as:
A. <u>Ideological</u>. **WHAT IS A GOOD EXAMPLE?** See also Up Close: The Libertarian Party: A Dissenting Voice.
B. <u>Protest Parties</u>. Usually involve an unsolved issue ignored by the major parties. **EXAMPLE??**
C. <u>Single Issue Parties</u>. **CITE TWO EXAMPLES. WHAT WAS THE SINGLE ISSUE FOR EACH?**
D. <u>Splinter Parties</u>. **CITE THREE EXAMPLES. WHAT PARTY WAS INVOLVED IN EACH CASE? WHAT PROVOKED THE SPLIT?**

TRUE-FALSE QUESTIONS:

1. A special interest group is more concerned with public policies than who wins political office.

2. To win in the Electoral College, one must receive more votes than any other candidate.

3. The principle motivation for the formation of the Republican party was to support big business.

4. The Republican Resurgence refers to the election of 1992.

5. Political parties are essential for a modern democracy.

6. For American political parties, winning the election is more important than standing on principles.

7. There is no reason for vote-maximizing parties to take strong policy positions in opposition to each other.

8. Most Americans strongly supported the Republican "Contract with America."

9. Independents are allowed to vote in most primary elections.

10. Most political candidates are nominated by caucuses or conventions.

MULTIPLE-CHOICE QUESTIONS:

11. The first political parties included one of the following:
    a. Republican party   b. Whig party c. Federalist party   d. Populist party

12. Which party was the main opponent of the Jacksonian Democrats?
    a. Republican party   b. Whig party c. Federalist party   d. Populist party

13. The phrase: "You shall not crucify mankind upon a cross of gold" is most associated with:
    a. William McKinley   b. Teddy Roosevelt c. Abraham Lincoln
    d. William Jennings Bryant

14. The New Deal Democrat party coalition consisted of all but one of the following groups:
    a. Working class and union members   b. Protestants
    c. Catholics and Jews   d. Black Americans

15. Which of the following were not part of the Reagan Coalition?
    a. Economic conservatives   b. Religious fundamentalists
    c. Southern whites   d. Social liberals

16. The Democratic Leadership Council would be most closely associated with:
    a. Neo-liberalism   b. Neo-conservatism   c. Libertarianism
    d. Liberalism

17. All but one of the following conditions would describe the "responsible party" model:
    a. a general, vague party platform   b. recruitment of candidates
    c. Educating the public about the issues d. Enact the party platform

18. The Republican party is perceived as doing the best job in all but one of the following areas:
    a. Foreign policy   b. National defense   c. Health Care
    d. Taxes

19. Raiding is most likely to take place in:
    a. caucuses   b. Closed primary   c. conventions   d. Open primary

20. Public officials would best describe:
    a. Party-in-the-Electorate   b. Party-in-government
    c. Party as organization   d. National party committee

21. National party conventions normally do all but one of the following:
    a. Nominate the presidential candidate   b. Approve the party platform
    c. Approve party rules   d. Elect the National Committee Chair

22. The process that describes the increasing number of independents is called:
    a. realignment   b. dealignment   c. critical election
    d. split-ticket voting

23. The Democratic party draws disproportionate support from all groups except one of the following:
    a. Protestants   b. Blue-collar workers   c. Black Americans
    d. Less-educated

24. The Republican party draws disproportionate support from all groups except one of the following:
    a. high income groups   b. whites   c. White-collar workers
    d. union members

25. Which of the third parties below received the most popular support in a presidential election:
    a. Bull Moose-Teddy Roosevelt
    b. Independent-Ross Perot
    c. Progressive-Robert LaFollette
    d. American Independent-George Wallace

CHAPTER SEVEN SAMPLE QUESTION ANSWERS

TRUE-FALSE QUESTIONS:

1. **TRUE.** While special interest groups support candidates with money, they are more concerned with who will support their issues rather than which party will govern. And they themselves are not interested in governing. See page 200.

2. **FALSE.** One must win by a majority of votes in the Electoral College. See Amendment Twelve to the Constitution. **WHAT HAPPENS IF NO CANDIDATE RECEIVES A MAJORITY?**

3. **FALSE.** While the Republican party is often associated with big business today, its original purpose was to prevent the spread of slavery into the Western territories. See page 201.

4. **FALSE.** 1992 was the year of Clinton. In 1994, the Republicans came storming back. See page 210.

5. **TRUE.** It would be hard to hold elections without party labels. See page 210.

6. **TRUE** With the multi-dimensional coalitions necessary to win elections, American parties must broaden their appeal to win and standing on principles could offend some of the coalition members. See page 211

7. **TRUE.** If the majority of voters lie in the middle of the political spectrum and both parties are trying to win their votes, their policy appeals will be very similar. See page 211.

8. **FALSE** Polls indicated that 80% of the American people were unaware of the Contract. See page 212.

9. **FALSE** One of the disadvantages of registering as an independent is that the voter forfeits their participation to chose the majority party candidates. See page 214.

10. **FALSE.** That used to be the method, but now primaries are the main tool. See pages 216-219

MULTIPLE-CHOICE QUESTIONS:

11. **C** The Federalist and Democrat-Republicans were the first organized political parties in the U.S. See page 200.

12. **B** The Whigs were the main opposition. Strange name for a party, no? See page 201.

13. **D** You can almost hear the thundering orator William Jennings Bryant saying those famous words now. See page 202.

14. **B** By and large, Protestant groups have remained with the Republican party. See page 203.

15. **D** Social liberals would be found in the Democratic party. See page 207.

16. **A** Neo-liberal-favoring economic growth to help solve society's ills. Refer to page 207.

17. **A** Parties would be expected to write clear, specific party platforms under this model. See page 211.

18. **C** Health Care is the answer. Clinton took the lead on the reform of health care and called it a right not an entitlement. See page 214.

19. **D** Open primaries permit voter cross-over which would facilitate raiding, See page 217.

20. **B** Public officials would be most likely found in the government. See page 220.

21. **D** The National Committee Chair is normally selected by the presidential candidate not the convention. See page 221

22. **B** A growing number of independents would certainly fit under the definition of dealignment. Refer to page 225.

23. **A** Catholics and Jews provide more support but not Protestants. See Figure 7-9.

24. **D** Union members are still in the Democratic camp, but many did support Reagan. See page 226.

25. **A** Teddy Roosevelt still has the title of third party champ! See Table 7-1.

CHAPTER EIGHT-CAMPAIGNS AND ELECTIONS

I. ELECTIONS IN A DEMOCRACY. If democracy is government by consent of the governed, then elections are the way that consent is given. Elections allow the governed to choose and pass judgment on officeholders who theoretically represent the governed.

   A. Elections as mandate? Since parties do not follow the responsible party model, it is difficult to support the idea that an election is a popular, majority mandate. Since parties and candidates support a number of issues, it is not clear which voter favored which issue. In addition, voters more often vote the candidate rather than the issue. Many candidates do not carry through with their campaign promises.

   B. Retrospective Voting. Voting can be either prospective (what the candidate will do-this is often determined from campaign promises) or retrospective (what the candidate did in office). Retrospective voting is probably more important for presidential elections than Congressional elections because while the President stands out (the buck stops here!), Congress is a large body and most voters have no idea how their Senator or Representative voted on issues. Retrospective voting seems more important on economic issues.

   C. Protection of rights. Elections provide a remedy from official abuse. The vote is our most important peaceful weapon in protecting our rights.

II. POWER AND AMBITION. Personal ambition is the driving force in politics. This ambition is fed by the prospect of power and celebrity. Power to get things done, change the world, etc. and celebrity for public attention, social status. These are more rewarding than money, leisure or privacy. Political ambition is the most distinguishing characteristic of public office holders. They are not necessarily the most intelligent, richest or most successful, but they do have ambition for power and celebrity. Most politicians would deny this ambition. Yet if there were no personal rewards in politics aside from money, few would run for office (Few get rich from public service). The following are some characteristics of office holders:

   A. Constitutional requirements for national office. Relatively few:
      1. President. A natural-born citizen of the U.S., a resident for 14 years and at least 35 years old.
      2. U.S. Senate. Citizen for 9 years, at least 30 years old and a resident of the state.
      3. U.S. Representative. Citizen for 7 years, at least 25 years old and a resident of the state.

   B. Political Entrepreneurship. The ability to sell oneself-raise money from contributors, organize people to work for the campaign, media savvy. Candidates recruit themselves; they seek out interest groups for money.

   C. Political Temperament. The willingness to work long hours, and live and breathe politics, sacrifice family life, etc. To be successful, one must like politics-the meetings, the handshakes, speeches, interviews, etc.

   D. Communication Skills.

E.   <u>Professionalism</u>. The idea of the citizen-officeholder is becoming less viable. Today, more office holders see politics as a full time occupation. It is more demanding to run for office and hold office.

F.   <u>Careerism.</u>

G.   <u>Lawyers in Politics.</u> The legal profession is well represented in political office holders. Some might say that the law lends itself to politics. Lawyers represent clients, politicians represent voters. Laws are statutes and lawyers interpret statutes. But more likely is that law and politics mix very well. Politics brings name recognition and contacts that can help the law office. Also many federal offices require a law degree-judgeships, federal attorneys and the justice department. Since politics is often a full time occupation, most politicians cannot practice law and politics at the same time. But upon defeat or retirement, most often a job is waiting in a law office.

III.   THE ADVANTAGES OF INCUMBENCY. An incumbent is one already holding office. Incumbents seeking reelection have a very high success rate. This is ironic since people have such a low opinion of government in general. Voters apparently distinguish between the institution and the officeholder.

A.   <u>Name Recognition.</u>

B.   <u>Campaign Finances.</u> Incumbents have an easier time raising funds. They are already in office and can do favors. A challenger is often an unknown. Individuals and organizations, including Political Action Committees (PACs) prefer incumbents. It is safer. Contributing to an opponent could make an enemy of the incumbent who could retaliate. Only when an incumbent has been very uncooperative will a PAC contribute to their opponent. Or if the incumbent appears particularly vulnerable to defeat. See Figure 8-1.

C.   <u>Office Resources.</u>

IV.   CAMPAIGN STRATEGIES. Campaigns for national office are largely media oriented and in the hands of professionals-public relation and advertising experts, pollsters, professional fund raisers, and media and political consultants. Marketing a commercial product strongly resembles a modern political campaign. Advertising is used to sell the product and the politician.

A.   The campaign strategy includes:
   1.   Computerized mailing lists for mail outs, fund raising and invitations to fund raiser functions-cocktail, barbecue, etc.
   2.   Campaign theme and candidate image
   3.   Continual polling to monitor progress
   4.   Production of TV tapes, newspaper ads, signs, bumper stickers, radio spots.
   5.   Selecting hairstyle and clothing for the candidate.
   6.   Writing speeches.
   7.   Scheduling appearances.
   8.   Planning the victory party.

B.   Selecting the theme

C.   "Defining" the Opponent. Essentially negative advertising. Seeks to identify the weaknesses of opponents and dramatize them in cleaver commercials. **Opposition research** and personal background investigations are undertaken by professional individuals or companies. They seek "dirt" and voting records. They look at tax records, court records, insurance claims and even seek medical reports.

D.   Using Focus Groups and Polling. **WHAT IS A "HOT BUTTON" ISSUE? WHAT IS A FOCUS GROUP?**

E.   Incumbent versus Challenger Strategies. Challengers attack the incumbent's record, conditions of the status quo, and stress the need for change. They frequently portray themselves as "outsiders" (not part of the Washington crowd) to appeal to voters turned off by government. The incumbent is a captive of current conditions. If the economy is sour, they may have a problem. Sometimes they will stick to the job claiming their responsibility as a public servant. The president can usually appear presidential-calming victims of the TWA flight, attending the Olympics, welcoming foreign dignitaries to the White House, etc.

F. <u>News Management</u>. Television is the battleground of the media campaign in national elections. Maximum "free" coverage of the news media is sought. Paid advertisements are used as well. Both should be coordinated with the campaign theme/s. News management is key to the media campaign. The candidate must be managed and placed at the "right spot" at the "right moment". Photo opportunities are highly prized. Words must be catchy and well crafted. Examples include: "End welfare as we know it" "Mend, but don't end affirmative action." Both are short but convey a message to different groups. For example, the latter expression might appeal to white male voters in the sense that affirmative action may be mended while the don't end it may appeal to women and minorities that benefit from affirmative action. Since coverage of the candidate will be short and his words allotted an even shorter period (7 seconds), what is said must be short and powerful. Thus, each day is a programmed activity of photo ops and sound bites interspersed with dinners and meeting with campaign financial contributors who pay for the TV campaign.

G. <u>Paid advertising.</u>

H. <u>Free Airtime</u>

V. MONEY IN ELECTIONS. The Professionalization of campaigning and heavy costs of a media campaign have driven up the costs of office seeking. In sum, in a presidential year, the costs of the presidential and Congressional candidates, political parties and independent political organizations tops $1 Billion. To raise these kinds of funds, requires much time and dedication.

    A. <u>Campaign percentage costs</u> for president or congressional seats approximate the following: **FILL-IN THE PERCENT:**
        1. Television Production-
        2. Television Time-
        3. Polling-
        4. Paid staff-
        5. Office overhead and candidate travel-
        6. Cost of fund-raising and solicitations-
    B. <u>Federal Election Commission</u>. Oversees all individual and organizational

campaign contributions and expenditures in federal elections. Composed of six members, appointed by the President to serve staggered six year terms. Traditionally, the six members are split equally between the Republican and Democratic parties.

C.   Presidential Campaign Costs. Contributions and expenditures are made by:
1.   Presidential campaign organization.
2.   Political parties
3.   Independent organizations not connected with the candidate or political party.

Normally a Presidential candidate must raise about $20M for the primaries and another $70M for the general elections.

4.   Congressional Campaign Costs. These depend on many variables-part of the country, size of the state, local cost of media, etc. However, most incumbent Senatorial candidates spend $5M and challengers $3M. The record was in 1994 in California for an open seat. The Republican candidate Michael Huffington spent $28M (mostly his own money) and the winner, Democrat Dianne Feinstein spend $12M. Thus, the total was about $40M. House incumbent members spend $550,000 and challengers about $225,000.

5.   Sources of Money. Individuals can contribute up to $1,000/ candidate/ election. Organization limits are $5,000/ candidate/ election. However, there are legal ways to contribute more. Each member of a family can give $1,000 /candidate/ election. Organizations can "bundle" individual donations of $1,000 and thereby exceed the normal $5,000 limit. Both individuals and organizations can give money to parties for "party building" and "voter registration drives" as long as this "soft money" is not directly spent on the presidential campaign. Independent organizations can spend unlimited money so long as it is not coordinated with the candidate's campaign. Finally, individuals can spend as much of their money as they wish, e.g. Huffington. Every candidate must file periodic reports listing contributions and expenditures. Individual contributors who give $200 or more must be listed by name, address, occupation and employer. All PAC and organization contributions must be listed whatever amount. See Table 8-1 for additional information.

6.   Fund Raising. Most campaign donations come from individuals. Depending on the survey, 7-10% of Americans say they have contributed to political campaigns. The characteristics of contributors is shown in Figure 8-2. **BASED ON THIS FIGURE, HOW WOULD YOU DESCRIBE THE TYPICAL INDIVIDUAL CONTRIBUTOR?** There are networks of contributors and with the aid of computers, mailing lists and telephone solicitations can be made of party and ideological supporters. Fund raising occupies more of the candidate's time than any other activity. This ranges from personal telephone calls to big

contributors, to fund-raising $1,000 plate dinners, cocktail parties, barbecues, fish-frys, etc. Tickets may be "bundled" or sold to organizations.

7. <u>Organizational Contributions</u>. Organizations must channel their donations through PACs, since corporations and labor unions are prohibited to contribute from company or union funds. Money may be solicited by company officers, stockholders, union members and their families. Trade and professional organizations also have PACs. See Figure 8-3 for money origin.

8. <u>Federal Funding of Presidential Elections</u>. Federal funds are available for primary and general elections. Candidates can qualify if they raise $5,000 from private donors of contributions no more than $250 from at least twenty states. To receive federal funds, candidates agree to FEC limits on campaign spending. Generally, Republican and Democratic candidates receive the same amount of funds. Ross Perot and Steve Forbes both rejected federal money and used their own. Federal funding covers 1/3 of primary costs and all of the official presidential campaign organization costs. Parties also receive federal funds for their nominating conventions and general election activities. Third party candidates can receive matching funds <u>after</u> an election in which they receive at least 5% of the vote. If they fail to receive this margin, they get nothing. These federal funds are generated by the one dollar/taxpayer check off on the income tax form. Only about 15% of taxpayers check-off this block. Checking the block does not affect the tax payment.

9. <u>Why People Contribute?</u> There are a variety of reasons:
   a. Ideological identification with the candidate or policy issues.
   b. Status seekers who like to hobnob with the famous.

VI. WHAT DO CONTRIBUTORS BUY? It is illegal to buy a vote. So there is no direct trade-off of a campaign contribution for a vote. Still, the contributor expects something for his money. A liberal or conservative contributor expects the candidate to support their respective views on policy.

A. <u>Access to Policy Makers</u>. Money opens the door so that the contributor has a chance to present their view directly to the politician. While most cannot legitimately expect to knock on door of the President, contact with key staff members is a possibility. Contributors have expectations of personal meeting with their Congressional representative; constituents get a letter.

B. <u>Assistance.</u> Contributors often with business connections expect some help with the federal bureaucracy. Politicians are asked to intervene and their interest can expedite the case or cause. Congressional interest tags are placed on files. These get more attention that a normal file. The bending of rules or regulations can often backfire if the opposition party learns of them.

VII. THE PRESIDENTIAL CAMPAIGN: THE PRIMARY RACE. Presidential fever-the willingness to endure a grueling, physically, mentally and emotionally exhausting campaign. Every aspect of one's life-family, friends, etc. is under the microscope.

A.   <u>Media Mentions</u>.

B.   <u>Presidential Credentials</u>. Refer to Table 8-2.

C.   <u>Decision to Run</u>. See Figure 8-4 for a typical campaign organization.

D.   <u>Primary Strategy</u>. Involves an appeal to party activists and ideologically motivated voters in key states.

E.   <u>The New Hampshire Primary</u>. First state to hold primary. Relatively unimportant for delegate strength, but receives unusual media coverage. Begins the winnowing process of candidate elimination. The horse race has begun. A good showing in New Hampshire receives favorable media coverage and encourages financial contributions. A poor showing does just the opposite.

F.   <u>The Front End Strategy</u>. Jimmy Carter was the first presidential candidate to adopt a front-end strategy which is a go-for-broke strategy. That is, spend all or most of your resources at the beginning of the race. Carter's campaign staff realized that Carter was a governor of an obscure state and to be taken seriously as a presidential candidate, he had to establish his credentials early. The decision of delegate rich states of California and New York to move up their primaries has only heightened the importance of striking early. While New Hampshire, a small state, facilitates "retail politics", that is, the person-to-person approach-door-to-door and handshaking, the states of New York and California are media campaigns and require money up front. Thus, there is even more emphasis today on candidates to raise "early" money.

G.   <u>Super Tuesday Southern Strategy.</u> **WHY WAS THIS STRATEGY ADOPTED? DID THE STRATEGY INITIALLY WORK? WHAT HAPPENED IN 1996 THAT MAY MAKE THE STRATEGY LESS VIABLE?**

H.   <u>Big State Strategy.</u>

72

I.   Convention Showplace.

VIII.   THE PRESIDENTIAL CAMPAIGN: THE GENERAL ELECTION BATTLE.
- A.   General Election Strategies. Presidential election campaigns must concentrate on the Electoral College count. Presidents are not popularly elected. State electoral votes are determined, in most cases, by a winner-take-all policy. A narrow plurality say 51% of the vote, wins 100% of the electoral votes. The winning candidate must win at least 270 electoral votes-California has 54, New York 33, Texas 32, Florida 25. Winning just these four states would give a candidate over 50% of the electoral votes needed to become president. Refer to Up Close-Understanding the Electoral College.
- B.   Targeting the Swing States. Candidates must identify which large electoral college vote states are winnable and concentrate his efforts there. States that are in his win column need some attention, just to show interest. States that are a definite loss, can be ignored. Marginal states are targets, but more attention will be given to those with large numbers of electoral votes.
- C.   Regional Alignments. **WHAT REGIONS ARE IMPORTANT TO REPUBLICANS? TO THE DEMOCRATS? WHICH IS THE MOST IMPORTANT SWING STATE?**
- D.   The Presidential Debates. More people watch these debates than any other campaign event. The candidate can appeal to their supporters and undecided voters. These are "image" more than issue debates. How well does the candidate communicate? Hold up under pressure? Candidates are "prepped" for the event. Dress rehearsals are used with stand-ins for the opponents. Anticipated questions are pre-answered. Short, one-liner "zingers" are written and rehearsed. "I knew John F. Kennedy and you are not a John F. Kennedy!" Senator Bentsen's famous one liner directed at Dan Quale. Media interpretation is very important, and the candidates "spin doctors" try to convince the media that their candidate came out on top. Dukakis when asked his reaction to the rape of this wife (a hypothetical question) gave a very bland, unemotional answer. His image as a cold, liberal intellectual was imprinted in the public's mind. To date, no candidate perceived as losing the debates has been successfully elected as president. For more information, refer to Up Close-The Presidential Debates.

IX.   THE VOTER DECIDES. There are many factors which explain why a voter casts their ballot for a particular presidential candidate:

ballot for a particular presidential candidate:

A.   <u>Party Affiliation.</u>   One of the most important explanations of voting. Figure 8-5 shows that Republicans largely voted for Bush and Democrats for Clinton in 1992. Since Democrats still outnumber Republicans, Republicans must receive independent and Democrat split-ticket votes to be successful. **WHO WON MORE INDEPENDENT VOTES IN 1992? IN 1988? IN 1984? WHO WON THE ELECTIONS IN THESE YEARS?**

B.   <u>Group Voting</u>.   As seen in chapter 7, certain groups appear to identify disproportionately with one party or the other. The same pattern exists in voting. Democratic presidential candidates receive more support from:
1.   Black Americans
2.
3.
4.
5.
6.   Union members.

Republican presidential candidates receive more support from:
1. Whites
2.
3.
4. Higher-income voters

There appears to be a serious <u>gender gap</u> affecting Republican candidates. Reagan received the majority of female votes, but Bush did not. Black-American voters strongly support Democratic candidates as do Hispanic voters, except for Latin voters in the South Florida area.

C.   <u>Candidate Image.</u>   Extremely important in presidential elections. Image is crucial and has been characterized by: warmth, compassion, strength, confidence, honesty, sincerity, good humor, appearance and "character" which can be interpreted as moral. In communications, there are <u>verbal</u> and <u>non-verbal</u> aspects. Many studies show that non-verbal makes a more lasting impression than verbal. There is an old saying: "Look into a person's eyes to see if they are telling the truth." This is an example of non-verbal communication. If a candidate appears to be uneasy, voters are likely to be uneasy about the candidate.

D.   <u>The Economy.</u>   People have a tendency to vote their pocketbooks or wallet. If they are unemployed, if disposable income is down, the party in power normally pays the price. Certain axioms have developed from a study of economic conditions and success/failure in presidential elections:
1.

2.

3.

      It appears that a voter's perception of economic conditions may be more important than their own particular economic condition.

      E.   <u>Issue Voting.</u> Most voters do not cast their ballot based on an issue. However, some do. For example, pro-choice voters would be careful to see if the Republican platform was anti-abortion and many would cast their vote on this issue alone. Gay rights advocates might so the same. But these would still be a minority of voters.

CHAPTER EIGHT SAMPLE QUESTIONS

TRUE-FALSE QUESTIONS:

1. Elections are not important for a democratic government.

2. Most elections can be interpreted by successful candidates as a mandate from the voters.

3. Without voting, governments would have very little incentive to respond to popular needs.

4. Personal ambition is the driving force in politics.

5. The most prevalent background occupation of politicians is businessperson.

6. "Defining" the candidate is often part of negative advertising.

7. A well-managed campaign will coordinate themes and images for both free news coverage and paid commercials.

8. For presidential and Congressional races, the majority of campaign funds are spent for television production and advertising.

9. Most campaign funds for federal elections come from organizational contributors.

10. Virtually all major party nominees for the office of president have had previous high public elected office.

MULTIPLE-CHOICE QUESTIONS:

11. All but one of the following are conditions for an election to be considered a mandate:
    a. Competing candidate offer clear policy alternatives.
    b. Voters cast their ballots based on these policy alternatives.
    c. Election results indicate voter policy preferences.
    d. Elected officials ignore their campaign promises.

12. John Jones has carefully analyzed the candidates for president. Noting that the economy is sluggish, Jones decides to cast his ballot for the challenger. This type of voting would be characterized as:
    a. Mandate voting   b. Retrospective voting   c. Image voting
    d. Prospective voting

13. Nancy Hanks is a naturalized citizen of the U.S., has lived in the U.S. for twenty years and is 45 years old and is a Republican. She would not be qualified to run for President because of:
    a. Citizenship status   b. Length of residency in the U.S.   c. age
    d. Gender

14. All but one of the following are important talents or skills of persons running for office:
    a. Political entrepreneurship b. Political temperament
    c. Communication skills   d. Citizen officeholder

15. Which of the following is not an advantage of incumbents?
    a. Name recognition b. Campaign finances   c. Franking privilege
    d. Status of an insider

16. Which of the following is not part of a campaign strategy?
    a. polling the marketplace   b. rejecting a campaign theme
    c. planning a victory party   d. compiling computerized mailing lists

17. The first negative advertisement on television was:
    a. The "Daisy girl" ad   b. the infamous Willie Horton ad
    b. ads against Jefferson   d. The ads against Lincoln.

18. A focus group would be associated with:
    a. group voting   b. Media advertising
    c. "Hot-button" issues   d. ethnic voters

19. The average cost for an incumbent Senator running for reelection would be:
    a. $28M   b. $12M   c. $5M   d. $3M

20. Among the reforms suggested for campaign finance are:
    a. Eliminate PACs   b. Public financing of elections
    c. Limited spending   d. Banning "hard" money

21. Federal funds for presidential elections are available if:
    a. the major party candidate raises $5,000 in donations of no more than $250 in twenty states.
    b. the minor party candidate raises $5,000 in donations of no more than $250 in twenty states.
    c. the major party candidate does not agree to FEC spending limits.
    d. the major party candidate receives at least 5% in the election.

22. Emily's list is a fund for:
    a. Minority candidates   b. Conservative candidates
    c. Women candidates   d. Male candidates

23. In which state is the nation's first primary for president?
    a. Vermont   b. California c. New Hampshire   d. New York

24. Super Tuesday refers to states in what region of the country?
    a. South   b. Far West   c. North   d. Mid-West

25. Which of the following would be a recommended strategy for a presidential campaign?
    a. Spend a lot of time in states where you have strong support.
    b. Spend a lot of time in states where you have weak support.
    c. Spend a lot of time in swing states.
    d. Spend some time in states where you have weak support.

CHAPTER EIGHT SAMPLE QUESTION ANSWERS

TRUE-FALSE ANSWERS:

1. **FALSE.** Elections are crucial for a democracy as they are the principal means to express "consent of the governed." See page 242.

2. **FALSE.** Considering the conditions necessary for an election to be mandate, very few elections if any can be considered a mandate. Page 242 refers.

3. **TRUE.** Democratic governments are more responsive to popular needs than other forms of government because voters remove unresponsive officials. See page 245.

4. **TRUE.** Whether for beliefs or celebrity status, the motivating force for political office is ambition. Page 245 refers.

5. **FALSE.** Although many politicians have a business background, lawyers tend to dominate the occupational background of politicians. See page 247.

6. **TRUE.** One of the purposes of "opposition research" is to dig up dirt that could be used in the campaign. Page 252 is pertinent.

7. **TRUE.** This is the essence of news management. See page 256.

8. **TRUE.** Both types of campaigns must make heavy use of the media and TV is where the action is. See page 257.

9. **FALSE.** Most campaign money comes from individual contributors. See page 259.

10. **TRUE.** The only exception is Dwight Eisenhower and one could argue that he held high public office-Supreme Commander during World War II and the first commander of NATO forces. But he did not have any previous elected office experience.

MULTIPLE-CHOICE ANSWERS:

11. **D** Candidates must be bound by their promises to meet the condition for a voter mandate.

12. **B** Voters that look at the performance of the incumbent which they evaluate as poor and then cast their vote for the challenger have retrospectively voted.

13. **A** A naturalized citizen cannot run for President, only a native-born individual can. What this means however, is unclear. Does one have to be born in the U.S.? Or does an individual born overseas to American parents qualify? Although we have never had a female candidate for president, there is no constitutional impediment for a female candidate. Refer to page 244.

14. **D** The increasing Professionalization of politics and careerism make it increasing unlikely that Jefferson's concept of the "citizen officeholder" is viable today. Refer to page 245.

15. **D** Many challengers try to tag the incumbent as a member of the status quo, especially if voters are turned off by government. Incumbents will sometimes campaign against the "status quo." All the other choices are definite advantage of incumbency. See pages 247-249.

16. **B** Selecting a campaign theme is a part of the strategy. The theme should become the paradigm of the campaign. Page 249 refers.

17. **A** The 1964 campaign featured the "Daisy Girl" ad suggesting the that Barry Goldwater, the Republican candidate, would be prone to use nuclear weapons. See Up Close-Dirty Politics, page 251.

18 **C** Focus groups are used to identify "hot button" issues which can then be used to frame campaign issues and themes. See page 252.

19. **C** The average cost of $5M means that some spend more and some less. The all-time record for a Senate race was in 1994 in California which equaled $40M for both candidates. Page 257. refers

20. **D** Banning "soft" money is a suggestion, but not "hard money" **WHAT IS THE DIFFERENCE?** See A Conflicting View-Reforming Campaign Finance. page 259.

21. **A** Answer D is not correct since the donations cannot be more than $250 from a donor. Donors must be from at least 20 states and the total raised would be $5,000. See page 260

22. **C** The fund is largely generated by professional women interested in electing liberal, pro-choice women to office. See Up Close-EMILY's List, page 264.

23. **C** Cold, small New Hampshire is where the official presidential race kicks off. Pages 267-268.

24. **A** Super Tuesday was a Southern strategy to help moderate democratic candidates against more liberal candidates. See page 269.

25. **C** Don't spend a lot or any time in states you expect to lose. Spend some time in states you expect to win, but not a lot. Reserve your time for marginal, swing states. See pages 272-273.

CHAPTER NINE-INTEREST GROUPS

I. **INTEREST GROUP POWER.** Organization concentrates power and concentrated power prevails over unorganized interests. **REMEMBER: INTEREST GROUPS <u>ARE INTERESTED</u> IN POWER TO INFLUENCE PUBLIC POLICY; THEY ARE <u>NOT INTERESTED IN EXERCISING</u> POWER. POLITICAL PARTIES ARE INTERESTED IN EXERCISING POWER AND IN SO DOING MAKE PUBLIC POLICIES.** The First Amendment gives us the right to organize to influence the government.

    A. <u>Electoral versus Interest Group Systems.</u> The Electoral System is organized geographically-state and congressional districts. The Interest Group System is organized to represent specific constituencies-economic, ideological, religious, racial, gender and specific issues, e.g. abortion. Both systems provide the individual with an avenue for participation in the political process. Interest group activity provides a more direct representation of policy preferences than electoral politics. Interest groups provide a concentrated focus on issues, while voters can only indirectly act through elected representatives.

    B. <u>Checking Majoritarianism.</u> Parties and the electoral system cater to majoritarian interests, while interest groups are much more narrow. In effect, they can help check the impulse of majoritarian politics. However, these special interests can obstruct the majority from exercising its will and can also be attacked as not representing the public interest, but rather a sectarian interest.

    C. <u>Concentrating Benefits while Dispersing Costs.</u> Interest groups often seek special benefits, subsidies, privileges and protections and also seek to pass the cost of these on to the taxpayers. When the cost is distributed so widely-it is rarely worth the time and effort of an individual taxpayer to organize to oppose the benefit. But if the benefit, etc. is odious enough, some group may organize to act against it. The diffusion of so many special favors over time results in <u>organizational sclerosis</u>-work, productivity, and investment are discouraged which, in effect, lowers everyone's standard of living.

II. **ORIGINS OF INTEREST GROUPS.** James Madison's "factions" are today called special interests. Madison viewed them as a necessary evil-they would compete against each other and prevent one interest from becoming all-powerful and thus help to preserve democracy.

    A. <u>Protecting Economic Interests.</u> Madison felt the cause of most factions was an unequal distribution of property. He therefore identified <u>economic interests</u> as the most prevalent in society. And indeed, business interests organized from his day to today to protect their interests. See Up Close-Superlobby: The Business Roundtable.

    B. <u>Advancing Social Movements.</u> **FILL-IN**

C.   Seeking Government Benefits. Expanded government activity creates more interest groups. Wars result in veteran interest groups. The growth of the welfare state spawned more interest groups such as the American Association of Retired Persons (AARP). The Professionalization of state and local governments and the expanded role of the federal government in state/local affairs created interest groups to lobby the federal government, i.e., one government level lobbies the other level government. Expansion of the government into education helped to create education interests-National Education Association, etc. See People in Politics-Marian Wright Edelman, Lobbying for the Poor.

D.   Responding to Government Regulation. **FILL-IN**

III.   THE ORGANIZED INTERESTS IN WASHINGTON. One of the most intensive studies of interest group activities in Washington was undertaken by two Boston College professors in the early 1980s. The results of their research was a book entitled Organized Interests and American Democracy. In 1981, they found 7,000 organizations that had an office in the capital or hired professionals to represent them. In addition, they found 3,000 PACs registered with the Federal Elections Commission. Thus, even several years ago, there was a substantial presence of interest groups in our nation's capital.

A.   Business and Trade Organizations. Economic organizations dominate special interest group politics in Washington.

1.   Business interests are represented by large umbrella organizations, such as:

a.   U.S. Chamber of Commerce-represents thousands of local chambers of commerce.

b.   The National Association of Manufacturers

c.   The Business Roundtable-represents the top 200 U.S. corporations

d.   National Federation of Independent Businesses-represents small businesses

2.   Trade Organizations. These represent specialized memberships. Among the most powerful are;

a.   American Banker Association

b.

c.

d.

e.

f.

g.

3. Many individual corporations and firms also open their own lobbying offices or hired experienced lobbying or law firms. <u>Table 9-1 lists by type major interest groups in Washington.</u>

B. <u>Professional Associations</u>. These rival business and trade organizations for influence in Washington. Some of the more prominent are:

1. American Bar Association (ABA)-includes virtually all of the nation's practicing lawyers, including the American Association of Trial Attorneys who <u>are not</u> interested in tort reform.

2. American Medical Association (AMA)-one of the highest spending lobbies. Opposes government efforts to regulate health care costs. Only about 45% of the nation's doctors belong to the AMA Many prefer to associate with specialized medical associations. <u>See Up Close: How Harry and Louise killed Hillary's Health Plan.</u>

3. National Education Association

C. <u>Organized Labor</u>. Union membership has declined over the years from 35% of the labor force to 16%. The American Federation of Labor-Congress of Industrial Organizations (AFL-CIO) is an umbrella group which represents more than 100 separate unions. The AFL-CIO has influence in Congress and the Democratic Party.

D. <u>Farm Organizations</u>. Farm population has decreased from 25% in the 1930s to about 3% today. Still, large producers remain a very strong force in Washington. The most powerful include The American Farm Bureau and National Grange and specialized groups, such as the National Milk Producers and National Cattlemen's Association. Small and low income farmers are represented by the National farmers Union.

E. <u>Women's Organizations.</u> **FILL-IN**

F. <u>Religious Groups</u>. **FILL-IN**. <u>See Up Close: The Christian Coalition: Organizing the Faithful.</u>

G. <u>Public Interest Groups</u>. Claim to represent a broad section of society and act to balance the narrow selfish interests of business, trade and professional organizations and unions. They are frequently allied with liberal ideological groups, civil rights organizations, and environmental groups. Their interests include Government regulation of:

1.   Consumer products
2.   Public Safety
3.   Campaign finance

Among the most influential are: Common Cause and Ralph Nader's organizations. <u>See People in Politics: Ralph Nader, People's Lobbyist.</u>

    H.   <u>Single-Interest Groups.</u> **FILL-IN** <u>See Up Close: NRA:Top Gun in Washington.</u>

    I.   <u>Ideological Groups.</u> Mostly conservative and liberal groups often with great passion and considerable financial resources. They are heavy users of computerized mailing lists. Some notable organizations include: the liberal Americans for Democratic Action (ADA) and conservative American Conservative Union (ACU). See Table 9-2 for ideological ranking of selected members of Congress.

    J.   <u>Government Lobbies.</u> State and local taxpayers foot the bill to lobby Washington to transfer federal taxpayer money to states and communities. Some example groups include: National Governor's Association, The National Council of State Legislators, The National League of Cities, the National Association of Counties, and the U.S. Conference of Mayors.

IV.   LEADERS AND FOLLOWERS. Every group needs a leader. The question often is: How well does organization leadership reflect the views of the membership?

    A.   <u>Interest Group Entrepreneurs.</u> Many recent interest groups of late have been started by entrepreneurs. Ralph Nader is a good example. Sometimes these groups can overcome a perennial problem-that of the free rider. In a collective group, unless there is some way to compel or attract members, some will prefer to collect the benefits, but not pay the costs to obtain the benefit. These types of individuals are called <u>Free Riders.</u> For example, if a teacher's union represents all teachers in collective bargaining with the school board but does not have a union shop (cannot compel teachers to join the union), all teachers will accept the pay raises and benefits obtained by collective bargaining, but many refuse to join the union.

    B.   <u>Marketing Membership.</u> Some entrepreneurs appeal to passion or emotion, especially ideological, public interest and single-issue organizations. An appeal is made to sense of duty and commitment to cause rather than material benefits. Business, trade and professional organizations usually offer members more tangible benefits, such as information, journals and newsletters, national generally easier to organize small, specialized economic interest groups than larger, general, non-economic ones. Larger organizations must rely on material benefits to attract members. For example, the AARP offers discount drugs, magazines, discounts for travel and lodging, etc as an inducement for membership. Members of large organizations often join for these benefits and rarely even know or care what policy positions the organization is pushing.

C. <u>Organizational Democracy and Leader/Member Agreement</u>. Most special interest organizations are run by a group of leaders and activists. Few are governed democratically. Relatively few members take an active part in meetings, etc. Leaders may or may not reflect member's views. An exception to this rule are single-interest groups which because of the intensity of the member's views require leaders to adhere closely to these views.

D. <u>Class Bias in Membership.</u> While Americans are joiners, most just claim membership in a church. Special interest group membership is closely tied to professional and managerial, college-educated, and high-income persons. The class bias of membership varies with the organization. Unions obviously recruit workers. Public interest groups draw heavily from the university educated. The same statement could be made about environmental groups. Business, trade and professional memberships obviously have a high socio-economic status (SES). Usually, leaders and activists have even a higher SES than members.

V. WASHINGTON REPRESENTATIVES: LOBBYISTS FOR HIRE. Washington is awash with firms and individuals lobbying the federal government-law firms and lawyers, private consultants, public and governmental relations firms, business, trade and professional associations, and advocates of special causes. More than 14,000 people are involved in this lobbying effort or 25 for every member of Congress.

A. <u>Who Are the Lobbyists?</u> Table 9-3 provides a listing of their affiliation. Lobbyist is a pejorative term connoting sleeze. For this reason, most lobbyists now use more benign titles-"government relations", "public affairs", "regulatory liaison", legislative counseling" or merely "representation." Many are "fixers" who try to influence government policies for a price. Many are insiders-former Congress members, cabinet secretaries, White House aides who "know their way around." They help to open doors for their clients and they are usually well paid for the service. One example is Michael Deaver who left the White House and within a year was known as the $18M man.

B. <u>Regulation of Lobbies</u> While the First Amendment protects lobbying, the government can regulate lobbying activities. The Regulation of Lobbying Act requires lobbyists to register and report how much they spend, but enforcement is weak. Some groups clearly engaged in lobbying have never registered, e.g. National Bankers Association, National Association of Manufacturers, etc. The law requires disclosure for lobbying Congress, it does not cover lobbying efforts in the executive branch or administrative agencies. Nonprofit agencies cannot engage in direct lobbying. Individual donors can deduct any contributions to a nonprofit from their taxes and the income of the nonprofits is tax free. If a substantial part of their activity is lobbying, they may risk losing their tax free status. For example, the FEC recently filed a suit against the Christian Coalition for engaging in political activities.

VI.   THE FINE ART OF LOBBYING. Any activity directed at a government decision maker with the hope of influencing the decision is lobbying. Lobbying is a continuous activity-congressional committees, congressional staff offices, White house staff offices, executive agencies, and Washington cocktail parties. If a group loses a battle, it does not necessarily lose the war. Losing in Congress, the lobbyist can try to influence the agency or executive department administering the law, or it can challenge the law in court. The following year, it can try to repeal the law, weaken it with amendments or reduce the agency's budget that administers the law. The fight goes on! The following are typical lobbying activities.

A.   <u>Public Relations</u>. **FILL-IN**

B.   <u>Access</u>. **FILL-IN**

C.   <u>Information</u>. Lobbyists provide technical and political information about pending legislation. They gather detailed information from various sources and provide the information to legislators who do not have the time or staff to become fully conversant with every piece of legislation. In this activity, honesty is primordial. Providing false or slanted info could backfire. If the legislator uses the info in making arguments and opponents show it is false, the legislator is embarrassed. The lobbyist is done-he will never be trusted again. And the word will be spread far and wide-don't trust so and so. It's time to look for another occupation. Table 9-4 provides a list of lobbyist activities. **WHAT OCCUPIES MOST OF THE LOBBYISTS TIME?**

D.   <u>Grass Roots Lobbying</u>. This is an "outside" activity. Organized interests can often mobilize their members to contact their legislator by providing pre-addressed post cards or even telephone numbers. The hope is to deluge the legislator's office and show public interest in a particular piece of legislation. However, legislators are aware of these tactics and while they must be sensitive to the callers, etc., they know it is an orchestrated effort. Lobbyists can also try to mobilize the media by providing newsclips, articles, etc. They may even buy advertising in the newspaper. Occasionally, there are full page ads in The New York Times by various groups. See Up Close: AARP: The Nation's Most Powerful Lobby. This piece shows that the AARP is a powerful voice for the elderly and a powerful player in Washington. **HOW MANY PAID MEMBERS ARE IN THE AARP? WHAT ARE THE DUES? WHAT MATERIAL BENEFITS ARE OFFERED MEMBERS? DOES THIS ARTICLE SUPPORT THE CONCEPT OF INTERGENERATIONAL WARFARE?**

E.   Protests and Demonstrations. **FILL-IN**

F.   Coalition Building. Just another name for networking. Groups that have similar interests may often band together to influence legislation. For example, veteran groups work together-officer and enlisted- to influence legislation affecting retired military personnel

G.   Campaign Support. Campaign contributions are the big, but not the only thing. Lobbyists sometime serve as part of the legislator's campaign staff-working the media or donor lists and sometimes serve as political consultants on tactics and issues. Most experienced lobbyists avoid making threats-support my bill or we'll help your next opponent. Irritating a legislator is not a way to gain support and besides the threat is largely an empty one and the legislator knows it. Bribery is against the law and legislators have gone to jail for accepting bribes. Better to ply the legislator with favors and thus gain their support.

VII. PAC POWER. Organized groups funnel their campaign contributions through PACs.

A.   Origins. PACs were initially started by labor unions as a means of getting around the prohibition against using union dues to finance elections. The Federal Election Campaign Act of 1974 gave encouragement to corporations to form their PACs and since then there has been a deluge of PACs of corporations, trade and professional, etc. Table 9-5 shows the growth of PACs and which group they represent. Table 9-6 list the big $$$$ PACs. Candidates soon learned to like PACs because it was like one stop shopping-that is, it is easier to collect $5,000 from a PAC than $1,000 individual donations.

B.   Regulation. **FILL-IN**

C.   Distribution of PAC Money. PAC contributions go overwhelmingly to

C.   Distribution of PAC Money. PAC contributions go overwhelmingly to incumbents of either party. Labor PACs favor Democratic candidates. Environmental and issue-oriented PACs tend to favor Democrats as well. Table 9-7 shows PAC contributions in the last two Congressional elections. PAC money is more important in the House of Representatives than the Senate.

VIII.   LOBBYING THE BUREAUCRACY. Lobbying does not cease after a bill is passed and signed into law by the President. The law still has to be implemented by the bureaucracy.

A.   Interest groups try to influence the bureaucracy in many different ways:
1.   Monitor regulatory agencies for notices of new rules and changes.
2.   Provide reports, testimony and evidence in administrative hearings.
3.   Submit contracts and grant applications and lobby for their acceptance.
4.   Monitor the performance of executive agencies.
5.   Influence the selection of personnel in the agency.
6.   Argue for strict or loose interpretation or enforcement of the law.

B.   Iron Triangles. The mutual interest of congressional committee members, organized groups, and bureaucratic agencies come together to form what has been called "The Iron Triangle." Each feeds the other. The Congressional committee approves budgets for the bureaucracy and makes the laws. It in turn is treated with deference by the bureaucracy and the group provides the finances for the committee members reelection. The bureaucratic agency works closely with the special group. It is a cozy relationship. This triangle works best in specialized policy areas. Conflict is more apparent when powerful, diverse interests are at stake, e.g. environment.

C.   Policy Networks. In place of cozy, iron triangles, many observers see networks of interested parties developing. The parties can include:
1.   Interest group leaders and lobbyists.
2.   Members of Congress and their staffs
3.   Executive agency officials
4.   Lawyers and consultants
5.   Foundations and think tank personnel
6.   Media personnel
These networks involve people normally working in the same policy area. They interact and communicate frequently. They know each other. They depend on each other. In short, it is a marriage of mutual convenience.

D.   Revolving Doors. This term is normally used to describe people who move from a government job to the private sector as a consultant, lobbyist or salesperson. They have a commodity that the private sector is willing to pay for-technical expertise, contacts and knowledge of the inner workings of the government agency. The down side is the suspicion that as they get closer to retirement or departure, they may made decisions favorable to their next employer. The Ethics in Government Act prohibits former members of Congress from lobbying Congress for one year. Former executive agency members cannot lobby their responsibility. President Clinton has required top officials in his administration to sign a pledge that they will not lobby former agencies for 5 years and never represent a foreign government as a lobbyist. However, this is just a pledge and has no force of law. See What do You Think: Is It What You Know or Who You Know?

IX. LOBBYING THE COURTS. Litigation has become a favorite instrument of interest groups.
  A. These groups bring issues to the court by:
    1. Furnishing lawyers to individuals who are parties to the case.
    2. Initiating class action suits.
    3. Filing amicus curiae (Friend of the Court) briefs. Table 9-8 list groups filing briefs in an abortion case before the U.S. Supreme Court. **HOW MANY BRIEFS WERE FILED? WERE MORE BY PRO OR ANTI ABORTION GROUPS?**
  B. Some of the interest groups have specialized legal staffs that concentrate on certain issues-e.g., the American Civil Liberties Union (ACLU) on First Amendment cases, The Environmental Defense Fund, etc.
  C. Direct lobbying of judges is forbidden. Lobbying about the selection of judges is not and interest groups are very active, especially when a Supreme court vacancy occurs.

X. POLITICS AS INTEREST-GROUP CONFLICT Pluralists argue that interest-group politics is a natural extension of the democratic ideals of popular participation in government, freedom of association and promotes competition over public policy.
  A. Pluralism represents that public policy is an equilibrium among various interest groups. The relative influence of the interest group changes over time and dependent on the issue. Accordingly, the goverment is passive and only referees the squabble between interest groups. Government acts as a honest broker.
  B. Balancing Group Power. Interest groups act to check each other, according to Pluralists.
    1. Countervailing power will protect everyone's interests.
    2. Overlapping group membership will moderate demands and lead to compromise.
    3. Latent interest groups will check the more radical ones.
  C. Interest-Group Politics: How Democratic? Democratic theory looks at public policy as the rational choice of individuals with equal influence who evaluate their needs and reach a majority decision with due regard for the rights of others. This traditional theory does not view public policy as a product of interest-group pressures. If there were true competition between interest groups it might be more acceptable, but accommodation is the rule rather than competition. Further, interest groups are not democratically governed but rather led by a small elite. Nor are interest groups at all equal-some are more powerful than others.
  D. Interest Group Politics-Gridlock and Paralysis. Democracies require a sense of community and common purpose. If the demands of special interest groups

displace the public interest, government cannot function well. Uncompromising claims by conflicting interest groups equal gridlock. One good example is health care. We have over 40M Americans with no health insurance and medical costs are climbing out of sight. Yet with so many special interests out to protect their slice of the pie, real reform of health care still waits. Interest group paralysis and the resulting inability of government to act decisively to resolve national problems weakens popular confidence in government. Over time, the continued buildup of special protections, privileges and treatments in society results in "institutional sclerosis" and economic stagnation.

CHAPTER NINE SAMPLE QUESTIONS

TRUE-FALSE QUESTIONS:
1. Organization is a means to power.

2. Interest group activity is more of an indirect representation of policy preferences compared to electoral politics.

3. If James Madison were alive today, he would call the factions of his day, special interest groups today.

4. Government activities spawn creation of new interest groups.

5. The Business Roundtable is a meeting to the top 200 business CEOs or their representative.

6. Organized labor speaks with an increasingly powerful voice as membership in unions have increased over the years.

7. The Federal government's grant-in-aid programs to state and local governments have resulted in one government body lobbying another government body.

8. Because of the larger membership, it is easier to organize large groups than small groups.

9. The socio-economic status of group membership shows a bias toward professional, managerial, college-educated and high-income persons.

10. Democratic candidates rely more on PACs than Republican candidates.

MULTIPLE-CHOICE QUESTIONS:
11. The right to organize for political purposes is guaranteed by which amendment to the U.S. Constitution?
      a. 7th amendment   b. 10th amendment   c. First Amendment
      d. 14th Amendment

12. An interest group attempts to:
      a. Diffuse benefits and concentrate the cost b. Concentrate the cost and benefits
      c. Diffuse the benefits and costs   d. Concentrate the benefit and spread the cost.

13. Madison believed that the primary cause of factions was:
      a. Unequal distribution of property b. human nature
      c. Competition   d. government

14. All but one of the following explain the origin of interest groups:
    a. Protecting economic interests   b. Response to government regulations
    c. Advancing social movements   d. media pressure

15. The American Medical Association (AMA) would be best identified as a:
    a. Business Organization   b. Trade organization
    c. Professional organization d. Public Interest Group

16. The American Petroleum Institute would be classified as a:
    a. Business Organization   b. Trade organization
    c. Professional organization d. Public Interest Group

17. The Americans for Democratic Action (ADA) would be classified as:
    a. Ideological group   b. Single-issue group
    c. Professional organization d. Public Interest Group

18. Hillary's Health Care Reform was killed by Harry and Louise. These ads were sponsored by:
    a. medical doctors   b. U.S. Chamber of Commerce
    c. religious churches   d. insurance industry

19. A person who enjoys the benefit of group membership, but refuses to contribute anything to the costs to obtain the benefit is called a:
    a. scoundrel   b. free rider
    c. elite leader   d. entrepreneur

20. If an interest group cannot compel paid membership, then it must rely on:
    a. material incentives   b. union shop
    c. appeal to patriotism   d. free riders

21. Lobbying activities include all but one of the following:
    a. cocktail parties   b. Public relations
    c. Running for office   d. Protests and demonstrations

22. The nation's largest interest group is the American Association of Retired Persons (AARP). Approximately, how many members does it have?
    a. 16M   b. 33M   c. 5M   d. 55M

23. Which interest group has the most PACs:
    a. Corporate b. Labor   c. Trade and Professional   d. Ideological

92

24. Interaction in a common policy area among lobbyists, elected officials, staff personnel, bureaucrats, journalists and private-sector experts is called:
  a. Iron Triangle
  b. Revolving Door
  c. Pluralism
  d. Policy Network

25. The purpose of government in pluralist theory is to:
  a. promote interest groups
  b. Act contra to the elite.
  c. Serve as an honest broker among competing interest groups
  d. Control the impulsive nature of man.

CHAPTER NINE SAMPLE QUESTION ANSWERS

TRUE-FALSE ANSWERS:

1. **TRUE**. Organization concentrates power and concentrated power prevails over unorganized interests. See page 287.

2. **FALSE**. Election politics means we elect representatives who may or may not act according to our wishes regarding public policies. Our influence is through this representative and thus is indirect. In fact, the representative has to be concerned with many issues. In an interest group, we could be a more active participant and the interest group normally concentrates on an issue and directly represent the group to the government. See page 288.

3. **TRUE**. Some political scientists think that factions are different than interest groups. But our textbook author, Larry Sabato of the University of Virginia and yours truly feel that Madison would have no problem labeling a special interest group a faction. Refer to page 288.

4. **TRUE**. The expansion of government into veteran, welfare, education, etc. helped to create special interest groups in these areas. See page 289.

5. **FALSE**. One of the unique features of this organization is its "firm rule" that the CEO cannot send a representative. See Up Close-Superlobby: The Business Roundtable.

6. **FALSE**. Labor union membership has declined as manufacturing jobs have been lost. Union membership has fallen from 35% of the workforce in the 1950s to about 16% today. Refer to page 295.

7. **TRUE**. State and local governments lobby the federal government and local governments lobby state governments. See pages 308-309.

8. **FALSE** Just the opposite. In a smaller group, people recognize their importance to the group and are more willing to support it.

9. **TRUE**. Although 90% of Americans belong to some group, for most it is their local church. Membership in most other groups shows a class bias. The only exception are labor unions which are supposed to represent the working class. See page 306.

10. **TRUE**. For example, most labor PAC contributions go to Democrats. See page 315.

MULTIPLE-CHOICE ANSWERS:

11. **C** The right to assemble and the right to petition the government are key ingredients of interest groups and these rights are part of the First Amendment. Refer to page 288.

12. **D** Concentrate the benefit for your membership, but spread the cost to every U.S. citizen if

you can. The is the <u>modus operandi</u> of most interest group benefits, subsidies, etc. See page 288.

13. **A** Economic interests then as well as now largely explain the existence of factions. Human nature explains the origin of factions but not the cause. Competition is operational, not a cause. Government activity does cause creation of new interest groups, but the prevailing cause is still economic. See page 289.

14. **D** Media pressure is scarce in covering interest groups and we could not claim that the media played any role in creating interest groups except in this own area of communications. See pages 293-297.

15. **C** Medical doctors are professionals. See page 294.

16. **B** Petroleum is a commodity and is bought and sold just like pizza. Both oil and pizza organizations are classified as trade associations. Refer to page 293.

17. **A.** The Americans for Democratic Action (ADA) is a liberal espousal group. See pages 302, 307

18. **D** While all the groups opposed Hillary's plan, it was the insurance industry which paid for the advertising campaign featuring Harry and Louise. Refer to page 296

19. **B** While a free rider may be regarded as a scoundrel, the proper terminology is free rider. See page 305.

20. **A** While ideological, single-interest and public interest groups may base appeals for paid members on commitment and sense of duty, most have to offer material incentives for membership. This would include most trade and professional organizations and many business ones as well. See page 305.

21. **C** Running for office is not an activity of a lobbyist. Organizing protests and demonstrations is not a frequent activity, but "outsider" groups may have to use this activity to gain attention to their cause. See pages 307-311.

22. **B** With 33 million dues paying members ($8.00/year), the AARP has income from just membership dues over $264M/year. See page 312.

23. **A** While corporate groups could be expected to be number one, a surprising number two are ideological groups. See Table 9-5.

24. **D** The participation of journalists and private-sector experts takes it out of the iron triangle concept. See page 316.

25. **C** Government's role as seen but the Pluralists is to act as a referee to help promote a point of equilibrium in public policy. See page 321.

CHAPTER TEN-CONGRESS

I.   THE POWERS OF CONGRESS. Madison argued that one task of legislators was to control "factions."

       A.   Constitutional Powers. The Founding Fathers saw the legislature as the first and most powerful branch of government. Article I, Section 8 of the Constitution laid out very specific areas of responsibility of the Congress. In addition to legislation, the House of Representatives will elect the president if no candidate obtains a majority in the Electoral College. The Senate is called upon for "advice and consent" for treaties and presidential nominations to the judicial and executive branches. The House has the power to impeach executive or judicial officials and the Senate tries the charges. Each chamber can conduct investigations, discipline its members and regulate its internal affairs. Table 10-1 provides a very good list of common powers of each chamber and some specific to one chamber.

       B.   Institutional Conflict. The Constitution was designed with "checks and balances" so that conflict between the branches of government was not only foreseen, but encouraged so that no branch would become too powerful at the expense of the others. Indeed, over our two hundred year plus history, power has flowed and ebbed between the branches. However, in this century, we have seen a steady, if not undramatic, shift of power toward the executive branch. Normally, it is easier for Congress to play an obstructionist rule, than be the source of policy initiatives. Thus, Congress defeats or modifies presidential proposals, tinkers with the budget, delays or reject nominees, investigates the White House or executive agencies, holds committee meeting to highlight improprieties, such as the White House travel office firings or improper use of FBI files. Very recently, the Congress has tried to seize the initiative in policy initiatives, especially in the Contract with America. But many of these policy initiatives were watered down or vetoed.

       C.   Dividing Congressional Power: House and Senate. **FILL-IN. WHAT DOES BICAMERAL MEAN? HOW MANY ARE IN THE HOUSE AND SENATE? HOW MANY PEOPLE DOES A REPRESENTATIVE HAVE IN THEIR DISTRICT? IN THE HOUSE, FROM WHERE ARE NON-VOTING DELEGATES? WHAT IS THE TERM OF OFFICE FOR A SENATOR AND HOUSE MEMBER?**

       D.   Domestic versus Foreign and Defense Policy. Congress is more powerful in the domestic policy area, and usually defers to the president in the foreign and defense policy areas. Congress has declared war only five times. **WHAT WERE THESE DECLARED WARS?** Yet the president has sent U.S. Armed Forces into military actions over 200 times. The Vietnamese conflict convinced the Congress to reassert its power and they passed the War Power Act over President Nixon's veto. This act sought to curtail the president's use of the Armed Forces in combat without Congress's approval, but it has proved to be largely ineffective. For example both the invasion of Grenada and Panama were made without Congressional approval.

E.   The Power of the Purse. **FILL-IN. BEGINNING IN JANUARY 1997, THE PRESIDENT WILL HAVE A LINE-ITEM VETO. HOW WILL THIS AFFECT CONGRESS'S POWER OF THE PURSE?**

F.   Oversight of the Bureaucracy. **FILL-IN. WHAT IS THE DIFFERENCE BETWEEN THE FORMAL AND REAL RATIONALE OF OVERSIGHT? HOW DOES CONGRESS CARRY OUT ITS OVERSIGHT RESPONSIBILITY? HOW DOES OVERSIGHT SOMETIME BEGIN?**

G.   Agenda Setting and Media Attention. Congressional hearings and investigations often involve agenda setting-bringing issues to the public's attention. However. without the media, this effort would not be very successful. Hearing are usually on a specific bill whereas investigations are usually into alleged misdeeds or scandals. The formal reason for congressional investigations is to seek information to assist in lawmaking. But often the investigations are used for political purposes:

1.   Rally popular support for policies or issues favored by legislators.
2.   Attack the president or other officials or plans or programs of the president.
3.   Seek media coverage for legislators.

Congress has many powers to assist it in hearings or investigations: Subpoena witnesses (compel them to appear), administer oaths, cross-examine witnesses,

criminal contempt charges (refusing to cooperate) and perjury (lying under   oath).
Congress cannot impose criminal penalties as a result of its investigations   but can refer
the matter to the Justice Department for prosecution.

      H.   <u>Conflict Management.</u> Congress provides a forum for venting-gives witnesses a
chance to explain their views or plead their policy preferences.

II.   CONGRESSIONAL APPORTIONMENT AND REDISTRICTING. While the
      Constitution requires a reapportionment every ten years in the House, it does not specify
      the number of representatives. This was done by Congress in 1910 when it fixed the
      membership at 435. It could be changed again tomorrow, but most likely will not.

      A.   <u>Apportionment.</u> This means that every 10 years in accordance with the latest
            census, the 435 seats must be divided up between the 50 states based on their
            population. This division is based on a formula devised in 1929 which has
            withstood court challenges and is still used today.

      B.   <u>Malapportionment.</u> The Constitution does not indicate how each state will
            apportion its number of representatives. Some states were notorious for
            malapportionment-some rural districts had very few people, but urban ones were
            loaded with people. Each district had one representative, but districts were
            different in population size.

      C.   <u>Supreme Court Enters.</u> Prior to 1962, the court had refused to intervene in
            malapportionment cases, holding that this was a problem of states and the federal
            courts should avoid this "political thicket." The Supreme Court decision in
            Baker v. Carr (1962) was a surprise when the activist Warren Court ruled that
            population inequities violated the 14th Amendments equal protection clause. In
            1963 in Gray v. Saunders. the Court ruled that equality meant "one man, one
            vote." Since then, congressional districts have had almost the exact same number
            of inhabitants.

      D.   <u>Redistricting.</u> After each decennial census, new congressional district lines may
            be redrawn based on the census. Some states because of population shift or
            growth may gain or lose House seats. <u>Across the USA: Apportionment of House
            Seats, 1990</u> shows the latest apportionment with the states that gained, lost and
            remained the same. **DO YOU SEE ANY PATTERN? DID ONE AREA OF
            THE COUNTRY LOSE AND ANOTHER GAIN SEATS?** State legislatures
            draw up the new boundaries subject to the governor's approval or override of his
            veto. Recently, the Justice Department and courts have been involved in
            redistricting issues, especially to determine whether redistricting disadvantages
            black or Hispanic minorities.

      E.   <u>Gerrymandering.</u> This is the drawing of district lines for political advantage.
            <u>Figure 10-2 shows the original gerrymandered district.</u> With sophisticated
            computer programs and precinct voting records, while still a technical task, it can
            be done much easier now. Figure 10-3 shows how a sample city could be divided
            to elect one Republican and two Democrats or instead elect three Democrats
            through a process known as <u>splintering.</u> It would depend on which party was
            doing the splintering. Another process is known as <u>packing</u> when one would try

to compact all of one party in one area and give the other party advantage in other areas.

  F. <u>Partisan Gerrymandering.</u> , The Supreme Court has upheld partisan gerrymandering unless it degrades a voter's or group of voters influence in the political process. This is very vague and allows much leeway.

  G. <u>Seats-Vote Relationship.</u> **FILL-IN.**

  H. <u>The Politics of Redistricting.</u> Party control of the legislature and governorship are the keys to redistricting. Since the Democratic party had more control at the state level after the 1990 census, they were better positioned to protect Democratic House seats. The Republicans turned to the courts and championed efforts to create black majority-minority districts hoping to "pack" Democratic members in a few districts and help Republicans to win in the other districts.

  I. <u>Racial Gerrymandering.</u> The Voting Rights Act of 1965 (VRA) required states that had a past history of voter discrimination to clear redistricting plans with the Justice Department to ensure there was no intent to discriminate against black, Hispanic, American Indian, Alaskan native or Asian voters. A 1982 amendment to the VRA changed "intent" to "effect" minority voting. A 1986 decision of the Supreme Court Thornburg v. Gingles interpreted the "effect" test to require state legislatures to draw district lines that would maximize minority representation in Congress and state legislatures. These are called majority-minority districts. This has been called <u>affirmative racial gerrymandering.</u> Following the 1990 census, redistricting plans where there were large minorities were closely scrutinized by the Justice Department and the courts. The creation of new majority-minority districts resulted in a dramatic increase of black American and Hispanic representatives in Congress. Yet in order to draw in a maximum number of minorities, the resulting districts in many cases were bizarre. Some ran for miles down a railroad track or highway. A closely divided Supreme Court has recently voided majority-minority districts in Texas, North Carolina and Georgia and a federal court did the same in Florida holding that using race as the predominant factor in drawing district lines was unconstitutional. This is still a viable issue and probably we have not seen the last word.

III. GETTING TO Capitol HILL. Most members of Congress are political entrepreneurs. They nominate themselves, raise their own campaign funds and organize their own campaign staff.

  A. <u>Who Runs for Congress?</u> Many are career politicians. Most have a background in law, business or prior public service. Many of the lawyers have not practiced law but rather practiced politics instead. Table 10-2 provides an occupational background list of the 104th Congress. **WHICH PARTY HAS THE MOST**

LAWYERS? See People in Politics: Sonny Bono: Celebrity Congressman.

B. Competition for Seats. Incumbents have a clear advantage. Name recognition, campaign funds, and resources of Congressional offices limit competition for seats. Any district won with more than 55% of the popular vote is considered a safe seat. More than 2/3s of Congressional seats thus are considered safe. Reelection rates of incumbents often is at the 90% level. The reelection rate for Senators is lower in the neighborhood of 75%. This high retention rate has led some to call for term limits. See What Do You Think: Term Limits for Members of Congress? **WHAT PERCENT OF AMERICANS FAVOR TERM LIMITS? WHAT ARE THE PRO/CON ARGUMENTS?** The best chance to win a Congressional seat is when it is open-either the incumbent retired or ran for higher office, or is the result of reapportionment.

C. Turnover. There has been a higher rate of turnover recently.

D. The Congressional Electorate. Congressional elections are not of high interest to many voters. Most people cannot even name both Senators from their state. Voter turnout in Congressional elections (non-presidential) is only about 35% and voter turnout for Congressional primary races is even lower at 15-20%. This low turnout normally favors incumbents. See What Do You Think: Why Voters Reelect Members of an Unpopular Congress? **WHY IS THERE SUCH A DISPARITY BETWEEN APPROVAL RATES OF OWN REPRESENTATIVE AND CONGRESS?**

E. Independence of Congressional Voting. Congressional voting is largely independent of presidential voting. Voters cast their ballots on differing expectations.

F. Congressional Campaign Spending and Fund Raising. In most incumbent v. challenger elections, the incumbent heavily outspends the challenger. In open elections, Democratic and Republican candidates spend about the same. See Table 10-3. **WHAT IS THE AVERAGE COST OF A HOUSE OR SENATE SEAT?** Raising over $500,000 for a House race or $4.6M for a Senate race occupies much time of an incumbent. Even incumbents without opposition raise large amounts of money-just in case. An incumbent with a large campaign fund chest is less inviting for a challenger. By and large, incumbents receive the vast bulk of PAC contributions.

G. The Historic Democratic Dominance of Congress. For forty years the Democrats had a strangle-hold on the House. The election of 1994 when the Republicans took control was a bombshell. In the Senate, Republicans took control in 1980, but lost it in 1986. They too regained control in the 1994 elections. Democratic control of the Congress has been attributed to:

1. Predominance of Democratic registered voters. Party affiliation is a large predictor of voting.

2. Many voted Democratic locally, but Republican nationally.

3. Many looked at their representative to "bring home the bacon" and Democrats were better at doing this.

4.   Democrats enjoyed the advantages of incumbency.

H.   <u>The Republican Revolution?</u> The sweeping Republican victory in 1994 surprised most observers. Why did it happen?

    1.   Gingrich and the House Republicans *nationalized* the election focusing voter attention on discontentment with government and its performance.

    2.   The Democrat boast of bringing home the bacon looked foolish in the era of budget deficits.

The Republican victory may be long-lasting. More citizens have begun to identify with the Republican party; more consider themselves more conservative than liberal; and the Republicans have been making big gains in the traditional Democratic South.

IV.   LIFE IN CONGRESS. Attention to your local constituency is the key to survival and success in Congress. Without attention to your base, you lose touch and become part of the "beltway." This was part of former Speaker Foley's problem.

A.   <u>The "Representativeness" of Congress</u>. A large majority of the Congress is still lily white. While Black American, Hispanic and women representation has gone up significantly in the past years, they are still underrepresented as a percent of their respective populations-Black representatives equal 9% of House but blacks are 12% of the population; Hispanics representatives equal 4% of House membership but Hispanics are 9 % of the population. There are now six women senators or 6% of the Senate. Women equal about 50% of the U.S. Population. For two profiles, see <u>People in Politics: Carol Moseley Braun and Ben Nighthorse Campbell, Minority Faces in Congress</u>.

B.   <u>Congressional Staff</u>. In the1950s, there were abut 3,000 staff and support personnel. Now there are more than 25,000. Each representative has a staff of about 20 headed by an administrative assistant with legislative assistants, secretaries, etc. Senators usually have even more staff of 30-50 people. All representatives have Washington offices and local offices; they receive more than $500,000 for office, travel and staff expenses. Senators receive even more-about $2M for expenses. Congress spends over $2B on itself! Staff personnel have great influence over legislation. They move the legislative process. They keep track of bills and amendments. They even handle negotiations over legislation with special interest groups, and other staff members. They also handle much of the contact with interest groups and constituents. In addition to personal staffs, each committee and sub-committee have their own staff which range in size from 25 to 200 personnel. These are subject to the Chairman's control; although some committee staff is reserved for the minority party. If there is a change in party control or chairperson control, some committee staff could be looking for a new position.

C.   <u>Support Agencies.</u> In addition to personal and committee staff, there are four Congressional support agencies to provide assistance to Congressmen: **FILL-IN**

    1.   <u>The Library of Congress and Congressional Research Service (CRS).</u>

2.   General Accounting Office.

2.   Congressional Budget Office

3.   Office of Technology Assessment (OTA).

The creation and growth of congressional support agencies is tied to the continuing struggle between the executive and congressional branches for power.

D.   Workload. Members of Congress put in 12 to 15 hour days and often take work home. A typical day will include:
1.   2-3 hours in committee work
2.   2-3 hours on the floor of the chamber
3.   3-4 hours meeting with constituents, interest group representatives and staff
4.   2-3 hours attending conferences, events or meetings.
Members introduce 10-50 bills/session. Co-sponsoring a bill is very popular. While thousands of bills are introduced, only 600-800 become law/year. There are 900-1,000 recorded votes during a session and each Representative is a member of two standing committees and four subcommittees; each Senator may be a member of 9-12 committees and subcommittees. Meetings of these committees and subcommittees are scheduled each month.

E.   Pay and Perks. In 1991, after passing a 41% increase in pay to $129,000 in the name of reform (since Congress could no longer receive payments from interest groups for appearances and speeches), many taxpayers were outraged since we were in the middle of recession. An amendment had been sent to the states in 1789 with no time limit for ratification that would require a House election to take place before a pay raise would become effective. The amendment was never ratified until 1992 when 3/4ths of the states approved the amendment which is now part of the Constitution. Even so, with Cost of Living Allowances (COL) which Congress voted themselves to take place automatically, but at the same time voted to delay veteran COL, the pay of Congressmen now is $133,600/year. In addition to the pay, Congress has voted itself perks-the House had its own bank which acted as a credit union and which members abused by overdrafts, travel

103

and office expenses, free medical care, free parking at the capitol and airports, free media studios for making self-promotional materials, free mailing privileges, subsidized dining, gift shop and barber shop.

V.   HOME STYLE. Refers to the activities of legislators in promoting their images among constituents and personally attending to constituent problems and interests.

A.   <u>Casework</u>. A form of "retail" politics. This refers to winning one vote at a time. Members of Congress can win votes by helping constituents on a personal level-trace or obtain Social Security cards, Medicare problems, IRS problems, federal job applications-the list is endless. Staff does most of the work, but the letter goes back with the member of Congress's signature (probably by machine). One study indicated House members processed 100 cases/week and Senators 300 cases /week.

B.   <u>Pork Barrel</u>. **FILL-IN. WHY IS PORK BARRELING LESS ADVANTAGEOUS TODAY?**

C.   <u>Pressing the Flesh</u>. Members of Congress spend about 100 days/year in their state or district. While there, it is important to be seen and heard, so they go to dinners, civic affairs, etc. Congress normally handles legislation on a Tuesday-Thursday schedule giving members the opportunity for long weekends at home.

D.   <u>Puffing Images</u>. **FILL-IN.**

VI. ORGANIZING CONGRESS: PARTY AND LEADERSHIP.

A.   <u>Party Organization in Congress</u>. The major party organizations in the Senate and House are the principal means for organizing Congress. Leadership position while nominally elected by the whole body, are really decided in party meetings. Party leadership can help an incumbent be reelected-the right committee assignment is very important. Each party also has a campaign organization which can help funnel funds to their incumbents. Cooperation rather than confrontation is the way to succeed to power and influence in Washington. While calls are heard for party leaders to discipline their members more (and they have the means to do so-committee assignments, support for legislation, denial of campaign funds, etc), this is done only in rare instances. Members of Congress cherish their independence.

B.   <u>In the House: Mr. Speaker.</u> The Speaker serves as both the presiding officer of the House and his party leader in the House. In the event of the death of the President and Vice-President, the Speaker would be next in line to assume the presidency. The Speaker has many powers:

1.   Recognizes speakers on the floor and rules on points of order.
2.   Rules whether a motion or amendment is germane (relevant).
3.   Assigns new bills to committee.
4.   Can delay or schedule votes on a bill.
5.   Names members of select, special and conference committees.
6.   Names the majority members to the Rules Committee.

Because the Speaker represents the whole body, he is expected to apply the rules fairly; however as head of his party he is expected to advance the interests of his party.

C.   <u>House Leaders and Whips.</u> The principal assistant of the Speaker in the House is <u>the Majority leader.</u> He helps formulate the party's legislative program, helps steer it through the House, persuades committee chairs to support the program and helps arrange the legislative schedule. The minority party selects a <u>Minority leader</u>. He essentially does the same as the Majority Leader except schedule legislation. Both parties have <u>whips</u> to keep track of party members, their vote, pressuring them to be present for roll-call votes, and try to determine how they will vote on bills. The whips are part of the power structure and are consulted on the legislative program and scheduling.

D.   <u>In the Senate: "Mr. President"</u>. The official presiding officer of the Senate is the Vice-President. This is his only constitutional duty. However, the Vice-President rarely presides over the Senate since it is boring. The only power of the Presiding Officer is to cast the deciding vote when the Senators' vote is tied.

E.   <u>Senate Majority and Minority leaders.</u> Real Senate leadership is in the hands of the Majority Leader; although he is not as powerful as the Speaker of the House. The Majority leader schedules the business of the Senate and is recognized as the first speaker in floor debate. He is also one of the chief media spokesman for the party. The minority leader represents the opposition party in negotiations with the majority leader.

F.   <u>Career paths within Congress.</u> Leadership is normally achieved by movement up in the party hierarchy. Leadership positions are usually decided by elections and sometimes someone gains entrance into the hierarchy without a prior leadership position.

VII.   IN COMMITTEE. Much of the real work in Congress is done in committees. Usually, the chamber floor is deserted. Only during roll call votes does everyone make an attempt to be on the floor. Many times debate on a bill is done by a few representatives of each side. The TV cameras focus on the speakers. If they panned the chamber, it would be empty.

A.   <u>Standing Committees.</u> Are permanent committees that specialize in some area of legislation. Committee sizes vary from 30-40 in the House to 15-20 in the Senate.

committee is chaired by a member of the majority party. The minority party is represented by the ranking minority member. The principal function of the committees is to screen bills-they serve as gatekeepers. Usually, a bill that does not muster a majority vote in a committee is dead. Most bills die in Committee by either receiving an unfavorable vote or simply by never being discussed. Committee staff and committee members also draft their own bills, offer amendments, and rewrite bills. See Table 10-5 for a list of Standing Committees.

B.   Decentralization and Subcommittees. Congressional subcommittees further decentralize the legislative process. The House has about 90 and the Senate 70 subcommittees-each headed by a Chairman. They are largely independent of their parent committee. They have their own staffs and budget. They meet and schedule their own hearings. But any bill approved by a subcommittee still has to go to the full committee which normally also approves it. This decentralization of power occurred in early 1970s as the result of younger Democratic House members who wanted more independence and power. Formerly, interest groups could concentrate on a few house leaders and chairpersons of standing committees. But now with power decentralized, interest groups must pay attention to virtually every subcommittee. Executive agencies must do likewise. The result has been a considerable increase of policy networks. Chairing a committee is an opportunity to exercise power, attract media attention, and improve reelection chances. Sometimes committee chairs run their committee or subcommittee like "fiefdoms" and jealously guard their power. The decentralization of power weakens responsible government because party leaders do not have the power to push their party's legislative agenda through. See Up Close: The House Tries to Reform Itself for new House reform rules.

C.   Committee Membership. Members strive for committee assignments that will give them influence, allow the exercise of power, and improve their reelection chances. Party leadership in each chamber largely determines committee assignments.

D.   Seniority. Although committee chairs are elected by the majority caucus, the seniority system is still largely followed. The seniority system has a long tradition in the Congress. It permits conflict-management which might result if everyone was jockeying for a chair; it increases stability in policies overtime, but it also rewards committee members from "safe" districts.

E.   Committee Hearings. The decision to hold public hearing on a bill signals congressional interest in a particular policy matter and sets the agenda. They allow interest groups and government bureaucrats to be heard for the record. Staff members plan the meeting under direction of the Chair and contact favorite lobbyists and bureaucrats and schedule their appearances. The purpose of the hearing is not so much to inform Congress as it is to rally popular support via the media.

F.   Markup. Once hearings are completed, the committee staff usually writes a report and drafts a bill. Both normally reflect the Chair's position. But the

106

committee members can markup the bill-that is consider it line by line and propose any changes they think necessary. Markup sessions are usually closed to the public and interest groups to expedite the process. This is where the detailed work of lawmaking takes place and this is where experience pays off. Consensus and deal making are the order of the day.

G. Discharge Petition. House members who have a bill bottled up in committee can try to remove the bill from the committee for further consideration by use of a discharge petition. If 218 members of the House sign the petition, it is removed from the committee and considered by the whole House. Because it requires a majority of House members to sign the petition, it is usually interpreted as a slap at the majority leadership and for that reason, very few are ever successful. It could happen where the leadership wanted a bill, but the committee chair for some reason did not and refused to cooperate with the leadership.

VIII. ON THE FLOOR. A favorable committee vote enables a bill to be placed on a calendar. Even this does not guarantee success, since many bills die on the calendar.

A. House Rules Committee. In the House, prior to consideration by the full membership, the bill requires favorable action by the Rules Committee. This committee may refuse to issue a rule for the bill which effectively kills it. Or it may attach a rule to the bill which is simply when the bill will be considered by the full House, how long it will be debated and whether any amendments will be allowed. A closed rule prohibits any amendments. A restricted rule allows a few, an open rules allows an unlimited amount. The bill comes to the floor with a proposed rule. Before debating the bill, the House must agree to accept the rule which it normally does with little debate. Most bills carry closed or restrictive rules. The House also has a germane rule-that is, a proposed amendment must be related to the bill.

B. Senate Floor Traditions. The Senate has no comparable gatekeeper Rules committee like the House, but instead relies on unanimous consent agreements negotiated between the majority and minority leader and their staffs. This agreement specifies when a bill will be considered, what amendment will be considered, and when a final vote will be taken. Any Senator can object to the agreement, but this happens rarely. The Senate also has the tradition of the filibuster which permits a determined minority to talk the bill to death. Senate rules also allow a Senator to place a hold on a bill-indicating their unwillingness to allow a unanimous consent agreement. To cut off a filibuster, sixteen Senators can petition to cut off debate. Two days must elapse before the petition introduction and the cloture vote. If 60 Senators vote for the petition, each Senator is allowed only one more hour of debate. The Senate does not have a germane rule and any Senator can propose an amendment to a bill which my be totally disconnected from the bill. For example, an abortion provision of law could be attached to an interior bill concerning national parks. The Senate traditions of unlimited debate and non-germane amendments gives Senators more legislative power than Representatives.

C.   Floor Voting. Key floor votes are usually on amendments. Sometimes "Killer amendments" are proposed with the objective of killing the main bill if they are adopted. Votes are by voice-yea/nay or recorded roll-call votes. In the House a roll call vote is done electronically, in the Senate bound by tradition, roll-call votes are by voice.

D.   Conference Committees. The Constitution requires that both chambers of the Congress pass a bill with identical wording. Sometimes one chamber will just adopt the other chamber's bill. But sometimes the differences are so great, that the bills must be assigned to a conference committee to be worked out. These are temporary committees and the leadership assigns the members, usually senior members of the standing committees that considered each bill. The task of the conference committee is to write a single compromise bill that will pass each house without amendments since none are allowed. Research indicates that the Senate provisions of the bill have tended to be adopted more than House provisions.

IX.   DECISION MAKING IN CONGRESS. There are various factors that have been used to analyze voting in Congress. Among them are:

A.   Party voting. This is when the majority of one party votes one way and the majority of the opposition party the other way. About half the roll call votes exhibit party voting and it appears more common in the House than the Senate. Party Unity is the percent of Republicans voting with Republicans and likewise for the Democrats. Over the past 20 years, Republican unity has been 75-85%. Democratic unity was less due to Southern Democrat defections, but now is less of a problem. **WHY?** One explanation of party unity is that the members in each party are ideologically likeminded-the Democrats more liberal and the Republicans more conservative. On many policy issues, there is bi-partisan support of the goal, but party disunity on the means. Welfare reform was a bi-partisan goal, but there was considerable difference over the details. Foreign policy used to be fairly bi-partisan, but this eroded during the Vietnamese War. Since parties organize the legislature, members of these parties have a vested interest in their party's fortunes and policies.

B.   Presidential Support or Opposition. Presidents always receive more support from his party members in the legislature. With divided government (where one party control the presidency and the other the legislature), presidential support or opposition is less operable and becomes more obstructionist. Presidential influence then is reduced by the other party, the electoral independence of legislators, and the decentralization of Congress. When negotiations break down, the President can try to appeal directly to the people via the media or threaten a veto.

C.   Constituency Influence. If an issue has attracted media attention and generates intense feeling among the legislator's constituency, members of Congress almost always defer to constituent's views regardless of party, leadership or even their own feeling. This even applies to representatives from safe seats. Economic issues are the most likely to generate constituency pressure. Also the member lives in the community and possibly grew up there-so they have absorbed and internalized the views of their community. On most issues, the constituents are not aware, and thus the legislator has considerable leeway as to their vote.

    D.   <u>Interest-Group Influence.</u> **FILL-IN. WHO IS A CASH CONSTITUENT?**

    E.   <u>Personal Values</u> **FILL-IN. WHAT IS THE DIFFERENCE BETWEEN A TRUSTEE AND A DELEGATE REPRESENTATIVE? WHERE DID THIS DESIGNATION OF REPRESENTATIVES ORIGINATE?**

X.   CUSTOMS AND NORMS. These are designed to help members work together, reduce interpersonal conflict, facilitate and promote compromise and make life a little more pleasant in Congress. The addressing of each other follows a decorum-"my colleague from Indiana" etc. But recently decorum has been breaking down and daily life in the Capitol has become more brutish.

    A.   <u>Apprentice Role.</u> One norm was for freshmen legislators to be subservient to more senior members-"be seen and not heard". This norm is dead! Freshmen are now "seen and heard".

    B.   <u>Specialization and Deference.</u> The committee and subcommittee structure facilitates specialization in certain areas. Party members are expected to give deference to party experts in these specialized areas. When the issue is technical or complicated or outside the members own area of policy specialization, the system works. On major public issues, it does not work.

    C.   <u>Bargaining.</u> This is central to the legislative process as it facilitates compromise. A member is not expected to violate their conscience in a bargain, but normally there is much leeway available for bargaining. Most bargains take place in committee meeting and are thus largely out of the public view. This system has also been compared to "horse trading". Bargains may be implicit-you vote for my bill, I'll vote for yours" or they may be explicit-"You support me now and I'll catch you later." Bargaining requires integrity. A deal is a deal. Members must stick to agreements.

    D.   <u>Reciprocity.</u> Another form of bargaining. "You keep out of my hair and I'll keep out of yours." The norm of reciprocity facilitates compromise and agreement and thus helps get the work of Congress done.

    E.   <u>Logrolling.</u> Another form of reciprocity. This is a mutual agreement to support projects that primarily benefit individual members of Congress and their constituents.

    F.   <u>Leader-Follower Relations.</u> Since members are largely independent and the means of discipline relatively few, leaders have to rely on their bargaining skills to get cooperation. There are some tangible benefits that can be granted or withheld-to be recognized as a speaker, favorable treatment of a bill, including a favorable Rule, good committee assignment, etc. In the long run, alienating a party leader is not a path to a successful career in the legislature.

XI. CONGRESSIONAL ETHICS. While some may consider "Congressional ethics" to be an oxymoron, morality is a relative term in regards to Congress. In times past, it was even worse. Railroad baron's representatives traveled to Washington, D.C. with suitcases of money to buy votes. Congress over the years has established not only ethic codes but Ethnic committees as well.

A. Some of the rules include:
1. Financial disclosure-All members must file annual personal financial statements.
2. Honoria-Now forbidden to accept fees for speeches or personal appearances.
3. Campaign Funds-surplus funds cannot be for personal use.
4. Gifts-Representatives cannot accept any gift more than $200; Senators are allowed a $300 limit.
5.
6.

These rules while an improvement has not restored confidence in Congress-the House Bank scandal and use of stamp funds for personal cash tarnished anew the credibility of Congress. See Up Close: The Keating Five: Service to Constituents, for what price?

B. Expulsion. Each chamber under the Constitution has the power to discipline its members for "disorderly conduct." What this means is anyones guess? Expulsion is the most severe penalty. It is not a criminal conviction. During the Abscam scandal FBI sting operation, several members of Congress were compromised and videoed accepting bribes which is against the law. Only one member of the House was expelled-the first since the Civil War. Most members resign rather than face expulsion which would cut off their pension-if they resign they may still get a pension. This was the case with Senator Packwood in 1995.

C. Censure. A lesser form of punishment, but still humiliating. The chamber votes a motion of censure and the object of the censure has to stand in front of the chamber as the motion is read and voted upon. Sometimes censure can be used by an opponent in the next election-but even with censure, some are reelected.

CHAPTER 10 SAMPLE QUESTIONS

TRUE-FALSE QUESTIONS:

1. It is easier for the Congress to obstruct the policy initiatives of the president than it is to assume policy leadership itself.

2. House members face reelection every four years.

3. A House member must live in the district he/she represents.

4. Congress is more powerful in domestic than in foreign and military affairs.

5. The War Powers Act of 1973 has greatly restrained the use of military power by the president.

6. The Line item veto for the president starting in January 1997, will probably weaken Congress's Power of the Purse.

7. Congressional hearings and investigations often involve agenda setting.

8. Congressional district lines are drawn by the House of Representatives.

9. Members of Congress are political entrepreneurs.

10. The best chance for an aspirant to a congressional career is when there is an open seat.

MULTIPLE-CHOICE QUESTIONS:

11. The House has the sole constitutional power to:
    a. Appropriate money   b. Originate tax bills
    c. Declare War   d. Try impeachments

12. Which of the following is not a characteristic of Senators:
    a. Minimum age 25   b. Six year term of office
    c. U.S. citizen for 9 years d. Resident of state they represent.

13. Which of the following was not a declared war:
    a. War of 1812   b. Mexican War in 1848
    c. Spanish-American War in 1898   d. Korean War

14. The real reasons for congressional oversight of executive agencies include all but one of the following:
    a. secure favorable treatment for friends and constituents.
    b. lay the groundwork for increases/decreases of agency budgets.

c. influence executive branch decisions   d. praise presidential appointees.

15. When congressional or state districts have grossly unequal numbers of people, this is called:
    a. Apportionment   b. Malapportionment
    c. Redistricting   d. gerrymandering

16. States are required to redistrict every:
    a. after every election   b. 5 years   c. 10 years   d. every 20 years

17. The Voting Rights Act extends special protection to:
    a. African-Americans   b. Hispanics
    c. Asians   d. All of the above

18. The most common occupational background of Representatives is:
    a. law b. business   c. Public Service   d. Journalism

19. A "safe seat" is where the incumbent wins reelection by a margin of:
    a. Over 70%   b. Over 65%   c. Between 55-60%
    d. Between 50-55%.

20. American confidence in various institutions is determined by various polls.
In 1996, the institution receiving the lowest confidence rating was:
    a. Law firms b. The press   c. Congress
    d. The executive branch

21. The average challenger for a congressional seat spends:
    a. Over $550,000   b. Over $588,000   c. Over $3M
    d. Under $240,000.

22. All but one of the following is a Congressional Support Agency:
    a. Office of Management and Budget   b. General Accounting Office
    c. Library of Congress   d. Congressional Budget Office

23. The annual base pay of a member of Congress is about:
    a. $99,000   b. $200,000   c. $133,000 d. Over $200,000

24. The presiding officer of the Senate is:
    a. Vice-President   b. Majority Leader   c. President Pro Tempore
    d. Majority Whip

25. When a committee goes over a bill line by line, this is called:
    a. Rule   b. Mark-up   c. bill drafting   d. hearing

CHAPTER 10 SAMPLE QUESTION ANSWERS

TRUE-FALSE ANSWERS:

1. **TRUE.** As Gingrich found out with the Contract with America, it is hard for Congress to assume policy leadership against the determined opposition of the President. See page 329.

2. **FALSE.** House members must run every two years. This means they work one year and run for reelection the second year. And we wonder why nothing every gets done in Washington? Reforms call for a 4 year term with elections to coincide with the presidential election. Refer to page 330.

3. **FALSE.** While most do live in their district, Article 1, Section 2 of the Constitution specifies that they need only be a resident of the state they represent.

4. **TRUE.** This has been true for since the very beginning because of the President's role as Commander-in-Chief. See page 330.

5. **FALSE.** It was passed over President Nixon's veto, but both Republican and Democratic presidents have ignored its restrictions. See page 331.

6. **TRUE.** Thus, it was with some surprise when Congress approved the line item veto for the president. Harry Truman speaking of the presidency said: "The buck stops here." With this type of veto, there will be a sole point of responsibility and accountability.

7. **TRUE.** Bringing issues to the attention of the media and public can get them on the national agenda. See page 332.

8. **FALSE**. They are drawn by state legislatures and approved by state governors.
See page 337.

9. **TRUE.** They sell themselves. Refer to page 338.

10. **TRUE.** About 10% of Congressional seats come open every election as incumbents retire or try for higher office. This is the best chance to win a Congressional seat for a challenger.

MULTIPLE-CHOICE ANSWERS:

11. **B** Appropriating money is not the same as originating tax bills and trying impeachments is not the same as bringing impeachment charges. The Senate has the sole power to try impeachments and shares power with the House in appropriating money. See Table 10-1.

12. **A.** The minimum age for a Senator is 30. Article I, Section 3 of the Constitution is

applicable.

13. **D** The Korean war was not a declared war but one conducted under UN auspices. See page 331.

14. **D** Rarely if ever is a congressional oversight for praise, but rather for embarrassment. Refer to page 331.

15. **B** The other answers are in the same topic area but refer to other things. See page 333.

16. **C** Redistricting is keyed to the decennial census done by the Commerce Department in conforming to Article I, Section 2 of the Constitution.

17. **D** Also to American Indians and Alaskan natives. See page 337.

18. **A** This is also true in the Senate. Refer to Table 10-2.

19. **C** Winning by 55 to 60% of the vote indicates the incumbent faced no serious challenge. See page 340.

20. **C** Congress is dead last just as in 1990. See page 345.

21. **D** See Table 10-3

22. **A** OMB is an executive agency, the rest belong to Congress. See page 352.

23. **C** This is just the tip of the iceberg. Twenty-six round trips/year back home are paid by the taxpayers. Congressmen have reserved parking at airports. They don't have to look for a parking space! See pages 353-354.

24. **A** The only Constitutional duty of the Vice-President is to preside over the Senate which is rarely done. That's why there is a position President Pro Tempore. But this officer does not preside either. Catch C-Span sometime when the Senate is in session and identify the Presiding Officer. Refer to page 358.

25. **B** The staff draft is subject to committee mark-up which is a line-by-line look at the draft's wording. See page 366.

I. PRESIDENTIAL POWER. There are many aspects to presidential power. Some are:
  A. <u>The Symbolic President.</u> The president is seen as the symbol of the nation. As the nation's leading celebrity, the office is the focus of public and world attention. The President also gives expression to the nation's pride in victories, whether it be the national champion football team or 1996 Olympians.
  B. <u>Crisis Manager.</u> Whether it is a flood in the mid-West or a Hurricane Andrew, people look to the president for words of concern and comfort.
  C. <u>Providing Policy Leadership.</u> The President is expected to set priorities for policies since most originate with the executive branch. As a political leader, the president must rally support for these policies, both with Congress and the general public.
  D. <u>Managing the Economy.</u> The American people hold the president responsible for a healthy economy. If it falters, he will be blamed rightly or wrongly. If the economy is good, the president will take credit for its performance. High unemployment, high interest rates, raising inflation and poor stock/bond markets are all warning signals to an incumbent president. The president must have a game plan to lower taxes, create jobs and economic growth, cut/raise spending, lower interest rates, and improve America's competitiveness in the global economy. Public expectation of the president's power far exceeds his actual power. In most cases, government action does not immediately correct the ills in the economy as there is a lag time.
  E. <u>Managing the Government.</u> As the CEO of a $1.6 trillion enterprise with over 2.8M employees, the president is responsible for implementing policy which includes:
    1. Issuing orders.
    2. Creating organizations.
    3.
    4.
    5.
    6. Evaluating results.
  F. <u>The Global President.</u> The president is the single voice in international affairs. The president is the commander-in-chief and it is this office that orders the armed forces into combat.

CONSIDERING THE ABOVE, NAME THE FIVE GREATEST AND FIVE WORST U.S. PRESIDENTS.

II. CONSTITUTIONAL POWERS OF THE PRESIDENT. Compared to Congress, the office of the president has fewer specified powers. But the presidents over time have used these powers quite well and expanded them to the fullest.
  A. <u>Who May be President?</u> Any thirty-five year old, natural-born citizen who has

been a resident in the U.S. for over 14 years is eligible. The original Constitution fixed the term of office as four years but did not specify how many terms a president could have. George Washington started the tradition of only serving two terms (8 years) which endured until Franklin Roosevelt ran for a third and fourth term. In reaction, the Republican controlled Congress in 1947 proposed the 22nd Amendment which was ratified in 1951. This amendment formally limits the president to two terms.

B. Presidential Succession. Although the original Constitution provided for the replacement of the President for death, resignation, removal or inability with the Vice-President, there was no provision for a serious presidential illness nor any procedure to replace the Vice-President who might have to take the President's place. The 25th Amendment allows the Vice-President and a majority of the cabinet to notify Congressional leaders in writing that the president is unable to discharge his powers and duties. The Vice-President becomes acting president. The President may inform Congress in writing that no inability exists. If the VP and majority of the cabinet disagree, Congress must decide the issue within 21 days. A two-thirds vote in each chamber is required to replace the President by the Vice-President. This procedure has never been used to date. But the amendment also provided for selection of a vice-president which was necessary to use. Vice-President Spiro Agnew resigned in the face of bribery charges. Nixon nominated Gerald Ford as Vice-President who was confirmed by a majority vote of each chamber. Later, Nixon resigned and Ford assumed the presidency. He nominated Nelson Rockefeller as Vice-President who was also confirmed by the Congress. In effect, we had neither a president or vice-president elected by the people.

C. Impeachment. The House of Representatives has the power to impeach the president and other executive officials; and judicial personnel for reasons of treason, bribery or other high crimes or misdemeanors. Political disagreements are not a cause. Once impeached, the accused would stand trial in the Senate which could vote to remove the official by at least a 2/3s majority. Once removed, the official is barred from ever holding federal office again. Only one president was impeached-Andrew Johnson. In the Senate trial, the majority of Senators voted for his removal, but their votes fell short of the 2/3 minimum, by one vote. President Nixon resigned rather than face impeachment.

D. Presidential Pardons. The Constitution gives the president the power to grant reprieves and pardons. This is an absolute power, not subject to congressional review or judicial action. The most modern controversial pardon was when President Ford granted former President Nixon a full, blanket pardon.

E. Executive Power. Is this executive power broad or limited? This is an ongoing debate between liberals and conservatives. History has generally supported an expansive view of this power. Some examples:
1. Washington's issuance of a Neutrality Proclamation in the war between France and England.

2.

3.

4.   Lincoln's blockade of Southern ports, declaration of martial law and Emancipation Proclamation.

5.   Franklin Roosevelt's temporary closing of the nation's banks during the Great Depression and incarceration of Japanese-Americans during World War II.

F.   <u>Checking Presidential Power.</u> President Truman's seizure of the nation's steel mills during the Korean War was declared unconstitutional by the Supreme Court.

G.   <u>Executive Privilege</u> Through the ages, the presidents have claimed the right to confidentiality to protect national security and sensitive discussions within the White House. Congress has never recognized this executive privilege. The courts have generally refrained from interfering, but did so in U.S. v. Nixon (1974) when it said the executive privilege did not cover criminal acts. But the Supreme Court did allow that this privilege might be invoked to cover military or diplomatic matters.

H.   <u>Presidential Impoundments</u> While the Constitution forbids the president to spend money not appropriated, it is silent whether the president has to spend money appropriated. Various presidents refused to spend certain appropriations, but in 1974 Congress passed the Budget and Impoundment Act which requires the president to spend appropriated money. He can propose <u>deferrals</u>-postpone spending or <u>recessions</u>-canceling the spending. Congress by resolution (not subject to presidential veto) may vote to restore the deferrals and a recession cannot proceed unless both chambers approve the recession.

I.   <u>The Constitution's Congressional Tilt</u>. The Constitution gives Congress the upper hand:

1.   Override of presidential veto by 2/3 majority in each chamber.
2.   Impeach and remove the president.
3.   Only Congress can appropriate $$$.
4.   Major presidential appointments require Senate confirmation.
5.   President must faithfully execute the laws.

Congress <u>constitutionally</u> dominates the American government, but the president <u>politically</u> dominates the nation's public affairs.

III.   POLITICAL RESOURCES OF THE PRESIDENT. The principle tool is the power to persuade. The president is center of focus and attention and can communicate directly to the American people.

A.   <u>Reputation for Power.</u> To be effective, the president must be perceived as powerful. One seen as weak will not be very effective.

B. <u>Presidential Popularity.</u> National opinion polls regularly track presidential popularity. This is usually very high at the beginning of the president's term of office, but is normally very brief. After this, it fluctuates up and down, but the overall trend is down. Presidents usually recover some popularity if they run for reelection. Presidential popularity rises during periods of crisis, especially facing an international threat or military conflict. President Bush's approval reached 89% during Desert Storm, but one year later he was defeated for reelection. On the other hand, major scandals hurt popularity and approval. e.g. Nixon and Reagan. Economic recessions hurt the incumbent president.

C. <u>Access to the Media.</u> The president dominates the news. The most skilled reporters are assigned to the White House. Presidential press secretaries brief reporters daily. The president can use press conferences to advance his agenda. Presidents can also make a national address during prime time. Some networks are reluctant to provide coverage and most include time for an opposition reply. In addition, the president can use addresses at national meetings, college and university commencements, etc. to maintain contact with the American people.

D. <u>Party Leadership.</u>   **FILL-IN**

IV. CHIEF EXECUTIVE. The president presides over a huge enterprise-2.8M employees, 60 independent agencies, 14 departments, and the large Executive Office of the President. Yet the president cannot command this bureaucracy like a military officer or corporation president.

A. <u>The Constitutional Executive.</u> The Constitution is rather vague about presidential power. It grants executive power to the president, and gives authority for the president to appoint principal officers with advice and consent of the Senate, and allows the president to require opinions in writing from these principal officers on subject matter in their departments. And the Constitution charges the president to faithfully execute the laws. But Congress also has great constitutional power over the executive branch-the power of the purse and impeachment. It can also establish or abolish executive departments, agencies, etc. and perform oversight over these executive departments, agencies, etc.

B. <u>Executive Orders.</u> Presidents issue about 50-100 such orders every year. They usually direct specific federal agencies to pursue the president's wishes or desired course of action. These orders may be based on the president's constitutional powers or powers delegated to the president by laws passed by Congress. While most are somewhat mundane, some stand out. President Truman's E.O. 9981 in 1948 ordering desegregation of the armed forces and President Johnson's E.O.

11246 requiring private firms with federal contracts to institute affirmative action programs.

C. Appointments The President can appoint only about 3,000 of the 2.8M civilian employees of the federal government. These are top officials such as: cabinet secretaries, agency heads, and White House staff. These people are selected because they share the president's policy views. However, a great many factors influence their selection: interest group support, unifying various parts of the party, rewarding political loyalty, finding jobs for unsuccessful candidates; seek a balance of gender, ethnic and racial representatives. Presidents have very limited power to remove independent regulatory agency members. Having a loyal follower at the head of an agency does not guarantee presidential control over the agency. Career bureaucrats have the knowledge, skill and experience to frustrate directives they do not like; rather than fight this bureaucracy, some appointees "go native" and yield to the bureaucrats, special interests and congressional committees that determine the agencies budget and future. Republican presidents have more of a problem in this area, since the majority of career bureaucrats are Democrats.

D. Budget. FILL-IN. **WHICH AGENCY IN THE EXECUTIVE OFFICE OF THE PRESIDENT IS IN CHARGE OF THE BUDGET?**

E. The Cabinet. FILL-IN. **WHY IS THE CABINET RARELY A DECISION-MAKING BODY?**

F. The National Security Council. Created in 1947 by the National Security Act. Chaired by the President, statutory members are the Vice-President, and Secretaries of State and Defense. The Director of the CIA and the Chairman of the Joint Chiefs of Staff are statutory advisors to the NSC. This body advises the President in matters involving foreign, defense and intelligence activities.

G. White House Staff. Contains the closest allies and advisors of the president. None are subject to Senate confirmation, so their loyalty is to the president. Positions include: Chief of staff, senior advisors, press secretary, National Security advisor, counsel to the president, director of personnel, etc.

V. CHIEF LEGISLATOR AND LOBBYIST. About 80% of the bills considered by

Congress are originated in the executive branch.

A.   Policy Initiation. The president uses the annual State of the Union address before a joint session of Congress as the principal opportunity to make a policy statement and address necessary legislation. This is followed by the president's recommended budget which contains the president's programs with price tags. While Congress will not rubber stamp the budget, it still sets the agenda for debate and further Congressional action. During the year, many other executive departments will draft legislation and transmit it to the White House for review and approval after which it will be sent to Congress for further action.

B.   White House Lobbying. The White House employs a legislative liaison section which tracks bills, attends committee hearings, arranges executive branch witnesses, and advises the president as to legislative status and which bills need help by the president. The White House is not without weapons. They have many favors at their disposal. Support for projects in Congressional districts or states, invitations to state dinners and ceremonies, speeches in one's district with an invitation to accompany the president on Air Force One. In addition, the president can "twist arms" of individual representatives or senators by personally calling them and appealing to party loyalty, etc.

C.   The Honeymoon. **FILL-IN   HOW LONG DOES THE HONEYMOON LAST?**

D.   Presidential "Scorebox". Of legislation in which there was a clear presidential interest, how did the president fare? The most important determinant is whether the president's party controls Congress. Where this is true, the presidential success rate is very high. See Figure 11-5. Where the opposition party controls Congress, the president's success rate falls dramatically.

E.   Veto Power.   **FILL-IN. WHAT HAPPENS IF THE PRESIDENT FAILS TO SIGN A BILL AFTER 10 DAYS (NOT INCLUDING SUNDAYS)? WHAT IS A POCKET VETO? IF THE PRESIDENT VETOES A BILL, WHAT THEN?** Table 11-3 shows the veto override % of various presidents. **OVERALL, WHAT % OF VETOES ARE OVERTURNED?**

F.   Line-Item Veto. Commencing in 1997, the president will have a line item veto. It will be interesting to see how and when this veto will be exercised and whether

120

Congress can override the line item vetoes.

VI.   GLOBAL LEADER. The president of the United States is the leader of the world's largest and most powerful democracy. In the new global order, the U.S. can no longer dictate its will, must still must provide necessary leadership. This leadership is based on the president's power of persuasion. This is enhanced by a strong economy, military forces and support of the American people and Congress. Abroad, the president is treated with respect and dignity; while at home he must contend with interest groups, opposition party resistance, hostile press, etc. It is little wonder presidents prefer their global role.

A.   Foreign Policy. The President has the power to make treaties (subject to Senate ratification), appoints U.S. diplomatic personnel (subject to Senate confirmation), and receives foreign ambassadors. The president exercises the power of diplomatic recognition which is the granting of legitimacy to a foreign government. The president's role in foreign policy is strengthened by his role as Commander-in-Chief because military force is the ultimate diplomatic language. The president is the official spokesman for the United States in the world community of nations.

B.   Treaties   **FILL-IN. HOW MANY SENATORS MUST RATIFY A PROPOSED TREATY? IN THE CASE WHERE A TREATY PROVISION INTERFERED WITH A PROVISION IN THE STATE CONSTITUTION OF NEW YORK, WHICH WOULD BE UPHELD?**

C.   Executive Agreements. Made by the president with another head of state. Do not require Senate ratification. They are based on president's constitutional power to execute the laws, command the armed forces and determine foreign policy. They cannot supersede laws of the U.S. or any state. Congress does not like executive agreements which are not discussed in the Constitution. Congress passed the Case Act of 1972 which requires the president to notify Congress of any executive agreement within 60 days.

D.   Intelligence. The president is responsible for the intelligence activities of the U.S. The Director of Central Intelligence is appointed by the president and confirmed by the Senate. The DCI directly supervises the Central Intelligence Agency (CIA) and coordinates the activities of the National Security Agency (NSA)-electronic surveillance and the National Reconnaissance Office (NRO)-satellite surveillance.

1.   CIA-responsible for the collection, analysis, preparation and distribution of intelligence information within the government. The CIA engages in covert intelligence collection which the employment of spies. The CIA also engages in covert operations which means that their sponsorship of

121

the activity is hidden. Covert intelligence and operations require a high degree of secrecy. As a result of the Watergate scandal, both the House and the Senate established intelligence oversight committees and require a written "Presidential finding" authorizing covert operations. The president does not have to obtain Congressional approval for covert operations, but Congress can halt such actions if it chooses. For example, the Boland amendments prohibited the administration spending federal funds to aid the contras in Nicaragua.

    2.   NSA-analyzes and distributes information derived from electronic sources-radar, radio, telephone. NSA is also in charge of <u>decryption</u>-deciphering coded transmissions from other nations and <u>encryption</u>-coding U.S. transmissions so that other nations cannot read our mail.

    3.   NRO-plans, orders and launches spy satellites. Receives information from them, analyzes it and promulgates it within the government.

VII.   COMMANDER-IN-CHIEF. The President can issue orders to the military. George Washington is the only president to have personally led troops into conflict in the Whiskey rebellion in 1794. The presidents have ordered U.S. troops into combat over 200 times. Congress has the sole power to declare war, but we have had only 5 declared wars.

    A.   <u>War Powers Act.</u> Passed in 1973 at the height of the anti-Vietnamese movement in this country, it was an attempt by Congress to control presidential use of the armed forces. The Act has four provisions:

        1.   In the absence of a congressional declaration of war, the president can use armed forces only:

            a.   To repel an attack on the U.S. or imminent threat of attack

            b.   To repel an attack on U.S. armed forces outside the country or forestall such an attack

            c.   Protect and evacuate U.S. citizens and nationals in another country if their lives are endangered.

        2.   President must promptly report the use of force to the Congress

        3.   Involvement must be no longer than 60 days unless Congress authorizes more time.

        4.   Congress can terminate a presidential use of force by a resolution, not subject to presidential veto.

    B.   <u>Presidential Non-Compliance</u>. There is some question as to the legality of the War Powers Act and presidents, both Democratic and Republican, have largely ignored it. For example, President Clinton's sending of troops to Haiti and Bosnia were not reported under the War Powers Act.

    C.   <u>Presidential Use of Military Force in Domestic Affairs.</u> The Constitution contemplates the use of federal armed forces in states facing domestic violence only when the state legislature or if not in session, the governor requests the help of federal troops. But what happens when states violate federal laws, court orders or constitutional guarantees? Presidents have, in the history of our country, used federal troops-Pullman strike in 1894, in Little Rock in 1957 to enforce a federal court order for desegregation are two good examples.

VIII. VICE-PRESIDENTIAL WAITING GAME. The principal responsibility of the vice-president is to be prepared to step into the president's shoes. Eight VPs have had to do so.

    A. <u>Political Selection Process</u>. Candidates were selected to give geographical balance to the ticket. Some effort is made for ideological balance. Obviously, one consideration in selecting the VP, is finding a candidate who can help the ticket win the White House.

    B. <u>Vice-President roles.</u> Largely determined by the president. The only official duty of the VP is to preside over the Senate. The political function of the VP is more important than the government function. The VP can serve as a "lightening rod" while the president can remain above the fight. VPs can help with fund raising. Lately, presidents have given their VP more responsibility and view them now as senior policy advisors.

    C. <u>The Waiting Game.</u> Most vice-presidents have further ambitions-the Oval Office. Yet they have to be very discreet. They have to support the administration, yet develop an independent organization and agenda. If the outgoing president is popular, the VP can try to run on his success. If the country is going to the dogs, the VP has to run against the administration. Only four VPs have successfully advanced to the White House. Counting four VPs who entered office upon the death of a president and Nixon who lost in 1960, but came back in 1972, in all only 9 VPs have made it to the White House or less than 20%. Obviously, VP is not the best route to the White House!

CHAPTER ELEVEN SAMPLE QUESTIONS

TRUE-FALSE QUESTIONS:

1. Popular expectations of presidential leadership far exceed the office's constitutional powers.

2. The minimum age to become president is 40 years old.

3. If the Vice-President and 6 cabinet officers certify in writing that the president in unable to discharge his duties, the Vice-President becomes acting president.

4. The President and other high executive officials can be impeached by the Senate.

5. More incumbent presidents were defeated for reelection than presidents who decided not to run for reelection.

6. Both liberals and conservatives favor a strong presidency.

7. Congress is constitutionally positioned to dominate the American government.

8. Presidential popularity with the American people is a political resource.

9. The president's ability to appoint executive branch officials gives the president firm control of the bureaucracy.

10. The honeymoon period of the presidency starts about mid-term.

MULTIPLE-CHOICE QUESTIONS:

11. All but one of the following have been rated as great presidents:
    a. Washington   b. Lincoln   c. J.F. Kennedy   d. Jefferson

12. All but one of the following have been rated as below average presidents:
    a. Grant   b. Harding   c. Jackson   d. Nixon

13. The president normally throws out the first baseball to start the season. This would be in his role as:
    a. Symbolic   b. Crisis Management   c. Policy leadership d. Managing the economy

14. The president attends a meeting of the Group of Seven in Paris. This would be in his role as:
    a. Crisis Management   b. Policy leadership c. Managing the economy
    d. global president
15. In the federal government, there are _____ million civilian employees.
    a. 1.0M   b. 2.0M   c. 2.8M   d. More than 3.0M

16. The presidential appointment of federal judges is part of the constitutional powers of the presidency, specifically:
    a. Chief Administrator   b. Chief Legislator   c. Chief Diplomat
    d. Chief of State

17. The president decides that a cabinet officer will not appear before a Congressional committee to discuss a pending treaty negotiation. This would be an example of:
    a. executive agreement   b. executive privilege   c. presidential independence
    d. insubordination.

18. What is the term of office of the president?
    a. 4 years   b. 8 years   c. 10 years   d. Unlimited

19. Which action seeks to cancel an appropriation?
    a. impoundment   b. deferral   c. rescission d. miscue

20. All but one of the following help to explain the president's reputation for political power.
    a. Presidential popularity   b. Access to the media
    c. Party leadership   d. Presidential impeachment.

21. Which Executive office agency gives the president good control of the budget process?
    a. CBO   b. OMB   c. Department of the Treasury
    d. Council of Economic Advisors

22. Which cabinet officer is considered the senior cabinet officer:
    a. State   b. Defense   c. Treasury   d. Attorney General

23. Which of the following is not a full member of the National Security Council?
    a. Vice-President   b. Secretary of State c. Chairman of the Joint Chiefs of Staff
    d. President

24. The president receives a bill and Congress adjourns six days later. If the president does not sign the bill it:
    a. is null and void   b. becomes law automatically
    c. can be kept until Congress comes back   d. must be sent back to the Congress.

25. Over the entire history of the presidency, about what percent of presidential vetoes have been overridden?
    a. 10%   b. 5%   c. 4%   d. Less than 2%

CHAPTER ELEVEN SAMPLE QUESTION ANSWERS

TRUE-FALSE ANSWERS:

1. **TRUE** Our expectations frequently exceed reality. See page 390.

2. **FALSE.** The Constitution states the minimum age is 35. But consider life expectancy in 1787. Thirty-five years old was old. The mortality age of men was about 45. See page390.

3. **FALSE.** The majority of the cabinet needs to sign the certification and 6 cabinet officers would not be a majority. See page 392.

4. **FALSE**. Impeachment is an action of the House not the Senate. See page 393.

5. **TRUE.** Ten presidents running for reelection were defeated while only 7 incumbents decided not to run for a second term. See Up Close-The Road to the White House

6. **TRUE**. See A Conflicting View: Liberals, Conservatives, and Presidential Power.

7. **TRUE**. But the President is better positioned to politically dominate the nation's public affairs. See page 401.

8. **TRUE**. An incumbent president popular in the polls is very hard to defeat for reelection. See page 402.

9. **FALSE.** Most the president cannot fire and as political appointees, they can be captured by career bureaucrats and "go native". See page 404.

10. **FALSE.** The period actually is very early in the term, usually the first 60 days or so. See page 413.

MULTIPLE-CHOICE ANSWERS:

11. **C** Kennedy is the answer. His time in office was very short-3 years. He had the reputation of a playboy. And his legislative accomplishments were not impressive. See Feature-How Would You Rate the Presidents

12. **C** Stonewall Jackson is usually rated as one of the best-the first president to bring the office to the people. See Feature-How Would You Rate the Presidents

13. **A** Clearly symbolic. See page 385.

14. **D** While managing the economy would be a close second, since this is a meeting of the heads of the leading industrialized nations, it is the president acting as a global leader. See page 386.

15. **C** 2.8 million civilian employees is a lot, but that's the payroll! See page 389.

16. **D** Although Chief Administrator seems appropriate, the correct answer is Chief of State. Refer to Table 11-1

17. **B** This would be executive privilege which was officially recognized by the Supreme Court in 1974.

18. **A** The term of office is 4 years. The number of terms was not limited until passage of the 22nd Amendment in 1947. Refer to page 390.

19. **C** Rescission is an attempt to cancel spending; unless both branches concur, the money must be spent according to the Budget and Impoundment Act of 1974. See page 399.

20. **D** Presidential impeachment is a weakness not a strength. See pages 401-404.

21. **B** Office of Management and Budget (OMB) is the answer See page 408.

22. **A** By tradition, the Secretary of State is considered the most senior cabinet official. If a horrible accident were to occur, killing the President, Vice-President, Speaker of the House and President Pro Tempore of the Senate, the next person in line to become president would be the Secretary of State. Refer to page 408.

23. **C** The Chairman of the JCS is a statutory advisor but not a participating member of the NSC. See page 409.

24. **A** A pocket veto essentially kills the bill-it is null and void. Congress can reintroduce the bill when it reconvenes. See page 414.

25. **C** Ninety-six percent of the time, Congress has failed to override the president's veto. Therefore, 4% have been overridden. See Table 11-3.

I.   BUREAUCRATIC POWER. Once a bill is passed by Congress and signed into law by the president, the journey does not end here. For then the law passes into the morass of bureaucracy which has to interpret and implement the law. Americans are very suspicious of bureaucratic power and big government that comes with it. See <u>What Do You Think: Do Bureaucrats have too much Power</u>. **WHAT BUREAUCRACY IS MOST DEEMED TO HAVE TOO MUCH POWER? WHICH LEVEL OF GOVERNMENT IS DEEMED MOST TO HAVE THE RIGHT AMOUNT OF POWER?** Bureaucracy is often associated with red tape, paperwork, duplication of effort, waste and inefficiency, yet government is not the only organization with a bureaucracy-churches, businesses, armed forces, etc.-all have established bureaucracies.

      A.   <u>Nature of Bureaucracy.</u> Max Weber rationalized bureaucracy as having these features:

           1.   Chain of Command-hierarchial and command flows downward.

           2.

           3.

           4.

           5.   Impersonality-equal treatment based on merit and rules.

      B.   <u>Growth of Bureaucracy.</u> Due to advances in technology and increase in size and complexity of society. The president and Congress do not have the time nor expertise to concern themselves with the myriad of details involved in legislation. Thus, "technocrats" are necessary to carry out the intent of the law. However, Congress is also to blame when they pass vague and ambiguous laws requiring bureaucratic interpretation. They can show symbolic support for the law, but if it works out badly, they can blame the bureaucracy. Also vague laws play into the hands of special interest groups who can help shape the law like they desire. Another factor is that a growing bureaucracy becomes a power in itself-it feeds on itself-power begets power. A growing budget and more personnel is a sign of power.

      C.   <u>Bureaucratic Power: Implementation.</u> Is the development of procedures and activities to carry out policies legislated by Congress. This may involve creating new agencies or assigning new responsibilities to established agencies, translate laws into operational rules and regulations and allocation of resources-money, personnel, offices and supplies. In some cases, bureaucracies act rapidly to implement the law; in other cases, they seek to delay by holding hearings, failing to allocate sufficient resources, etc.

      D.   <u>Bureaucratic Power: Regulation.</u> Is the writing of formal rules for implementing legislation. The federal government publishes about 60,000 pages of rules annually in the <u>Federal Register.</u> The EPA is probably the most prolific agency in writing rules. There is a procedure established by the Administrative Practices Act of 1946 which governs rule writing:

           1.   Announcement in the <u>Federal Register</u> that a new regulation is under

consideration.

2.

3.

4.

5.

6. Publish the new regulation in the <u>Federal Register.</u> These published regulations have the force of law. Congress can try to amend them, but once published, it is a difficult to change them.

E. <u>Bureaucratic Power: Adjudication.</u> **FILL-IN.**

F. <u>Bureaucratic Power: Administrative Discretion.</u> Most laws have loopholes. Some cases may not fit the law, or rules may conflict. The IRS has thousands of rules, yet there is not uniformity in their administration. Bureaucrats can be helpful or hinder-it depends on their mood??

G. <u>Bureaucratic Power: To What End?</u> Most bureaucrats strongly believe in the value of their programs and their importance. But thcy also seek what most seek-higher pay, greater job security, added power and prestige. Most rarely do bureaucrats request a reduction of authority or budget, or elimination of a program. In fact, it is just the opposite. See <u>Up Close: Why Government Grows, and Grows and Grows.</u> **WHICH REASON DO YOU THINK BEST EXPLAINS THE GROWTH OF GOVERNMENT?**

II. THE FEDERAL BUREAUCRACY. The federal bureaucracy which is concentrated in the executive branch consists of 2.8M civilian employees and 1.4M members of the Armed Forces. It is organized into 14 cabinet departments, 60 independent agencies and the Executive Office of the president. All government spending-federal, state and local equals about $2.5 trillion of which $1.65 trillion is spent by the federal government alone which equals 2/3s of all government spending. This represents 23% of GDP. At the beginning of this century, federal spending was only 2% of GDP. This gives you some idea of how the federal government has grown. One should exercise a note of caution in looking at <u>Compared to What: The Size of other Governments.</u> The U.S. is a federal government where states and local government have independent taxing and spending authority. In contrast, many of the countries listed have unitary govcrnmcnts with centralized national government taxing and spending.

A. <u>Cabinet Departments.</u> These employee about 60% of federal workers. **WHICH DEPARTMENT HAS THE LARGEST BUDGET? WHY? WHICH DEPARTMENT HAS THE LARGEST NUMBER OF PERSONNEL?**

1. <u>State Department</u> (1789) Formulates and executes foreign policy;

negotiates treaties and agreements, represents the U.S. in the UN and more than 50 international organizations; maintains U.S. embassies abroad, issues U.S. passports to U.S. citizens and visas for foreign citizens

2.   Treasury Department (1789). **FILL-IN**

3.   Defense Department (1947) Absorbed the War Department (1789) and Navy Department (1798). Provides military forces to deter war, protect U.S. national security and provide the muscle for U.S. foreign policy.

4.   Interior Department (1849) Public lands and natural resources; American Indian reservations; national parks and historical sites.

5.   Justice Department (1870) Enforces federal laws; including consumer protection, antitrust, civil rights, drug, immigration and naturalization, maintains federal prisons.

6.   Agricultural Department (1889) **FILL-IN**.

7.   Commerce Department (1913) **FILL-IN.**

8.   Labor Department (1913). **FILL-IN.**

9.   Health and Human Services (1953). Administers social welfare for the elderly, children, and youths; protects from unsafe and impure foods, drugs, and cosmetics; operates the Center for Disease Control; funds Medicare and Medicaid programs and Social Security.

10.   Housing and Urban Development (1965) **FILL-IN**

11.   Transportation Department (1966). Nation's highway planning, development and construction; urban mass transit; railroads, aviation, and

safety of waterways, ports, highways, oil and gas pipelines.

    12. <u>Energy Department</u> (1977). Research, development and demonstration of energy technology; marketing federal electric energy; energy conservation; nuclear weapons and materials; regulation of energy production and use; collection and analysis of energy data.

    13. <u>Education Department</u> (1979). Administers and coordinates federal assistance for education.

    14. <u>Veterans Affairs</u> (1989). Administers veteran's programs, including education, housing, medical and burial.

B. <u>Independent Regulatory Commissions</u>. Designed to regulate some sector of society or the economy. They both make, enforce and adjudicate rules. Most organizations are headed by commissions of 5-10 members. They are appointed by the president and confirmed by the Senate. Usually membership is balanced by partisan identification. The president cannot remove a commissioner. They serve staggered terms. While most are outside any cabinet department, there are a few which are within a cabinet department-Food & Drug Administration with HHS, Occupational Safety & Health (OSHA) with Labor and IRS within the Treasury Department. <u>A list of the most prominent regulatory agencies is included in Table 12-2</u>.

C. <u>Independent Agencies</u>. These are outside any cabinet department and are headed by an administrator (not a commission). Administrators are appointed by the president and confirmed by the Senate, <u>but can be dismissed by the president.</u> Thus, they are not truly independent, but report directly to the president. The most powerful independent agency is the EPA.

D. <u>Government Corporations.</u> Relatively very few as compared to most other countries. The Tennessee Valley Authority (TVA) was established during the depression to provide work. It essentially built a series of lakes and dams to generate electrical power and sell it at inexpensive rates to inhabitants in the mid-South. The power capacity of the TVA was crucial for the fabrication of nuclear materials that were used in the atomic bomb. AMTRAC was created by Congress in 1970 to take over the ailing passenger rail lines. It is now profitable and may be sold to private investors. Finally, the U.S. Postal Service was a cabinet department and the source of many patronage jobs. But in 1971, it was made a government corporation with a mandate to at least break even.

E. <u>Contractors and Consultants</u>. While government employee levels have been relatively constant, the growth of government spending has been in this area. Roughly 1/5th of all federal government spending flows through private contractors for supplies, equipment, services, leases, and R&D. Consultants in "think tanks" form an army personnel in the so-called "beltway bandit" areas surrounding our nation's capitol. There are an estimated 150,000 federal contracting offices in nearly 500 agencies that oversee outside contractors and consultants.

III.   BUREAUCRACY AND DEMOCRACY. Should the federal bureaucracy be staffed by people loyal to the president or by nonpartisan people selected on the basis of merit and protected from political influence?

A. The Spoils System. To the victor goes the spoils-so said Senator William Marcy in 1832. The Spoils system is closely associated with the administration of Andrew Jackson elected in 1828. From what started as a policy of rewarding loyal party members, it grew to the bartering and selling of government jobs with attendant scandal. The assassination of President James Garfield by a disgruntled officer seeker set the stage for reform of the spoils system.

B. The Merit System. Passage of the Pendleton Act of 1883 initiated the career federal service and established the Civil Service Commission. Based on competitive examinations, the system initially covered only 10% of federal government employees. By 1978, more than 90% of federal workers were covered by civil service or other merit systems. About 2/3s are under the General Service system and the other third are part of "excepted services" such as the CIA, FBI and Postal Service. The Armed Forces also have their own recruiting and personnel systems. The Civil Service general service system consists of two types of levels-General level with grades from GS-1 to GS-15. College graduates normally enter at the GS-5 level. GS-9 thru GS-12 are technical and supervisory positions. GS-13 thru GS-15 are middle management and highly specialized positions. The other level-Executive Service are GS-16 to GS-18 levels with the GS-18 level being equivalent to a Major General of the Armed Forces. When an opening occurs, the three highest testing individuals are sent to the agency with the opening. The agency is supposed to hire one of the three, with the other two going to a waiting list. by defining the job with very particular requirements, the agency can give special preferences to the chosen few. Once hired and successfully completing a probationary period, an employee can only be fired for "cause." The procedure to fire is lengthy and burdensome. See page 455 for the detailed procedure.

C. The Problem of Responsiveness. **FILL-IN.**

D. The Problem of Productivity. Most federal workers receive pay raises almost automatically. Poor performance seldom is punished. Only 1/10 of 1% of federal employees are fired. Given this situation, there is little incentive to become more productive.

E. Civil Service Reform. President Carter in 1977 pushed through the Civil Service Reform Act of 1978 which abolished the Civil Service Commission and replaced it with the Office of Personnel Management (OPM). The act also streamlined dismissal procedures, established merit pay for middle managers, and created a

Senior Executive Service (SES) for the 8,000 top managers. The SES might be given salary bonuses, transferred among different agencies or demoted, if performance was lacking. Top civilian managers were often seen by their political appointee bosses as impediments to change and the idea of the reform was to move them around, so they could not become an immovable fixture in the agency. Like many reforms, intentions did not become reality. Congress never appropriated any money for merit pay increases. SES personnel have not been transferred and dismissal rates have not essentially changed.

F. <u>Bureaucracy and Representation</u>. In general, the federal bureaucracy mirrors the American population. However, as Table 12-3 shows, top management positions are <u>unrepresentative</u> of the general American population.

IV. BUREAUCRATIC POLITICS. Who does the bureaucracy really work for?

A. <u>Presidential Plums.</u> About 3,000 jobs are directly controlled by the president. Some 700 of these positions are considered "policy making." These include cabinet and sub-cabinet officials, judges, U.S. attorneys, U.S. marshals, ambassadors, and various commissions and boards. There are also "Schedule C" jobs which are described as "confidential or policy determining."

B. <u>Whistleblowers</u>. **FILL-IN.**

C. <u>Agency Culture.</u> **FILL-IN.**

D. <u>Friends and Neighbors.</u> Most bureaucratic hirings take place through the "old boy" network of personal friends and professional associates. The inside candidate learns of the position and can tailor his resume. Sometimes, the individual is requested by name; other times the personal request is tailor made for the applicant.

V. THE BUREAUCRACY AND THE BUDGETARY PROCESS. The annual budget battle is the heart of the federal government. The budget is the single most important policy statement of any government. The president's proposed budget frames the issues. While Congress occasionally frets and fumes, the reality is that final congressional appropriations rarely deviate more than 2 or 3 % from the president's proposed budget. Thus, the president and the OMB in the Executive office have real budgetary power.

A. <u>Office of Management and Budget</u> (OMB). This office has several responsibilities:
1. Preparation of the budget.
2. Improve the organization and management of executive agencies.

133

3.   Coordination of the extensive statistical services of the federal government.

4.   Analyze and review proposed legislation.

Budget preparation begins 16-18 months before the beginning of the fiscal year. The government's fiscal year begins October 1st and ends the following September. The specific fiscal year is keyed to the September year, i.e. the FY 98 budget would end on September 30, 1998. OMB after consultation with the president and his staff develops spending targets or ceilings. Agencies are then instructed to prepare budget submissions in accordance with these targets. After internal coordination, the proposal are sent to OMB which performs its own analysis. Since some budget submissions are over target, OMB has to say NO! The agency head can then try to appeal to the president for relief. But since this is a WIN-LOSE situation (if the agency's budget is increased, some other agency's budget must be cut), appeal to the president is rarely successful.

B.   The President's Budget. By December, the President and OMB spend considerable time looking over the budget submissions, making last minute changes, etc. By late January, the president sends his proposed budget to the Congress. This gives the Congress about 9 months to finish the budget before the beginning of the fiscal year in October.

C.   House and Senate Budget Committees. The president's budget is sent to these committees which rely on the Congressional Budget Office (CBO) to review the president's budget, especially the revenue assumptions. These committees draft a first budget resolution (due May 15th) which sets forth goals or targets to specific committees for their use in the authorization process. If proposed spending by these committees exceeds these targets, the first budget resolution comes back as a reconciliation measure and a second budget resolution (due September 15th) sets binding budget figures for committees.

D.   Congressional Appropriations Committees. Congressional approval of the budget takes the form of 13 separate appropriations bills covering broad areas-defense, commerce, etc. These are first started in sub-committees of the Appropriations committees where agency witnesses, lobbyists, etc. get a change to discuss the bills.

E.   Appropriations Acts. An authorization bill establishes a program and how much money it requires. It does not actually allocate any money. Authorizations for programs may be for a single year or multiple years, e.g. an aircraft carrier. The appropriations bill is for a single year and actually allocates $$$ for the programs. The allocation is frequently less than the authorization. These acts include obligational authority (permission to enter into contracts that require government payments over several years, e.g. aircraft carrier) and outlays (which must be spent in the fiscal year in which they are appropriated.

F.   Continuing Resolutions (CRA) and Shutdowns. Since the fiscal year begins in October, all 13 appropriation bills should be finished before that date. This rarely happens. Up until 1974, the fiscal year began in July. Congress felt it did not

134

have enough time to complete its work by June, so it extended the fiscal year until September so it could complete its work on time. So much for good intentions which is a good illustration of the Peter principle that work expands to fill the time allotted. Constitutionally, no government agency may spend money which has not been appropriated. Thus, if an appropriation bill is not finished, the agency faces a shutdown. To prevent this from happening, Congress normally passes a CRA to provide money for a specified period of time at roughly the same level as the last fiscal year. Sometimes the heat of the budget battle results in a CRA expiration with the executive and legislative branches still engaged in combat. In the FY 1996 budget battles between President Clinton and the Republican Congress, the government shut down a number of times. It really never shuts down completely so temporary layoffs are for "non-essential or non-critical personnel." Since Congress usually provides funds to cover the layoff periods, it amounts to a paid vacation for some government workers.

VI. THE POLITICS OF BUDGETING. Some of the bureaucratic strategies used in the politics of budgeting as shown in <u>Up Close- Bureaucratic Budget Strategies.</u>

    A. <u>Budgeting is Incremental.</u> The most important factor in determining this year's budget is last year's budget. Usually, last year's is used as a base and only changes and increases are really looked at. The result of this <u>incremental budgeting</u> is that many programs and expenditures continue long after there is no need for them. When new needs arise, rather than kill a current program, the needs are added to the budget. **WHY DOES SUCH A SYSTEM EXIST? HOW WOULD YOU EXPLAIN IT? WHAT REFORMS HAVE BEEN SUGGESTED? WHY HAVE THEY FAILED?**

    B. <u>Budgeting is Nonprogrammatic.</u> **FILL-IN. WHY WOULD PROGRAM BUDGETING BE RESISTED BY THE BUREAUCRACY?** See <u>What Do You Think? - How Much Money does the Government Waste?</u>

VII. REGULATORY BATTLES. Virtually every aspect of American life is regulated by some bureaucracy-whether it be interest rates by the Federal Reserve, automobile and airline safety, racial and sexual discrimination in the workplace, etc. Federal regulatory agencies have quasi-executive, legislative and judicial powers-all wrapped into one. They make the rules, investigate complaints and conduct inspections, hold hearings, issue corrective orders, levy fines and penalties.

    A. <u>Traditional Agencies: Capture Theory.</u> **WHAT ARE SOME SPECIFIC EXAMPLE AGENCIES AND WHO ARE THEY CAPTURED BY?**

B.   The Newer Regulators: The Activists. New activist regulatory agencies were created by Congress in the civil rights, environmental and consumer protection areas. Unlike other agencies, these do not concentrate on one industry, but rather regulate activities over a broad spectrum. Examples include: the EPA, Equal Employment Opportunity Commission (EEOC), and Occupational Safety and Health Administration (OSHA). Businesses do not like these activist agencies.

C.   Deregulation. In the 1980s, there was much public pressure to deregulate based on the heavy costs of compliance with regulations, the burdens these placed on innovation and productivity and the adverse impact on global competitiveness. The cost of regulatory compliance is estimated to be $300-$500B annually or approximately 1/4 of the federal budget. This cost is not borne by the government, but rather by business and ultimately the consumer. See Up Close-The Invisible Costs of Regulation. One of the first industries to be deregulated was the airline industry. While there is little doubt that this deregulation led to lower prices and more travelers, it also resulted in less service to outlying areas and the loss of some airlines. The Interstate Commerce Commission established in 1887 was abolished in 1995. Thus, the first regulatory agency was also the first to be abolished.

D.   Reregulation.   **FILL-IN.**

VIII.   CONGRESSIONAL CONSTRAINTS ON THE BUREAUCRACY. Bureaucracies are unelected hierarchial organizations and in a democracy must be responsive to the people. Although, the president is the nominal boss of executive agencies, Congress has its power also in the budget and its power to establish or abolish agencies. Congress can expand or contract the authority of an agency.

A.   In addition, Congress has passed specific legislation which governs the bureaucracy:

1.   Administrative Procedures Act (1946)-requires notification of proposed rules, publication in The Federal Register and the holding of public hearings.

2.   Freedom of Information Act (1966)-allows private inspection of public records, with some exceptions.

3.   Privacy Act (1974)-Requires agencies to observe confidentiality regarding personnel records of individuals.

B.   Senate Confirmation of Appointments. The Senate has the opportunity to scrutinize appointees and ascertain their views. If in disagreement, they can refuse to confirm or delay the confirmation indefinitely.

C.   Congressional Oversight. **FILL-IN**

D.   Congressional Appropriations. **FILL-IN**

E.   Congressional Investigations. **FILL-IN**

F.   Casework. Responding to calls, letters, faxes, telegrams, etc from constituents in their state or district requesting information or action, legislators frequently contact regulatory agencies for their assistance. Congressional requests are handled expeditiously and when possible every effort is made to respond favorably to the Congressional inquiry.

G.   Legislative Veto. Congress will often pass vague legislation. A legislative veto was a provision in the legislation that required the executive agency to submit regulations to Congress before they were implemented. Congress could then veto the proposed regulation by passing a resolution in either branch. The purpose was the review and reverse executive decisions. The Supreme Court in INS v. Chadha (1983) ruled the legislative veto unconstitutional.

IX.   INTEREST GROUPS AND BUREAUCRATIC DECISION MAKING. Interest groups pay more attention to the bureaucracy than the president or Congress because their interests are often directly impacted by the bureaucracy. These interest groups focus on the agency in their particular policy field. The American Farm Bureau monitors the Agricultural Department. Veteran groups monitor the Veteran's Department. Some bureaucracies were created by the pressure of interest groups-the EPA and EEOC are examples. Interest groups lobby the bureaucracy directly or thru Congress. Sometimes, they try to influence the bureaucracy through appeals in federal courts. For example, it is almost certain that the tobacco industry will appeal the FDA rules affecting tobacco advertising by filing law suits in federal courts challenging the rules.

X.   JUDICIAL CONSTRAINTS ON THE BUREAUCRACY. Judicial oversight is another check on bureaucracy.

A.   Judicial Standards of Bureaucratic Behavior. Judicial review of bureaucratic actions normally focuses on two issues:

1. Did the agency exceed the authority given by Congress?
2. Did the agency abide by procedural fairness-given proper notice of hearings, etc.?

If the answer is No to the first question and YES to the second question, the courts will normally not interfere.

B. <u>Bureaucratic Success in Court.</u> Overall, bureaucracies have been very successful in defending their actions in court. One study indicated the Federal Trade Commission at 91%, NLRB at 75%, and IRS at 78%. Only the INS had a poor record at 56%. Independent agencies enjoy greater success than departments. This success is explained by the battery of attorneys employed by the agencies who are paid by public funds and are specialized in an area of law. It is very expensive for individual citizens to undertake litigation and businesses and special interest groups must use a cost/benefit analysis to determine whether it would be useful to litigate. The long delay in court proceedings might cost more than a victory.

TRUE-FALSE QUESTIONS

1. Most people think their municipal or local government has about the right amount of power.

2. Bureaucracy is a form of social organization found not only in government, but also in corporations, churches, military forces, etc.

3. Bureaucratic power has grown with advances in technology and increases in the size and complexity of society.

4. Regulatory rules that appear in The Federal Registry are advisory only.

5. Of the total spending by all levels of government, the federal government spends about 64%.

6. Government spending constitutes a great deal of gross domestic product in the U.S. compared to other industrialized countries.

7. Cabinet departments employ about 60% of all federal workers.

8. Independent regulatory agencies differ from cabinet departments because only cabinet secretaries are political appointees.

9. Compared to other countries, the U.S. has a great number of government corporations.

10. The problem of bureaucratic responsiveness refers to citizen inquiries and complaints.

MULTIPLE CHOICE QUESTIONS:

11. Which is the most feared government bureaucracy?
    a. FBI   b. CIA   c. IRS   d. Alcohol, Tobacco & Firearms

12. Max Weber indicated that a rational bureaucracy would have certain characteristics. Which of the following is NOT one of these characteristics?
    a. Generalized labor   b. Chain of Command   c. Specification of authority
    d. Impersonality.

13. All but one of the following factors explain the growth of the federal bureaucracy:
    a. Neither the president nor Congress has the necessary time to be concerned with details.
    b. The increasing complexity and sophistication of technology requires technical experts.
    c. Congress writes specific and detailed laws.
    d. Bureaucracy is its own source of power and growth.

14. The federal bureaucracy publishes about _____ pages of rules in <u>The Federal Register</u> each year:

    a. 30,000   b. 40,000   c. 50,000   d. 60,000

15. The growth of government has been explained by many factors including all but one of the following:

    a.   Incrementalism   b. Citizen pressures
    c.   Wagner's Law of Societal Demands   d. Wars and Crisis

16. All but one of the following describe the federal bureaucracy:

    a. 2.8 million civilian employees   b. 20 cabinet departments
    c. 60 independent agencies   d. Executive Office of the President

17. Which of the following cabinet departments is the newest?

    a. Defense   b. EPA
    c. Education   d. Veterans

18. What is the principal difference between a regulatory commission and an independent agency:

    a. Members of the former are appointed by the president while the latter are designed by Congress.
    b. Independent agency heads can be fired by the president.
    c. Only regulatory commission members are confirmed by the Senate.
    d. Regulatory commissions are more important.

19. The spoils system selected persons based on all but one of the following:

    a. party loyalty   b. merit   c. electoral support   d. political influence

20. The civil service system established a uniform General Schedule of job grades. A college graduate could expect to enter at grade:

    a. 16   b. 12   c. 5   d. 1 or 2

21. Which of the following statements is correct regarding government workers and the general population?

    a. Blacks are under represented in the federal work force.
    b. Hispanics are over represented in the federal work force.
    c. Females are over represented in the lowest pay grades
    d. Both females and minorities are under represented in executive levels in the federal work force.

22. The federal government fiscal year begins:

a. January 1st   b. July 1st   c. October 1st   July 15th

23. Which of the following is responsible for the preparation of the president's budget:
    a. Department of the Treasury   b. OMB
    c. Council of Economic Advisors   d. CBO

24. Congress uses _____appropriation bills to provide funds for this fiscal year:
    a. 1   b. 13   c. 5   d. 14

25. All but one of the following are bureaucratic budget strategies:
    a. Spend it all b. Always ask for more   c. Cut vital programs
    d. Avoid new programs.

CHAPTER 12 SAMPLE QUESTION ANSWERS

TRUE-FALSE ANSWERS:

1. **TRUE.** The same answer would be true for the U.S. military. See page 432.

2. **TRUE.** Any hierarchy is indicative of a bureaucracy. See page 432.

3. **TRUE.** This was a pretty easy question. You got it right, no? See page 432.

4. **FALSE.** These published rules have the effect of law and the regulatory agencies have the power to ensure compliance. Refer to page 435.

5. **TRUE.** Total spending is $2.5T. The federal government budget is about $1.6T which is 64%. See page 438.

6. **FALSE.** Government spending by governments in the U.S. equals 32.2% of GDP which is fairly low compared to other countries. See Compared to What: The Size of Government in other Nations, page 440.

7. **TRUE.** The Defense department is the largest employer. See Table 12-1 and page 443.

8. **FALSE.** Both cabinet secretaries and regulatory commissions and heads are politically appointed. The main difference is that the president can remove a cabinet secretary but cannot remove a regulatory commission member or head.   See page 444.

9. **FALSE.** In reality, we have very few-3 in total. See page 444.

10. **FALSE** This refers to the power of the bureaucracy to be non-responsive and obstructive to presidential directives. Refer to page 448.

MULTIPLE-CHOICE ANSWERS:

11. **C** The IRS strikes terror in the hearts of taxpayers. See page 433.

12. **A** A bureaucracy would stress specialized workers to improve productivity. Refer to page 435.

13. **C** The fact that Congress writes vague and ambiguous laws requires a bureaucracy to interpret and implement these laws. Refer to page 435.

14. **D** It's incredible to think but 60,000 pages of rules is the answer. See page 435.

15. **B** Interest group pressures are a cause but not individual citizen pressures. See Up Close-Why Government Grows, Grows, and Grows, pages 437-438.

16. **B** There are only 14 cabinet departments. See page 438.

17. **D** While President Clinton desires to elevate EPA to a cabinet department, it has not happened yet, so the Veteran's department created under President Reagan remains the newest. See page 443.

18. **B** Like cabinet secretaries, agency heads serve at the pleasure of the president. Answer D. may appear to be correct, except that the EPA is extremely powerful, arguably more so than any regulatory commission. See page 444.

19. **B** Merit was a secondary consideration. See pages 447.

20. **C** College grads would be looking at grade 5 or slightly above. See page 447.

21. **D** At the highest level of the federal work force there are not many women or minorities. Refer to Table 12-3.

22. **C** It used to be July 1st, but was changed in 1974 to October 1st to give Congress more time to complete appropriation bills. See page 454.

23. **B** The Office of Management and Budget (OMB) has the key responsibility. See page 454.

24. **B** Lucky 13 is the magic number. See page 456.

25. **D** Bureaucrats do not avoid suggesting new programs, but present them in an incremental fashion so as to not arouse opposition. See Up Close: Bureaucratic Budget Strategies, page 458.

CHAPTER 13-COURTS

I. JUDICIAL POWER. Many political questions are eventually turned into judicial questions.

 A. For example, the courts have taken the lead in deciding many contentious political issues, such as:

 1. Elimination of racial segregation and decisions about affirmative action.

 2.

 3.

 4. Defining free speech and press and deciding such issues as obscenity, censorship and pornography.

 5.

 6. Defining the rights of criminal defendants and preventing unlawful searches.

 7. Decisions about capital punishment.

 B. Constitutional Power. Article III of the Constitution grants judicial power to the Supreme Court and other courts as established by Congress. These courts are independent. Judges are appointed, not elected. Their term is for life, barring any impeachable offense. Their salary may be increased but not cut.

 C. Interpreting the Constitution: Judicial Review. Since the Constitution is the supreme law of the land and takes precedence over federal and state laws and since the interpreter of the Constitution are the courts, this gives the judiciary great authority. Judicial review-the power to invalidate congressional or state laws- is not mentioned in the Constitution but was discussed in the Federalist Papers. But it was the historic decision in the case of Marbury v. Madison (1803) that officially established the power of judicial review. See People in Politics: John Marshall and Early Supreme Court Politics for an excellent summary of the case and its importance. The legal reasoning of Marshall is outlined on page 484. The power of an unelected body to overturn the decisions of democratically elected officials is troubling to some observers who view this power of the court as undemocratic.

 D. The Use of Judicial Review. Recognizing that overuse of judicial review might be prejudicial, the Supreme Court has used the power very sparingly. Table 13-1 illustrates this conservatism. For example, during the period 1803-1859, the court invalidated only one federal law. Indeed, considering that over 60,000 laws have been passed by Congress since the beginning of our government in 1789, only 127 have been declared by the Supreme Court as invalid or roughly 0.2%. While use has been circumspect, some of the overturns were critical. In 1857, the Supreme Court ruled in Dred Scott v. Sandford that slaves were property and the Missouri Compromise of 1820 which restricted introduction of slaves into U.S. territories was unconstitutional. This decision was one of the sparks of the Civil War. The Court also ruled many of President Franklin Roosevelt's New Deal laws unconstitutional, prompting Roosevelt in 1936 to suggest legislation

144

increasing the number of Supreme Court justices from 9 to 13. Presumably, the four additional justices appointed by Roosevelt would be more accommodating. This plan meet resistence in the Congress and one of the Justices changed his position, prompting the saying: "A switch in time saved nine." The Supreme Court has ever been more reluctant to challenge presidential power. This first instance was in Ex Parte Milligan (1866) declaring President Lincoln's suspension of the writ of habeas corpus unconstitutional. In 1952, the Court invalidated President Truman's seizure of steel mills and in 1974 it ordered President Nixon to turn over the White House tapes concerning Watergate. The Court has used the power of judicial review much more in invalidating state laws.

    E.   <u>Interpreting Federal Laws</u>. Not only do the courts interpret the Constitution, but they also are called upon to interpret statutory laws written by Congress. Sometimes vague or ambiguous language is used-such as fairness, good faith, probable cause, etc. and the courts are called upon to give specific meaning to these phrases.

    F.   <u>The Supreme Court's Policy Agenda.</u> The overwhelming number of cases decided by the Supreme Court fall into three areas:

        1.   civil right and treatment of minorities and women.

        2.   procedural rights of criminal defendants

        3.   The First Amendment-especially freedom of religion and speech.

The Court is also active in determining the meaning of American federalism. Finally, the Court gives considerable attention to governmental regulatory activities-environmental, banking and securities, and labor-management issues. The Court has been noticeably absent in areas of national defense and international affairs, leaving these areas for the Congress and president to resolve.

II.   ACTIVISM VERSUS SELF-RESTRAINT. Justice Felix Frankfurter once said that the only check on judicial power was the sense of self-restraint.

    A.   <u>Judicial Self-Restraint.</u> This doctrine holds that judges should not read their own philosophy into the Constitution and should avoid confrontations with the other branches of government where possible.

    B.   <u>Wisdom versus Constitutionality.</u> A law may be unwise or even stupid, but that doesn't mean it is unconstitutional. Yet there is the suggestion that the Supreme Court indeed often equates wisdom with constitutionality.

    C.   <u>Original Intent.</u> Should the Constitution be interpreted in terms of the values of the Founders or should the Constitution be considered a "living document" which must be interpreted by today's standards and values? If the latter, whose interpretation and values should prevail? Those favoring original intent suggest that the Constitution should be interpreted using the values of the founders. Judges that decide cases using their own views of today's standards are simply substituting their own morality for that of elected bodies. Such actions are illegitimate in a democratic society.

    D.   <u>Judicial Activism.</u> **FILL-IN**.

E.	Stare Decisis. The rule of precedence is very important in the law. This rule provides continuity and stability in the law. It essentially means that a previous decision should stand in a present case, the facts and issue being essentially the same. Thus, if the Supreme Court decided an issue 20 years ago, and the same issue is before the Court again with different Justices, these Justices are bound to observe the previous ruling. Those favoring judicial activism do not give much credibility to state decisis. The Supreme Court has overturned some of its previous rulings, i.e. violated precedence, e.g. Brown v. Board of Education.

F.	Rules of Restraint. The Supreme Court does exercise some self-restraint:

1.	It does not issue advisory opinions to Congress or the President; it only rules on actual cases of legislation.
2.	It does not decide hypothetical cases or issues.
3.	The Court tries to apply the narrowest interpretation possible.
4.	The Court will not decide a constitutional question, if the case can be disposed of using some other means, procedural or structural.
5.	A plaintiff must show injury to have standing.
6.	A plaintiff must exhaust all other remedies at lower levels before the Supreme Court will accept the case for review.
7.	
8.	
9.	

III.	STRUCTURE AND JURISDICTION OF FEDERAL COURTS. The federal court system consists of three levels:

A.	Federal District Courts. There are 89 federal district courts in the 50 states and one each in Puerto Rico and the District of Columbia. There are over 600 federal judges that serve in these courts who were appointed by the president, confirmed by the Senate and serve for life. There is also a U.S. marshall for each district whose staff carries out the orders of the court and provides order in the courtroom. District courts serve as the entry point for a federal case, that is, they have original jurisdiction. They handle both criminal and civil cases. Each district also has a U.S. Attorney and staff representing the Department of Justice. Charges are presented by the U.S. Attorney to a Grand Jury which hears evidence and decides whether an individual should be indicted and tried. If they so decide, the defendant is tried before a Petit Jury which determines guilt or innocence. District courts hear about 300,000 cases/year, including about 50,000 criminal cases.

B.	Courts of Appeal. There are 12 regional federal Courts of Appeals and one for the District of Columbia. They have appellate jurisdiction only. That is, they hear appeals from district court decisions. They do not hold another trial, but consider only the written record of the district court and oral or written arguments

146

(briefs) submitted by attorneys. Federal law grants everyone the right of appeal. Appellate judges estimate that 80% of the appeals are without merit. There are more that 100 federal appellate judges, again appointed by the president, confirmed by the Senate and serving for life. Generally, appeals are heard by a panel of three judges. More than 90% of cases end at this level. Appeal to the Supreme Court is not guaranteed. See the feature <u>Across the USA: Geographic Boundaries of Federal Courts.</u>

    C.   <u>U.S. Supreme Court.</u> The only court specifically mentioned in the Constitution. The number of justices is not fixed by the Constitution, but by Congress. The current number is 9. The Supreme Court has <u>both original and appellate jurisdiction</u>. Its original jurisdiction is rather limited: cases between states, cases between a state and the federal government, and cases involving foreign dignitaries. This later instance is really null and void since the Congress of Vienna in 1815 which recognized diplomatic immunity. Now a foreign dignitary who was charged with a crime would be declared <u>persona non grata</u> and expelled from the U.S. <u>Most cases that reach the Supreme Court involve appellate jurisdiction.</u> The Court is in session from October to the following June and hears oral briefs, receives written briefs, confers and renders decisions. The Supreme Court also has appellate jurisdiction over state supreme court decisions, but it exercises this jurisdiction rarely. Congress has also placed some limits on federal jurisdiction, for example, disputes between citizens of different states may not be heard in federal court unless the amount in dispute is over $50,000. <u>A summary of the jurisdiction of all the above courts is given in Table 13-2.</u>

    D.   <u>Federal Cases.</u> About 10M civil and criminal cases are begun every year. There are more than 805,000 lawyers in the U.S. compared to 650,000 physicians. Of these 10M cases, fewer than 300,000 begin in federal courts. There are about 5,000 cases appealed to the Supreme Court, but it accepts only about 200. Thus, the vast bulk of cases are heard in state/local courts. Federal caseloads have risen over the past years (See Figure 13-2). This has been caused by greater activity of the FBI, DEA, ATF and IRS as well as Congress expanding the list of federal crimes.

IV.   THE SPECIAL RULES OF JUDICIAL DECISION MAKING. Unlike the other branches, the courts employ highly specialized rules for decision making.

    A.   <u>Cases and Controversies.</u> Courts do not initiate action on cases; someone must bring the case to them. A case must involve two disputing parties and must involve real damage. The vast majority of cases do not involve important policy decisions, but rather determinations of guilt or innocence, contract claims, and negligence civil suits.

    B.   <u>Adversarial Proceedings.</u> **FILL-IN.**

C. Standing. To bring an issue to court, one party must have standing-must be directly harmed by a law or action. Anyone prosecuted by the government automatically has standing. Federal courts in recent years have liberalized the definition of standing. The party suffering the damage is the Plaintiff. The party against whom the suit is filed becomes the defendant. The doctrine of sovereign immunity means that one cannot sue the government without its consent. By law, the U.S. government has granted this consent in contract and negligence cases. Citizens can also sue to force a government official to perform their duty or for acting contrary to the law.

D. Class Action Suits. Suits that are filed not only by an individual but for a whole group of people similarly situated in being damaged by the same defendant. One of the earliest class action suits was Brown v. Board of Education. Class suits mushroomed in popularity, especially fed by lawyers. Individuals charged excessive rates for insurance, interest or utility charges would normally not be in a financial position to file a law suit to collect $10. But a sharp lawyer could sue for all the victims and collect a nice fee. Lawyers were able to file a suit without even notifying all the victims, but now they are required to do so.

E. Legal Fees. It costs money to go to court. Criminal defendants are guaranteed services of an attorney without charge if they are poor. But if you have money you have to pay the bill. OJ Simpson was found innocent by a jury, but the criminal trial cost him more than $5M. In civil cases, both parties must pay legal fees. The most common arrangement for the plaintiff is the contingency fee-plaintiffs will pay the expenses of the lawyer and share 1/3 to ½ of any award for damages if the case is won or settled out of court. If the case is lost, the attorney gets zero. Lawyers will not accept contingency fee cases unless they think they have a good chance of winning.

F. Remedies and Relief. Judicial power has greatly expanded through court determinations of remedies and relief that go beyond a prison sentence, fine or cash judgment. Federal judges have supervised the operation of schools, ordered forced bussing, local authorities to build low cost housing in a specific area, supervision of a state prison system, and ordered a school board to raise taxes to pay for a desegregation plan.

V. THE POLITICS OF SELECTING JUDGES. All federal judges are appointed by the president and confirmed by the Senate. Judicial recruitment is a political process. Almost always presidents appoint judges of their own party. More than 80% of federal judges held some political office prior to appointment. Political philosophy also is now an important criteria.

A. The Politics of Presidential Selection. Since judicial appointments are made for life, presidents have a strong motivation to select judges that share their political philosophy. However, presidents have been surprised about 25% of the time when their appointees deviated their expected judicial philosophy. See Table 13-3 for additional information.

B. Political Litmus Test. In general, Democrat presidents and senators prefer more liberal judges while Republicans prefer more conservative judges. A litmus test refers to the judicial candidate's position on a single issue. More recently, this has been the abortion issue. Another issue could be capital punishment.

C.   Competence and Ethics.   **FILL-IN.**

D.   The Politics of Senate Confirmation. Presidential nominations are sent to the Senate Judiciary Committee which holds hearings, votes on the nomination and then reports it to the full Senate. The custom of senatorial courtesy has been used to screen nominees. If a senator from the same party as the president objects to the nomination of a judge for his state, normally his colleagues in the Senate would disapprove the nomination. Note that this courtesy applies only to judges in a state-it would not apply to appellate judges or Supreme Court justices. Supreme Court nominations receive unusually strict scrutiny. Over the first two centuries, the Senate refused to confirm or rejected 20% of the president's nominations. In this century, only 5 nominations have been defeated. The general rule is to respect the president's nomination and unless some extraordinary circumstance exists, e.g. financial scandal, racial or religious bias, etc., the Senate usually concurs with the nomination.

VI.   WHO IS SELECTED. In spite of differing views on the law, the Constitution and its interpretation, the background of Supreme Court justices is remarkably similar.

A.   Law Degrees. While there is no constitutional requirement that Supreme Court justices be lawyers, every one has been one. Moreover, the majority have attended the most prestigious law schools-Harvard, Yale and Stanford.

B.   Judicial Experience. About half of the justices have been federal or state judges prior to appointment to the court. About 1/4 have come from private practices. Many have served as U.S. Attorneys. Relatively few have been elected politicians-two notable exceptions are Sandra Day O'Connor who served in the Arizona legislature and William Howard Taft who was president before taking his place on the court.

C.   Age. In the fifties seems to be the magic age.

D.   Race and Gender. Until President Johnson appointed Thurgood Marshall, no black American had been a justice. Until President Reagan appointed Justice O'Connor, no woman served on the court. When Marshall retired, President Bush decided to appoint another black American to the court who proved to be very controversial-Justice Clarence Thomas. President Clinton added another woman to the bench when he appointed Ruth Bader Ginsburg.

E.   Class. With these exceptions, Supreme Court justices have been white, male, Protestant, Anglo-Saxon, high social status, urban, and from well to do families. See Table 16-6 for the background of Supreme Court Justices.

VII.   SUPREME COURT DECISION MAKING. Except for original jurisdiction cases, the Supreme Court decides what cases it will hear. More than 5,000 cases come to the Court each year, yet the court accepts for opinions only about 200 or in other words about 4%. In another 150 or so cases, the Court decides the case summarily (without opinion) either affirming or reversing the lower court decision.

A.   Setting the Agenda: Granting Certiorari. The party losing a case at the appellate level may petition the Supreme Court for a Writ of Certiorari or Cert for short.

B.   In effect, this petition requests the Supreme Court to require the lower court to turn over its records for review. The decision to grant cert depends on the Rule of Four. Four justices have to agree to accept the case. **WHAT EXPLANATIONS ARE OFFERED WHY FOUR JUSTICES WOULD ACCEPT A CASE?**

1.   The issue is one the justices are interested in-it may be abortion, or free speech.

2.   When there is conflict in the court system. Two Courts of Appeals have decided cases exactly opposite.

3.   A lower court has either ignored a Supreme Court decision or misinterpreted it.

4.   The U.S. Government is a party in the case.

C.   Hearing Arguments. Once the Supreme Court accepts a case and places it on its calendar, attorneys for both sides prepare written briefs citing applicable law and previous cases. The Court may also allow other interested parties to file amicus curiae (friend of the court) written briefs. This is the only opportunity for interest groups to influence a judicial decision. The U.S. government will frequently submit these briefs when it is not a party to the case. Oral arguments are scheduled after the justices have had time to read the written materials. Usually attorneys for the parties are allowed from ½ hour to one hour for the oral presentation which is strictly controlled. Judges can interrupt at any time with questions-some of which may be friendly and others hostile. Some court observers try to guess the eventual decision in the case by the tenor and identity of the justice asking the questions.

D.   In Conference. The justices meet in private conference (no public, reporters or law clerks) on Wednesday and Friday afternoons and discuss the cases of the week. The Chief Justice presides. A vote is taken to determine who wins or loses the case or whether the lower court case is affirmed or reversed.

E.   Writing Opinions.   **FILL-IN   WHAT IS A MAJORITY, CONCURRING AND DISSENTING OPINION?**

F. <u>Voting Blocs.</u> The most prominent bloc involves the liberal-conservative axis. Sometimes an activist-judicial restraint axis is employed; although there is a high degree of correlation with the liberal-conservative axis. Table 13-7 provides the bloc position of various justices in the Warren, Burger and Rehnquist courts.

VIII. CHECKING COURT POWER. As unelected members of a powerful branch of government, there is some concern about the possible abuse of power. There are, however, some check on this power:

A. <u>Legitimacy as a Restraint in the Judiciary.</u> The courts do not have the power to enforce its decisions. With only a few thousand marshalls, the court must depend on the executive for enforcement of its decisions. Although the courts decided that Mississippi, Arkansas, and Alabama schools had to integrated, federalized troops were required to accomplish the task. Most Americans feel that court decisions are authoritative and that citizens have a duty to obey the decisions whether they agree with them or not. Widespread opposition to a decision can delay its implementation as integration of schools and the banning of school prayer demonstrate.

B. <u>Compliance with Court Policy.</u> Lower federal judges and state courts are obliged to follow Supreme Court decisions in their courts. Sometimes courts will express their disapproval of the decision, but they still must follow it. Sometimes they will try to narrowly interpret the decision when they disagree with it. Public officials who defy Court rulings risk lawsuits and court ordered compliance. Failure to comply will result in fines and penalties. Even the president must comply with Court orders. Failure to do so could result in impeachment.

C. <u>Presidential Influence on Court Policy.</u> **FILL-IN. HOW CAN THE PRESIDENT INFLUENCE THE COURT??**

D. <u>Congressional Checks on the Judiciary.</u> Congress has the power to establish or disestablish inferior courts. Congress can increase or decrease the number of Supreme Court justices. Congress can increase or decrease the number of federal district or appellate judges. Congress can limit the jurisdiction of the courts and can specify in legislation how any appeals will be made. For example, in flag burning legislation, the Congress specified that if a federal district court held the law to be unconstitutional, the appeal would go direct to the Supreme Court without any hearing at the Appellate level. Article III of the Constitution states: ...The Supreme Court shall have appellate jurisdiction, both as to law and fact, with such exceptions, and under such regulations as the Congress shall make.   In 1866, the Reconstruction Congress passed a law that specifically prohibited the Supreme Court from adjudicating the law. This is the only instance in history where Congress specifically limited the Supreme Court. Were it used too often, the Court might proclaim the limitation to be unconstitutional. Often the Court is called upon to interpret the meaning of a law. If the court interprets the law to Congress's disliking, Congress can always amend the statutory law. In terms of the Court interpreting the Constitution to Congress's dislike, the only remedy is to amend the Constitution. In 1895, the Court held that a federal income tax was unconstitutional. So Congress passed the 16th Amendment. Attempts by Congress to amend the Constitution to overturn a Supreme Court decision are rarely successful, e.g., school prayer, prohibiting flag burning, etc. In theory, Congress could impeach Justices, but only for committing a crime, not for a decision. So in reality, the threat of impeachment has no real influence over judicial policy making.

CHAPTER 13 SAMPLE QUESTIONS

TRUE-FALSE QUESTIONS:

1. Courts are "political" institutions.

2. Federal judges salaries can be increased but not decreased during their term in office.

3. The power of judicial review is contained in Article III of the Constitution.

4. Federal courts have used judicial review to invalidate far more federal laws than state laws.

5. The Supreme Court has challenged legislation more than executive actions.

6. An unwise law is a prime candidate to be found unconstitutional.

7. Believers in original intent feel that the Supreme Court should not set aside laws made by Congress unless they conflict with the original intent of the Founding Fathers.

8. If Congress is in doubt about the constitutionality of a proposed law, the judiciary committees can ask the Supreme Court for an advisory opinion.

9. In the U.S., there are more lawyers than doctors.

10. Most trials take place in state/local courts.

MULTIPLE-CHOICE QUESTIONS:

11. The courts have decided issues in all the following areas except:
    a. Civil rights
    b. Voting rights
    c. Reproductive rights
    d. Medical care rights.

12. The Supreme Court has invalidated federal laws in all but one of the following areas:
    a. Prohibition of the expansion of slavery into the western territories.
    b. FDR's New Deal laws.
    c. Banning of PACs
    d. Limiting personal spending in federal campaigns.

13. The number of Supreme Court justices is:
    a. 7   b. 9   c. 11   d. 13

14. The Supreme Court has been most active in three of the following areas. Which area is not correct?
    a. Civil rights   b. Rights of criminal defendants   c. Rights of criminal victims
    d. First Amendment rights

15. The Supreme Court has also been very active in other policy areas. Which of the following is not one of these areas:
    a. overseeing activities in defense and international relations.
    b. refereeing the struggle for power between the executive and legislative branches.
    c. determining the nature of federalism
    d. governmental regulatory activity.

16. A justice believes that in making a ruling, he should avoid where possible confrontations with the Congress and president. This justice could be said to believe in:
    a. Judicial activism   b. Judicial restraint
    c. The living Constitution   d. Stare decisis

17. A judge who was liberal would be likely be a practitioner of:
    a. Judicial restraint   b. Judicial activism   c. Original intent
    d. None of the above.

18. The federal district courts are an example of:
    a. Original jurisdiction   b. Appellate jurisdiction   c. Mixed jurisdiction
    d. Petite juries

19. The U.S. Supreme Court is an example of:
    a. Original jurisdiction   b. Appellate jurisdiction   c. Mixed jurisdiction
    d. Grand jury

20. Which court does not involve a trial or receive any new evidence:
    a. District court   b. Appellate court   c. Supreme Court   d. County court

21. Driving the litigious nature of American society are all but one of the following:
    a. Product liability claims   b. Third-party suits   c. Joint and Several Liability
    d. Contingency fee limits.

22. What is the name of the doctrine that states that individuals may sue the government only with the later's consent:
    a. Stare decisis   b. Class Action   c. Sovereign immunity
    d. Amicus curiae

23. Which of the following is not a member of the Supreme Court:
    a. Robert Bork   b. Clarence Thomas   c. Antonia Scalia

d. Ruth Bader Ginsburg

24. To grant a writ of certiorari requires the approval of:
    a. all justices   b. A minimum of 4   c. 2/3s of the justices
    d. 3/4s of the justices

25. Most Supreme Court justices have been:
    a. Catholics   b. 51-60 when appointed   c. Republicans
    d. Females

CHAPTER 13 SAMPLE QUESTION ANSWERS

TRUE-FALSE ANSWERS:

1. **TRUE.** The courts decide who gets what. See page 474.

2. **TRUE.** A great job if you can get it! See page 474.

3. **FALSE.** The Supreme Court said it had this power in the case of Marbury v. Madison. Refer to page 474.

4. **FALSE.** The opposite is true. State courts have no way to respond to federal courts-if the courts invalidated many of Congress's laws-it might be a different story. See Table 13-1.

5. **TRUE.** The instances of challenges to the president have been very few. See page 478.

6. **FALSE.** Wisdom does not equal constitutionality. Some think it does, but the court tries to avoid such a relationship. See page 479.

7. **TRUE** They also believe that words in the Constitution should be interpreted in their historical context. See page 480.

8. **FALSE.** This is an example of Supreme Court restraint. They will not rule on hypothetical questions. Refer to page 481.

9. **TRUE** Strange as it sounds, eh? 805,000 lawyers v. 650,000 doctors. See <u>A Conflicting View-America Drowning Itself in a Sea of Lawsuits.</u> Pages 486-487.

10. **TRUE.** Only 3% take place in federal courts. Page 488 refers.

MULTIPLE-CHOICE ANSWERS:

11. **D** So far the Court has not found a right to medical care in the Constitution-in all the other areas it has. See pages 473-474.

12. **C** It is doubtful the Supreme Court would invalidate a law banning PACs. However, this is a hypothetical question since there is no such law. See page 477.

13. **B** Nine is not a magic number. The number is determined by Congress. The number of nine has been in place since 1869, so it would unlikely to change any time soon. See page 477.

14. **C** Strange as it may seem criminals have more rights than victims. See page 478.

15. **A** Thus far, the Court has stayed out of this area. See page 479.

16. **B** This would be a clear case of judicial restraint. See page 479.

17. **B** There is a high correlation between liberalism and judicial activism. The same is true for conservatism and judicial restraint. See page 479.

18. **A** District courts are courts of first instance, i.e., original jurisdiction or where the rubber hits the road. See page 481.

19. **C** The Supreme Court has both original and appellate jurisdiction or mixed. See page 482.

20. **B** Appellate courts just look at the trial record and questions of law not evidence. See page 483.

21. **D** While contingency fees have a limit, they are far too high. See A Conflicting View-America Drowning Itself in a Sea of Lawsuits. Pages 486-487

22. **C** The name gives the answer away. You didn't miss this one???? See Page 490.

23. **A** The nomination and rejection of Judge Bork was because of his conservative views. See Up Close-the Bork Battle.

24. **B** The Rule of Four is applicable. See page 499.

25. **B** This is the magic age for most appointments. See Table 13-6.

CHAPTER 14-POLITICS AND PERSONAL LIBERTY

I.   POWER AND INDIVIDUAL LIBERTY. Liberty or freedom was the most sacred value
        to the founders of our country who saw government as a mechanism for preserving
        liberty.
        A.   Authority and Liberty. In order to secure their liberty., citizens willingly give up
                some for a government which will protect the liberty of all. However, this sets up
                a dilemma-people must create laws and government to protect their liberty, but
                the laws and government restrict freedom.
        B.   Democracy and Personal Liberty. If democracy is defined only as a decision-
                making process, there is little protection for liberty. But it must also be defined to
                include substantive values-the dignity of the individual and equality under the
                law. The purpose of the Constitution and Bill of Rights was to limit government
                power over the individual and place personal liberty beyond the reach of
                government. See Table 14-1
        C.   Nationalizing the Bill of Rights. Originally, the provisions in the Bill of Rights
                applied only to the national government. Most state constitutions contained
                similar provisions, but these were enforceable in state courts only. With the
                passage of the 14th Amendment and its due process and equal protection of the
                law provisions, there was a question whether these general phrases incorporated
                the Bill of Rights and made them applicable to states. At first, the Supreme Court
                did not agree with this idea. But gradually, beginning in 1925, case by case, the
                Supreme Court has incorporated almost all of the provisions of the Bill of Rights
                in making them applicable to both the federal government and lower
                governments. See Table 14-2
II.   FREEDOM OF RELIGION. Americans not only believe in freedom of religion, but they
        also practice their religion more than people in any other industrialized country. The
        First Amendment established two specific provisions regarding this freedom:
        Government shall not establish a religion, nor prohibit the free exercise of religion.
        A.   Free Exercise of Religion. Although the working of this provision seems
                absolute: Congress shall make no law... , Congress has passed laws that restrict
                the practice of religions and some of these have been upheld by the Supreme
                Court. One of the earliest was a law to ban polygamy in Utah. The Court
                distinguished between faith and behavior. Congress also passed a law to ban all
                religious schools-but the court struck down this law. Beliefs are absolutely
                protected, but religious practices are not. If government has a valid secular (non-
                religious) reason for banning a religious practice, it may be upheld. E.g. human
                sacrifice or ceremonial use of illegal drugs. The court upheld the right of Amish
                parents to remove their children from public schools after the 8th grade, allowed
                the IRS to revoke the tax-free status of Bob Jones University because of its rules
                against interracial dating or marriage, and also struck down a local ordinance
                banning the sacrifice of animals.
        B.   No Establishment of Religion. Interpretations of this clause range from simply

prohibiting the state from establishing an official religion to building a wall of separation between church and state. The court has allowed provision of public school bus transportation to religious schools and pupil releases to attend private religious instruction.

C.   What Constitutes Establishment . One of the most vexing problems for the Supreme Court because our money has the words In God, we trust, sessions of Congress begin with prayers, the Armed forces builds chapels and pays for chaplains. The Supreme Court uses a test for establishment that it fashioned in the Lemon v. Kurtzman case. The three prongs of this test are:

1.   **FILL-IN**

2.

3.

Using this test, the court has struck down paying for teacher's salaries or instructional material in parochial schools, but upheld the use of public funds to purchase non-religious textbooks, lunches, and transportation in church-related schools, and the use of federal grant money to church-related universities and colleges. The Court has also sanctioned tax exemptions for churches, allows student religious groups to meet in public school classrooms after school hours, allows deductions from federal income taxes for church contributions, allows states to close stores on Sunday, and allows Nativity scenes on public property if these have some secular connection=reindeers and Santa.

D.   Prayer in School. The question of prayer and the reading of the Bible in school has been the most controversial involvement of the Supreme Court with freedom of religion. In spite of the long history of prayer in school, in 1962 the Court declared this practice to be unconstitutional. In 1963, they said the same about reading from the bible. The majority opinion held that the Bible could be studied as part of a secular course, but not used in religious ceremonies. When Alabama mandated a moment of silence for meditation or silent prayer, the court struck this down as well. In a stinging dissent, Chief Justice Burger accused the court of abandoning neutrality toward religion and substituting hostility.

E.   Religious Freedom Restoration? Congress passed the Religious Freedom Act in 1993 which exempts persons from government laws or regulations that burden religious freedom, unless the government can prove the burden is the least restrictive means of furthering a compelling government interest.

III.   FREEDOM OF SPEECH. Again, although the First Amendment is absolute- Congress shall pass no law... , the Supreme Court has never agreed that all speech is protected by the First Amendment.

A.   Clear and Present Danger. If speech creates a serious and immediate danger such as crying out FIRE in a crowded theater, it is not protected speech. This doctrine was used by the government to stifle speech during World War I when it passed the Espionage Act of 1917 and the Sedition Act of 1918.

B.   Preferred Position Doctrine.   **FILL-IN.**

C.   The Cold War Challenge. The passage of the Smith Act made it unlawful to advocate the overthrow of the U.S. government. In 1949, the federal government prosecuted 11 members of the Communist Party of the U.S. They were convicted and the Supreme Court upheld their convictions. Since then, the Court has returned to more stringent clear and present danger position. A democracy must not become authoritarian to protect itself from authoritarianism. In later cases, the Court held that mere advocacy of revolution without any unlawful action is protected speech. Later cases struck down federal laws requiring communist organizations to register with the government, the requirement of loyalty oaths , prohibition of communists working in defense plants, and laws stripping the passports from Communist leaders.

D.   Symbolic Speech. **FILL-IN. HOW DO HATE CRIME LAWS CONFLICT WITH SYMBOLIC SPEECH??**

E.   Speech and Public Order. Can authorities ban a speech because the audience may become unruly? Generally, the Court says no! However, authorities can require sponsors to post a bond or to take out a permit, or even be charged for extra police protection.

F.   Commercial Speech. While allowing some protection of commercial speech, the Court is far more forceful in protecting political speech. States had banned advertising by professionals and listing of prices by pharmacies. These the court banned. But the Court upheld federal laws banning or controlling liquor and cigarette advertising.

G.   Libel and Slander. These have never been considered protected speech. Libel is defined as damaging falsehood. Public officials must not only prove the speech was libel but that it was made with actual malice.

IV.   OBSCENITY AND THE LAW. Although obscenity can be banned, the main problem is defining what is meant by obscenity. Is nudeness obscene? Pornography is simply a synonym for obscenity. Soft-core porn usually denotes nakedness and suggestive poses. Hard-core porn is usually more explicit.

A.   A Narrow Definition of Obscenity: The Roth Standard. What an average person applying contemporary community standards would find obscene. This test became very difficult to use in cases. Community standard later became society at large. The work as a whole had to be obscene. There could be no redeeming social or literary merit.

    B.   <u>A Broader Definition of Obscenity: The Miller Standards.</u> Because of the difficulty in interpreting the Supreme Court's slippery standards, the Court again looked at this issue in 1973 in the case of Miller V. California. Local community was now the determining mechanism and they defined prurient as patently offensive representations or descriptions of various sexual acts. Instead of a test of utterly without redeeming value, we now have lacks serious literary, artistic, political or scientific value. Of course, what does the word serious mean?

    C.   <u>Child Porn.</u> Generally, the Court has come down much harder on child porn. The mere possession of child porn material is evidence that a crime has been committed.

V.   FREEDOM OF THE PRESS. The idea of a free and independent press is deeply rooted in the evolution of democratic government.

    A.   <u>No Prior Restraint Doctrine.</u> This is the censorship of written material by government authorities. It was quite common in England before the American Revolution. In 1931, the Court struck down a Minnesota law that prohibited the publication of a muckraking publication. The Court suggested that prior restrain might be applicable in time of war. This issue came to the court in New York Times v. Sullivan-the case of stolen top secret Pentagon papers. Could the government prevent the NY Times and *Washington Post* from publishing this stolen material? The Court majority said NO.

    B.   <u>Film Censorship.</u> The Supreme Court has not given the film industry the same prior restraint protection as the press. The Court approved government censorship for obscenity, but the industry adopted its own system of rating films to head off the government.

    C.   <u>Radio and Television Censorship.</u> Since radio and TV uses the public airways, and there is a problem with frequency allocation and usage, the Federal Communication Commission has been given much more control over this medium. The Court upheld fairness and equal time requirements of the FCC, for example.

    D.   <u>Media Claims for Special Rights.</u> The news media argues that they would be ineffective as reporters unless they can provide sources confidentiality. The Supreme Court has rejected this argument, but news organizations have pressured state governments to pass shield laws which allow them this confidentiality at the state level.

    E.   <u>Conflicting Rights .</u> In order to protect witnesses, a court places a gag order on attorneys and parties to the trial. This gag order is a restriction of free speech and press. Thus, there is a conflict between the right of a free and impartial trial and free speech and press.

    F.   <u>The Information Highway.</u> Cyperspace has opened a new area of First Amendment rights. Does the government have the right to ban obscene or racial slurs, or bomb making instructions?

VI. FREEDOM OF ASSEMBLY AND PETITION. The right to organize political parties and interest groups is derived from freedom of assembly. Freedom to petition protects most lobbying activities.

    A. Right of Association. Freedom of assembly includes the right to join organizations and associations. The Court has included student organizations within this right.

    B. Protests, Parades, and Demonstrations. Also protected by the freedom of assembly right. Authorities have the right, within reasonable limits, to make restrictions as to time, place, permits and manner of assembly to protect public order, but must apply these restrictions in an impartial manner.

    C. Picketing. Public property for the above protests, etc. are one thing, but private property is another. Shopping malls may regulate these activities, but airports are another problem since in most cases, they are publically owned. Opponents of abortion have tried to use this right to picket abortion clinics. Generally, the courts have upheld restrictions of this activity to ensure free movement to and from the clinics. In 1994, the federal government passed a law guaranteeing access to abortion clinics, since abortion is a recognized constitutional right. Again, another case of conflicting rights. See What Do You Think-Freedom of Assembly for Whom?

VII. THE RIGHT TO BEAR ARMS. This is certainly one of the most volatile issues in public policy today.

    A. Bearing Arms. When this amendment was adopted there was a fear that despotic governments would try to seize the arms of citizens. Also, citizen soldiers were the armed forces.

    B. State Militias. An alternate interpretation is that the writers of this amendment were interested in the maintenance of well regulated state militias. Thus, there is no right for private groups or individuals to bear arms.

    C. Citizen militias . In 1912, National Guard units replace state militias. Recently, there have been self-styled citizen militias that have formed which have an anti-government mentality, and engage in training in military tactics and small arms practice. They see themselves as modern-day decedents of American patriot militias who fought in the Revolutionary War. These units frequently come into conflict with various federal agencies like the ATF.

VIII. CRIME, VIOLENCE, AND THE CONSTITUTION. In suppressing these, democratic government must balance remedies with constitutional rights. Government repression, police brutality, invasions of privacy are evils at least as dangerous as crime and violence.

    A. Crime in American. **FILL-IN. HAVE CRIME RATES GONE UP IN THE 1990S? WHAT % OF CRIMES ARE DRUG RELATED?**

B.   <u>Victimization</u>.   **FILL-IN. ARE VICTIMIZATION CRIME RATES HIGHER OR LOWER THAT OFFICIAL ESTIMATES?**

IX.   RIGHTS OF CRIMINAL DEFENDANTS. While society needs protection by the police, also important is to protect society from the police. <u>See Table 14-4 for limitations on the power of policy and the rights of the accused.</u>

    A.   <u>The Guarantee of the Writ of Habeas Corpus.</u> Part of English common law, this is a court order requiring officials to deliver the prisoner to the court and explain the reasons for detention. If unlawful, or insufficient evidence exists, the judge can order the prisoner's release. The courts have been very diligent in protecting this right, declaring in <u>Ex Parte Milligan</u> that Lincoln acted unconstitutionally is suspending the writ during the Civil War.

    B.   <u>The Prohibition of Bills of Attainder and Ex Post Facto Laws.</u> **FILL-IN.**

    C.   <u>Unreasonable Searches and Seizures</u>. **FILL-IN. ARE SOME SEARCHES ALLOWED WITHOUT A WARRANT?**

    D.   <u>Arrests.</u> Generally warrants are not required for arrests, except in the case of entering the home of someone to arrest them. If the owner gives his consent, a warrant is not required.

    E.   <u>Indictment.</u> **FILL-IN. ARE A DEFENDANT'S RIGHTS PROTECTED DURING A GRAND JURY?**

F.   Self-incrimination and the Right to Counsel. The right to avoid self-incrimination is predicated on the assumption of innocence and to prevent torture being used to obtain confessions. The 5th Amendment covers this right. Taking the Fifth is when a witness refuses to testify. Failure to testify cannot be used to influence a jury regarding a verdict. Witnesses not the subject of criminal prosecution can be compelled to testify by a grant of immunity from prosecution. Nothing a witness says can be used against him/her, therefore, they cannot refuse to answer questions. The Warren Court greatly strengthened self-incrimination and right to counsel: **SUMMARIZE THESE RIGHTS IN THE FOLLOWING CASES:**
1.   Gideon v. Wainwright (1963):

2.   Escobedo v. Illinois (1964):

3.   Miranda v. Arizona (1966):
It does not appear that the granting of these rights has hampered successful prosecutions.

G.   The Exclusionary Rule.   **FILL-IN.   DOES THE TEXT AUTHOR AGREE THAT CONTAMINATED EVIDENCE SHOULD NOT BE USED? WHAT REMEDY DOES HE SUGGEST FOR SUCH EVIDENCE?**

H.   Bail Requirements. While the 8th Amendment does not establish the right to bail, the Supreme Court held that one should not be held until trial except in unusual circumstances. Pretrial bail can be denied for heinous crimes, the untrustworthiness of the defendant, or to protect the safety of the community. Most people do not have the cash for bail, so they have to use the services of a bail bondsman who charges a hefty fee for the service. If the defendant shows up, the bond is returned. If the defendant flees, the bondsman has the fee, but loses the bond. They then send out mercenaries to find the defendant.

I.   Fair Trial. The right to such a trial is guaranteed by the 6th Amendment. Specifically guaranteed are:

1.   Right to a speedy and public trial.
2.
3.
4.   Right of the accused to compel favorable witnesses to appear.
5.

Trials follow a fairly regular format. The prosecution makes the opening statement, followed by the defense attorney. The prosecution then attempts to prove the crime by calling witnesses and presenting evidence. The accused is in the court room. His defense attorney will try to impeach the veracity of the witnesses or evidence. After the prosecution rests, the defense presents its case. To place the accused on the stand is a large decision. Once the defendant is sworn, he/she must answer questions not only of the defense attorney, but also the prosecution. After the defense presents its case, the attorneys have a chance to summarize their cases in concluding remarks. The defense attorney goes first and the prosecutor has the last word. After the judge issues his instructions to the jury regarding appropriate law, the jury retires to render its verdict. Federal trials have 12 jurors. A unanimous verdict is required. If the jury is deadlocked, a mistrial is declared, and it is up to the prosecution to decide to reprosecute the case.

J.   Plea Bargaining. More than 90% of criminal cases are plea bargained. In return for concessions from the prosecutor, such as dropping the more serious charges or agreeing to a lighter sentence, the defendant pleads guilty and waives the right to a jury trial. The process has many critics who argue that it is a form of leniency and loses any deterrent effect. They also charge the process violates the right to self-incrimination and trial by jury. Supporters argue it saves the state money and any other policy would result in clogged courts.

X.   THE DEATH PENALTY. One of the key issues in criminal justice. Does capital punishment violate the 8th Amendment's prohibition of cruel and unusual punishment. There is little doubt that the death penalty is applied in a capricious way. A large percentage of those executed have been poor, uneducated, and black.

A.   Prohibition Against Unfair Application. Prior to 1971, the death penalty was in use in about half of the states. Federal law also called for the death penalty in certain crimes. In Furman v. Georgia (1972) the Court declared the death penalty to be unconstitutional because it was not applied uniformly. After this decision, many states rewrote their laws to conform to the guidance in the Supreme Court decision. They called for its mandatory use for certain crimes of violence-murder committed during rape, robbery, hijacking, murder of prison guards, murder with torture and multiple murders. Two trials were established-one to determine guilt and the other to present aggravating or mitigating circumstances to determine the sentence.

B.   Death Penalty Reinstated. In 1976, the Court upheld the death penalty. They used many different rationales-framers of the Bill of Rights accepted it, most state legislatures rewrote their laws and hundreds of juries have imposed the death penalty. It has social purposes of retribution and deterrence. The Court also called for the automatic review of any death sentence by the state supreme court and also disapproved of state laws that made the death penalty mandatory for all first-degree murders.

C. <u>Racial Bias.</u>   **FILL-IN.   HAS THE SUPREME COURT ALLOWED STATISTICS TO BE USED TO PROVE RACIAL BIAS?**

D. <u>Delays</u>   Delayed justice is mislaid justice. The average time between sentence and execution is over 7 years. Prisoners file appeal after appeal at the state level and federal level. Recent legislation will now limit appeals to one.

CHAPTER FOURTEEN-SAMPLE QUESTIONS

TRUE-FALSE QUESTIONS:

1. For the authors of the Declaration of Independence, individual liberty was inherent in human nature.

2. Democracy is both a decision-making process and a system of government that includes substantive values.

3. Nationalizing the Bill of Rights refers to legislation passed by Congress that made them applicable in the 50 states.

4. Statistical discrepancies of racial bias can be used to challenge the death penalty.

5. More than 90% of criminal cases are plea bargained.

6. Defense attorneys have the first and last word in a trial.

7. The exclusionary rule refers to the peremptory challenge to jurors in a trial.

8. The grant of immunity from prosecution waives the right to self-incrimination.

9. Prior to trial on in a federal felony case, one must be indicted by a grand jury.

10. The percentage of population 12 years or older reporting the use of drugs has been declining since 1988.

MULTIPLE-CHOICE QUESTIONS:

11. Which amendment protects a person from self-incrimination?
    a. First   b. Fourth   c. Fifth   d. Sixth

12. Congress passes a criminal law and makes it retroactive. This would be an example of:
    a. Writ of Habeas Corpus   b. Ex Post Facto law   c. Bill of Attainder
    d. Stare Decisis.

13. Regarding the establishment of religion, the current Lemon doctrine has all but one of the following tests:
    a. The law may be acceptable if the majority of those affected agree with the law.
    b. As its primary effect, the law must neither advance nor inhibit religion.
    c. The law must have a secular purpose.
    d. The law must not foster an excessive government entanglement with religion.

14. Which of the following is protected absolutely:
    a. Religious practices   b. Freedom of speech
    c. Freedom of press   d. Religious beliefs.

15. A wall of separation between church and state would be interpreted as:
    a. Government cannot establish an official religion.
    b. Government may not prefer one religion over another.
    c. Government should not endorse, aid, sponsor, or encourage religious activities.
    d. None of the above.

16. Which of the following best describes the Supreme Court's position on religion in schools:
    a. Only non-denominational prayers are allowed.
    b. Only voluntary school prayers are allowed.
    c. Studying the Bible in public schools is allowed.
    d. A moment of silent prayer is allowed.

17. Which of the following best describes the Supreme Court's position on obscenity?
    a. A local community standard is allowed.
    b. An average person standard is used.
    c. The obscene piece must be without redeeming merit.
    d. The Court looks at sex and obscenity the same.

18. The prior restraint doctrine is most applicable to:
    a. The press   b. Books   c. The film industry   d. Radio and televison

19. In order to protect the confidentiality of sources, the press relies on:
    a. Court orders   b. Police cooperation c. Shield laws
    d. Editorial discretion.

20. Freedom of assembly and petition is important to all but one of the following:
    a. Political parties   b. Interest groups   c. Student organizations
    d. Government organizations

21. Authorities may do all but one of the following in regulating protest, parades and demonstrations:
    a. Specify the time when they will be allowed
    b. Require a permit for a parade
    c. Deny a permit to a group that is radical
    d. Specify the place for the activity.

22. All but one of the following are considered to crimes against property:
    a. Burglary   b. Robbery   c. Auto theft   d. Larceny

23. Which of the following best describes U.S. crimes rates?
    a. From 1965-1975, went up 50%.
    b. In the early 1980s, crime rates went down.
    c. The leveling continued in the 1990s.
    d. Increasing crime rates appear related to cocaine and use of other illegal drugs.

24. The United States leads all industrialized countries in all but one of the following:
    a. Victimization rates   b. Murder rates   c. Incarceration rates
    d. Gun control laws

25. All but one of the following are used to ensure a fair trial:
    a. Speedy and private trial   b. Impartial jury
    c. Right to counsel   d. Right to cross-examine witnesses

CHAPTER FOURTEEN SAMPLE QUESTION ANSWERS

<u>TRUE-FALSE ANSWERS</u>:

1. **TRUE.** Liberty is considered one of our inalienable rights. See page 515.

2. **TRUE.** If democracy is defined only as a decision-making process, there is little protection for personal liberty. Refer to page 516.

3. **FALSE.** The Bill of Rights was made applicable for the states not by an act of Congress, but rather by a series of Supreme Court decisions. See pages 517-518 and Table 14-2.

4. **FALSE.** Only racial bias against the defendant can be used to challenge. See page 551

5. **TRUE.** Incredible as it may seem-see page 550.

6. **FALSE.** The prosecutor has this honor. See page 549.

7. **FALSE.** It refers to the exclusion of contaminated evidence in a trial. See page 547-548.

8. **TRUE.** If so granted, a witness can be compelled to testify. See page 547.

9. **TRUE.** This is a right guaranteed by the 5th Amendment. See page 542.

10. **TRUE.** See <u>A Conflicting View-Legalize Drugs to Control Crime.</u>

<u>MULTIPLE-CHOICE QUESTIONS</u>:

11. **C** This was fairly easy-Taking the Fifth Amendment-refusing to answer questions. See Table 14-1.

12. **B** If you know Latin, this would be an easy question. Ex post facto-after the fact. See Table 14-1.

13. **A** The constitutionality of a law is not subject to a vote. See pages 521-522.

14. **D** Only beliefs are protected unconditionally. See page 520.

15. **C** Jefferson used the words wall of separation and it was intended to mean barring any government assistance to religion. See page 521.

16. **C** When studying the Bible is part of a secular education course in public school, it is allowed by the Supreme Court. See pages 522-523.

17. **A** From an average person standard, the Court retreated to a local community standard. See pages 531-532.

18. **A** The press enjoys the most protection under the no prior restraint doctrine. Refer to pages 533-534.

19. **C.** The press has been active in pressuring state legislatures to pass shield laws to protect their sources. See page 535.

20. **D** This freedom is not applicable to government organizations. See pages 535-536.

21. **C** Authorities have to be even handed in applying the same rules to all groups. See page 536.

22. **B** Robbery is considered a violent crime. See Table 14-3.

23. **D** After leveling off in the 1980s, crime rate began to increase in the 1990s, apparently to the increased use of illegal drugs. See page 540.

24. **D** Many other nations have more stringent gun control laws-England for example. Unfortunately, the U.S. leads in all the other categories. See Compared to What-Crime and Punishment.

25. **A** You have a right to speedy and public not private trial. See page 547.

CHAPTER 15-POLITICS AND CIVIL RIGHTS

I.   THE POLITICS OF EQUALITY. Equality is the very essence of our democracy: "All men are created equal..." Traditionally equality meant "of opportunity"-to develop individual talents and abilities and to be rewarded for work, initiative, merit and achievement. Over time, there has been a shift to equality of result-an equal sharing of income and material rewards. This requires government action to modify the effects of equality of opportunity, i.e. policies to redistribute income, wealth, jobs , promotions, admissions, etc. A related issue is whether equality applies to individuals or groups. Traditionally, equality was seen as fair treatment of all individuals, rather than treatment afforded to particular groups-racial and ethnic minorities, women and the handicapped. Inequality as a member of a group takes on even greater political significance than inequality among individuals. Table 15-1 lists some of the most important milestones in civil rights.

II.   SLAVERY, SEGREGATION AND THE CONSTITUTION.

    A.   Slavery and the Constitution. The Constitution recognized and protected slavery. Article I stated that slaves were to be counted as 3/5ths of a person for purposes of representation in Congress and taxation. Article IV guaranteed the return of escaped slaves to their owners. The majority opinion in the Dred Scott case clearly stated the inferiority of the Negro race who could be treated as mere property.

    B.   Emancipation and Reconstruction. The abolition movement totally disagreed with the Dred Scott decision. The election of 1860 was a four man race which was won by Lincoln. Although personally opposed to slavery, Lincoln promised during the campaign not abolish slavery where it existed. Southerners were not convinced and three months after Lincoln was inaugurated, South Carolina seceded from the Union and the Civil War began. This was to be our nation's bloodiest war. Northern Republicans joined the abolitionists in calling for the emancipation of the slaves to punish the South since its economy depended on slave labor. Lincoln also realized that if the war was being fought to free slaves, British intervention to help the South was less likely. So on September 22, 1862, Lincoln issued his famous Emancipation Proclamation. While this freed the slaves in the seceding states, the 13th Amendment freed slaves in all the country. The 14th Amendment required states to "provide equal protection to all citizens" and the 15th Amendment prohibited the federal and states government from abridging the right to vote on account of race, color or previous condition of servitude. These amendment and civil rights laws passed during the 1860s and 1870s guaranteed the newly freed slaves protection in the exercise of their constitutional rights. Between 1865 and the early 1880s blacks made much progress-holding federal and state offices, and admission to theaters, eating places, hotels and public transportation.

    C.   The Imposition of Segregation. Political support for Reconstruction was eroding. .Because of the close, disputed election of 1876, a deal was struck. In return for

Southern support to elect the Republican Rutherford B. Hayes, the national government would withdraw its troops from the South. As white southerners regained political power and blacks lost the protection of federal forces, the Supreme Court also struck a blow by declaring federal civil rights laws preventing discrimination by private individuals to be unconstitutional. This essentially paved the way for the imposition of segregation as the prevailing social system in the South. During the 1880s and 1890s white southerners imposed segregation in public accommodations, housing, education, employment, and almost every other sector of public and private life. By 1895, most southern states had passed laws requiring segregated schools. Government was the principal instrument of segregation, which was reinforced by individuals and businesses and lynch mobs if necessary. From the blacks in the South there was a cradle to grave system of segregation.

D. Early Court Approval of Segregation. In the Plessy v. Ferguson, The Supreme Court held that segregation of the races did not violate the Equal Protection Clause of the 14th Amendment so long as people in each race were treated equally. Schools that were separate but equal were constitutional. In a lone dissent, Justice Harlan argued for a color-blind standard.

III. EQUAL PROTECTION OF THE LAW. The initial goal of the civil rights movement was to eliminate segregated education and then fight against segregation and discrimination in all sectors of American life. Both public and private.

A. The NAACP and the Legal Battle. The NAACP and its Legal Defense and Education Fund fought to abolish lawful segregation. Led by chief legal counsel Thurgood Marshall, his strategy was to attack the separate but equal doctrine. The NAACP was able to win a series of court cases when they could prove facilities were not equal, but Marshall's goal was to attack the issue of segregation as unequal. His goal was a reversal of Plessy v. Ferguson. Marshall's task was to locate a school district that was segregated, but where there was equality between white and black schools. He found such a district in Topeka, Kansas and in 1952, the NAACP filed a suit on behalf of Linda Brown. Marshall wanted a case where the court could not simply order measures to achieve equality and then wash their hands of the case. Rather, he wanted the courts to squarely face the issue of segregated education.

B. Brown v. Board of Education of Topeka. In 1954, a unanimous Supreme Court held that separate education facilities are inherently unequal and reversed Plessy v. Ferguson. This decision was of critical importance to the civil rights movement.

C. Enforcing Desegregation. The Brown ruling struck down the laws of 21 states and the District of Columbia. Such a far reaching ruling clashing with very strongly held social views was bound to meet resistence. For this reason the Supreme Court did not order immediate desegregation, but rather required state and local authorities operating under the supervision of federal judges to proceed with "deliberate speed." Still it was at least 15 years before segregated schools

173

were on their way out.

D. <u>Busing and Racial Balancing.</u> Federal judges have been given wide freedom to fashion remedies for past or present discriminatory practices caused by government action. However, in 1971, the Supreme Court pulled in the reins somewhat. In the case of Swann v. Charlotte-Mecklenburg County Board of Education, the Court held that forced busing of students was not required to integrate schools unless the racial imbalance was caused by past or present government action. In other words, in the absence of any government action contributing to racial imbalance, states and school districts are not required by the 14th Amendment to integrate their schools. In 1974, the Court threw out a federal judge's order for massive busing between Detroit and 52 suburban schools. If schools are predominantly of one race because of residential patterns, cross-district busing is not required to achieve racial balance.

IV. THE CIVIL RIGHTS ACT. The early civil rights movement effort was to eliminate <u>public</u> discrimination and segregation practiced by government. For this remedy, they turned to the courts. When <u>private</u> discrimination was faced-private owners of restaurants, hotels, motels, stores, private employers, landlords and real estate agents, the movement took its fight to Congress.

A. <u>Martin Luther King, Jr. and Nonviolent Direct Action.</u> King was the leader of the fight in the streets-the tactic of nonviolent action-the breaking of "unjust" laws in an open, "loving," nonviolent fashion. Publicity was key to the success of this tactic. King picked the city of Birmingham, Alabama-the most rigidly segregated city in the South-as a test case. In the Spring of 1963, thousands of blacks led by King were met by Police Chief Eugene ""Bull" Connor and police and firefighters who met the demonstrators with fire hoses, cattle prods and police dogs. All on prime time media. The event was designed to touch the conscience of white Americans. Later in 1963, King led a march on Washington, D.C. which attracted 200,000 white and black participants where he gave his famous "I Have a Dream" speech. President Kennedy proposed a Civil Rights bill in 1963 but was killed before he could see it enacted. As a tribute to the fallen president, President Johnson pushed Kennedy's civil rights bill through Congress in 1964. King was honored by receipt of the Nobel Prize for Peace in the same year.

B. <u>The Civil Rights Act of 1964.</u> This acts stands alongside the Emancipation Proclamation, the 14th Amendment and the Brown case in importance to the civil rights movement.

    1.   Title II-forbids discrimination in any facility serving the public.

    2.   Title VI-Every federal department or agency was to end discrimination in all programs or activities receiving federal support, which could include termination of financial assistance.

    3.   Title VII- **FILL-IN**

C. <u>Civil Rights Act of 1968.</u>   **FILL-IN**.

V. EQUALITY: OPPORTUNITY VERSUS RESULTS. The gains of the civil rights movement in the 1960s were mostly in the area of opportunity; racial politics today concerns actual inequalities between whites and blacks in incomes, jobs, housing, health, education, etc.

    A.   <u>Continuing Inequalities.</u> Table 15-2 shows that there is still a gulf of inequality between blacks, Hispanics and whites. Blacks are less likely to hold prestigious executive jobs or many skilled craft jobs.

    B.   <u>Policy Choices?</u> What should be done to achieve equality? Should color-blind standards be used or should the government take affirmative action to remedy the results of past unequal treatment of blacks by giving preferential treatment in university admissions and scholarships, jobs and promotions, etc.

    C.   <u>Shifting Goals in Civil Rights Policy.</u> From equal opportunity, the goals shifted to affirmative action involving the establishment of "goals and timetables" to achieve greater equality. While avoiding use of the word "quota," the notion of affirmative action observes whether blacks achieve admissions, jobs, and promotions in proportion to their numbers in the population.

    D.   <u>Affirmative Action.</u> These programs were initially developed in the federal bureaucracy. President Johnson signed Executive Order 11246 in 1965 which required all businesses that contracted with the federal government to implement affirmative action programs. In 1972, the U.S. Office of Education issued guidelines which mandated goals for university admissions and faculty hiring of minorities and women. Federal officials generally measure "progress" in terms of the number of disadvantaged group members hired, admitted, employed, etc. The pressure to show "progress" can result in a relaxation of traditional measures of qualification, such as test scores. Advocates of affirmative action argue that these are not valid since they are biased in favor of white culture.

VI. AFFIRMATIVE ACTION IN THE COURTS. The constitution question involved is whether affirmative action programs discriminate against whites in violation of the Equal Protection Clause of the 14th Amendment and the Civil Rights Act of 1964. The Court has not developed thus far any clear-cut answers.

    A.   <u>The Bakke Case.</u> Allan Bakke applied for medical school at the University of California. For two years he was denied admission, even though minorities with lower GPAs and medical aptitude tests were admitted. A special program reserved 16 of the 100 annual admissions for minority students. The university argued that its programs were designed to help minorities. The Supreme Court in University of California Regents v. Bakke ruled that while race could be a factor, it could not be the sole factor and ordered Bake's admission. To use race as a sole factor would be a violation of the Equal Protection Clause of the 14th Amendment. Both opponents and supporters of affirmative action claimed victory: Race was upheld as a legitimate factor in affirmative action. Bakke was admitted.

B. Affirmative Action as a Remedy for Past Discrimination. The Court has continued to approve affirmative action programs designed to remedy past discrimination. The Court upheld in 1979 a training plan designed to help minorities into skilled technical jobs. Weber who was white was denied this training opportunity while blacks with less seniority and fewer qualifications were accepted. In 1987, the Court upheld a rigid 50% quota system for promotions in the Alabama Department of Safety. The court felt that whatever burdens were placed on innocent parties were over weighed by the need to correct the effects of past discrimination.

C. Cases Questioning Affirmative Action. In 1984, the Court ruled that a city could not lay off white firefighters in favor of black firefighters with less seniority. In 1989, the Court ruled that the City of Richmond Virginia's 30% minority set-aside program violated the Equal Protection Clause.

D. Absence of a Clear Constitutional Principle. There is no clear rule of law, or legal test, or constitutional principle that tells us what is permissible and what is prohibited in racially conscious laws and practices. Still, over time some general tendencies have appeared:

   1. Response to a past proven history of discrimination.
   2. Narrowly tailored.
   3. No absolute bar to white competition or participation.
   4. Serve clearly identified, compelling and legitimate government objectives.

VII. AFFIRMATIVE ACTION IN CONGRESS. Congress has also played a role in affirmative action. Mindful of the public's support of affirmative action in the abstract, but resistence to "quotas and preferences," Congress has tried to steer a middle course.

A. Getting into Specifics. The CRA of 1964 bars racial or sexual discrimination in employment. Can statistical under representation of minorities or women prove discrimination absent any specific concrete evidence of direct discrimination? If an employer uses a job requirement or test that has a disparate effect on minorities or women, who has the burden of proof to show that the requirement or test is relevant to effective job performance? In 1989, a closely divided Court held that statistical imbalance by itself was insufficient and that plaintiffs had the burden of proof.

B. Civil rights and Women's Equity Act of 1991. Civil rights groups alarmed at the Supreme Court's narrowing of the CRA sought help from Congress to rewrite the section of the CRA to restore these protections. Businesses fought to avoid quotas. Congress in writing the bill specifically outlawed the use of quotas. Other important provisions include:

   1. Statistical imbalance   **FILL-IN**

2. <u>Disparate Employment Practices</u>   **FILL-IN**

3. <u>Penalties</u>   **FILL-IN**

VIII. NEW DEBATES OVER AFFIRMATIVE ACTION.
    A. <u>Individual Rights versus Group Rights.</u> Over time, the civil rights movement has shifted its focus from <u>individual rights</u> to <u>group benefits.</u> Affirmative action programs classify people by group membership. Racial and gender preferences are currently used in hiring and promotion in private and public employment, including colleges and universities.
    B. <u>Rising Opposition to Preferences.</u> Blacks and whites have different opinions about the extent of discrimination. <u>See Up Close: Black and White Opinion on Affirmative Action.</u> There is increasing resentment against preferential treatment for minorities. The stereotype "angry white male" has emerged. Some argue that the disadvantages in society today are class not race based and preferences should be based on economic disadvantage. Some black Americans opposed affirmative action because it negatively stereotypes blacks as unable to advance based on merit alone. The black Americans argue that affirmative action has been more harmful than helpful.
    C. <u>The California Civil Rights Initiative.</u>   **FILL-IN.**

IX. GENDER EQUALITY AND THE FOURTEENTH AMENDMENT. The Supreme Court has never interpreted the Equal Protection Clause to give the same level of protection to gender as to racial equality. Indeed, in 1873, the Supreme Court specifically rejected arguments that this clause applied to women.
    A. <u>Early Feminist Politics.</u>   **FILL-IN**

177

B.   Judicial Scrutiny of Gender Classifications. Early in the 1970s, the Court became responsive to arguments that sex discrimination may violate the Equal Protection Clause of the 14th Amendment. In 1971, the Court ruled that sexual classification must be reasonable not arbitrary. Since then, the Court has also ruled:
1.   The state cannot set different gender ages to become legal adults or purchase alcohol.
2.   Women cannot be barred from police or firefighting jobs by arbitrary height and weight requirements.
3.   Insurance and retirement plans for women must pay the same benefits.
4.   Men and women coaches must receive the same pay in high school sports.

C.   Continuing Gender Differences. The Court has upheld statutory rape laws which make it a crime for an adult to have sex with a female under the age of 18, regardless of her consent. The Court upheld the draft registration of men only. Women in the military can serve in air and naval combat units, but remain excluded from combat infantry, armor, artillery and special forces.

X.   GENDER EQUALITY IN THE ECONOMY. As cultural views of women have changed and family budgets need two wage earners, women's participation in the work force has increased. With this, feminist political activity has shifted toward economic concerns-gender equality in education, employment, pay. etc.

A.   Gender Equality in Civil Rights Laws.
1.   Title VII of the CRA of 1964 prohibits sexual discrimination in employment, pay, and promotions. The EEOC bars stereotyping of men's and women's jobs.
2.   The Federal Equal Credit Opportunity Act of 1974 prohibits gender discrimination in credit transactions.
3.   Title XI prohibits sex discrimination in education. This bars discrimination in admissions, housing, financial aid, faculty and staff recruitment and pay and athletics.

B.   The Earning Gap. Women earn on average 71% of what men earn. This wage difference is attributable to the labor market division of traditionally male and female jobs with the former paying more. See Figure 15-1 and Compared to What: the Earnings Gap in Democratic Countries.

C.   The Dual labor market and "Comparable Worth." The dual labor market with male-dominated "blue collar" jobs distinguishable from female-dominated "pink-collar" jobs remains a major obstacle to pay equality between men and women. Women's choices of employment have been limited by cultural stereotyping, social conditioning, and training and education. Recognizing that wage equalities may be more a result of occupational differentiation rather than discrimination,

178

some feminist organizations have called for <u>comparable worth</u> in the labor market. Advocates recommend that jobs should be evaluated by their responsibilities, effort, knowledge and skill requirements and that jobs judged "comparable" should be paid the same wages. This approach raises many issues-who selects the standards? Who decides what wages should be equal? So far, the comparable worth has been rejected by the EEOC and federal courts, but has been accepted by a few state governments and employers.

D. The "Glass Ceiling". **FILL-IN. WHAT ARE SOME OF THE EXPLANATIONS USED TO THIS CEILING?** See also feature <u>What Do You think?: What Constitutes Sexual Harassment?</u>

XI. HISPANIC POLITICS. The term Hispanic includes: Mexican-Americans, Puerto Ricans, Cubans and others of Spanish speaking ancestry and culture. Percentages follow the same order-the largest number of Hispanics are Mexican-Americans, etc. Median family income for Hispanics is higher than blacks but lower than whites. The same is true of poverty levels and unemployment rates. The percent of Hispanics completing high school is lower that blacks or whites. Yet the term Hispanic masks substantial differences among the various groups.

A. <u>Mexican-Americans.</u> **FILL-IN. WHY DOES MEXICAN-AMERICAN POLITICAL POWER NOT MATCH THEIR POPULATION PERCENTAGE?**

B. <u>Puerto Ricans.</u> **FILL-IN. WHAT EXPLANATION IS OFFERED TO EXPLAIN THE LOWER MEDIAN INCOME AND POVERTY OF PUERTO RICANS?**

C. <u>Cuban-Americans</u>. **FILL-IN. HOW DO CUBAN-AMERICANS COMPARE ECONOMICALLY WITH OTHER HISPANIC GROUPS?**

179

D. Hispanics in Congress. **FILL-IN. ARE MOST HISPANIC REPRESENTATIVES DEMOCRATS OR REPUBLICANS?**

XII. NATIVE AMERICANS: TRAILS OF TEARS. It is estimated that 7 to 13 million native Americans lived in the U.S. and Canada before the arrival of the Spanish. Twenty-five more million lived in Mexico. There was not a single Indian nation, but rather hundreds of separate cultures and languages. The native population of the Americas was devastated by wars, disease and famine. Overall, the population declined by 90%, the greatest disaster in human history. Diseases brought from Europe were the most effective killers-small pox, measles, bubonic plague, influenza, typhus, etc. By 1910, there were only 210,000 native Americans in the U.S. Since then, the population has climbed to 2.2 million, which is less than 1% of the American population.

A. The Trail of Broken Treaties. In the Northwest Ordinance of 1787 and the Intercourse Act of 1790, the U.S. government promised to respect the territorial integrity of Indian lands; yet these promises were repeatedly violated by white invasions of these lands with subsequent wars that led to further loss of Native lands.

B. Indian Territories. **FILL-IN. WHAT HAPPENED TO THE INDIAN TERRITORIES?**

C. Indian Wars 1864-1890. The continuing encroachment of Indian territories by white settles and hunters who decimated the buffalo herds led to malnutrition and demoralization of the Indian Plains peoples which resulted in a long period of war. The most historic battle was that of the Little Bighorn River where Civil War hero General George Armstrong Custer and elements of the 7th Calvary were destroyed by Sioux and Cheyenne Indians lead by Chief Crazy Horse. The Apaches under Geronimo also fought hard, but by 1890 Indian resistence was at an end.

D. The Attempted Destruction of Traditional Life. The Dawes Act of 1887 governed federal policy toward Native Americans for decades. It broke up traditional Indian lands into homesteads to encourage the Native Americans to become farmers instead of hunters. Traditional native culture, traditions and language were to be shed for English and traditional schooling. The net effect was the loss of 50% of native lands suffered greatly. The Bureau of Indian Affairs which was

180

supposed to look after the Native Americans was corrupt and poorly managed. It encouraged dependency and interfered with native religious affairs and customs. The native Americans suffered high infant mortality rates, poverty and alcoholism.

E. The New Deal. **FILL-IN. WHAT WERE THE EFFECTS OF THE INDIAN REORGANIZATION ACT OF 1934?**

F. The American Indian Movement. The Civil Rights movement in the 1960s inspired Indian activists. The American Indian Movement (AIM) was founded in 1968 and occupied Alcatraz Island and the site of the Wounded Knee battle. Several Indian nations pressed their claims in Congress and the federal courts to win back lands or compensation for lands taken in violation of treaties. Native culture was revitalized and best selling books were written of the Indian's plight.

G. Native Americans Today. **FILL-IN. WHAT IS THE STATUS OF NATIVE AMERICANS? ARE THEY ANY BETTER OFF TODAY?**

XIII. THE RIGHTS OF THE DISABLED AMERICANS. Disabled Americans were not included in the landmark Civil Rights Act of 1964. Yet they have long suffered obstacles to participation in education, employment and access to public accommodations. The Americans with Disabilities Act (ADA) of 1990 prohibits discrimination against disabled people in private employment, public accommodations, and telecommunications. The act is vague in many parts providing lawyers and bureaucrats with much employment over the next several years. Specifically, the ADA provides:

A. Employment. Employers should make reasonable accommodations for disabled employees, but are excused if these accommodations would cause undue hardship to the employer.

B. Government programs. The disabled cannot be denied access to government programs or benefits. New taxis, buses, and trains must be accessible.

C. Public accommodations. **FILL-IN. WHAT TYPE OF ALTERATIONS MUST BE DONE TO ACCOMMODATE THE HANDICAPPED?**

D.   Telecommunications. Devices must be available for the hearing or speech impaired to the extend possible.

XIV.   INEQUALITY AND THE CONSTITUTION. Americans often claim rights that are not based on the Constitution-medical care, education, retirement benefits and jobs. The Constitution is designed to limit the government, not mandate that it governs justly or wisely.

A.   Constitutional versus Legal Rights. All the benefits mentioned above come from laws passed by Congress, i.e. are legal rights.

B.   "Reasonable" Classifications. Government programs may classify people by income, age, illness, disability or any other "reasonable" standard. The Equal Protection Clause of the 14th amendment has been interpreted by the Supreme Court to prohibit "invidious discrimination" by the government, but does not prohibit "reasonable classifications" of individuals. The Equal Protection Clause does require that once such a classification is made, those meeting the eligibility must receive the same benefits. These benefits are legal requirements not constitutional. Therefore, Congress could change the benefits or eligibility as they desire.

C.   Protection for Poor Americans. The Constitution does provide some protection for the poor's legal and political rights. Included among these rights are:

1.   Free legal counsel in criminal cases.

2.   No tax or financial requirement for voting.

But the poor cannot demand government funding as a constitutional right to exercise other rights. For example, the Hyde Amendment in 1977 denied government funding for Medicaid abortions. The Supreme Court recognized that abortions were a constitutional right, but that federal funding of them was not required by the Constitution.

D.   Income Inequality. The government does not have any Constitutional requirement to eliminate inequality of wealth or income. In fact, the Founding Fathers thought that any such requirement would violate the right to property. Minority groups have charged that unequal public school spending discriminates against poor children. But the Supreme Court disagreed holding the spending differences based on dependence on property taxes and the value of property did not violate the Equal Protection Clause. Some state courts have held that such inequalities do violate state constitutions.

CHAPTER 15 SAMPLE QUESTIONS

TRUE-FALSE QUESTIONS:

1. The equal sharing of income and wealth would be described as equality of opportunity.

2. Traditionally equality was reserved for individuals rather than groups.

3. The Civil Rights Act of 1957 was the first civil rights legislation passed by Congress since Reconstruction.

4. The Emancipation Proclamation freed slaves throughout the United States.

5. The Compromise of 1877 denationalized desegregation efforts to in the South.

6. Once the Supreme Court in the Brown case announced that segregated schools were unconstitutional, integrated schools were rapidly operated in their place.

7. The Constitution does not govern the activities on private individuals. Only Congress at the national level could outlaw discrimination in the private sector.

8. The Comparable Worth doctrine was developed to help bridge the gap between white and black earnings.

9. Puerto Ricans comprise the largest Hispanic minority group.

10. Approximately, about 50% of Native Americans live below the poverty line.

MULTIPLE-CHOICE QUESTIONS:

11. The amendment that contains the Equal Protection Clause is the:
    a. 13th b. 14th c. 15th d. 16th

12. What legislation prohibits discrimination in the rental or sale of housing?
    a. Civil Rights Act of 1957   b. Civil Rights Act of 1964
    c. Civil Rights Act of 1968   d. Civil Rights Act of 1871.

13. Which Supreme Court case supported the idea that blacks were inferior to whites?
    a. Dred Scott v. Sandford   b. Plessy v. Ferguson
    c. Brown v. Board of Education   d. Griswold v. Connecticut

14. Which of the following Supreme Court cases upheld state segregation laws:
    a. Civil Rights cases of 1883.   b. Plessy v. Ferguson

c. Brown v. Board of Education   d. South Carolina v. Kazenbach

15. Which of the following black leaders was in favor of accommodation with white supremacy?
     a. Booker T. Washington   b. W.E.B. DuBois
     c. Oscar de Priest   d. Thurgood Marshall

16. Which of the following black leaders was influential in the founding of the NAACP?
     a. Booker T. Washington   b. W.E.B. DuBois
     c. Oscar de Priest   d. Thurgood Marshall

17. In the important Swann v. Charlotte-Mecklenburg County Board of Education, the Supreme Court upheld all but one of the following:
     a. Racially balanced schools and assignment of pupils to schools based on race.
     b. Court ordered bussing to achieve racial balance.
     c. Close scrutiny by judges of schools that are of one race.
     d. Using the above remedies when past or present government action did not contribute to racial unbalance.

18. Which title of the Civil Rights Act of 1964 prohibits discrimination or segregation of public accommodations?
     a. Title II   b. Title VI   c. Title VII   d. Title VIII

19. In most socio-economic measures, Blacks compared to Hispanics are less favorably placed except in one of the following measures:

     a. % completing college.   b. Median family income
     c. % below poverty level   d. Unemployment rate

20. Which of the following Supreme Court cases addressed minority set-aside construction programs?
     a.. University of California v. Bakke
     b. United Steelworkers of American v. Weber
     c. United States v. Paradise
     d. City of Richmond v. Crosen Co.

21. While the Supreme Court has failed to develop a clear constitutional standard in the area of affirmative action, there are some guidelines that have been observed. Which of the following is not one of these guidelines?
     a. Adopted in response to past discrimination
     b. Narrowly tailored
     c. Absolute bar to whites or males
     d. Serve compelling and legitimate government objectives.

22. Among the more important provisions of the Civil Rights Act of 1991 are all but one of the following:

    a. Statistical workforce imbalance does not prove discrimination.

    b. Quotas are permissible for certain industries.

    c. Employers bear the burden of proving that a job disparate impact bears some relationship to effective job performance.

    d. Victims of discrimination can obtain both compensatory and punitive awards.

23. Black and white public opinion is most divided on the issue of:

    a. Job training for minorities to qualify them for better jobs

    b. Set aside minority scholarships at public colleges.

    c. Provision of special education classes to prepare minorities for college.

    d. Set aside minority admissions at schools.

24. Since 1971, the Supreme Court has issued many rulings dealing with gender disparities. All but one of the following areas were included in such court rulings.

    a. legal age to purchase alcohol.

    b. height and weight requirements for police or firefighters.

    c. monthly payments for insurance benefits.

    d. equal availability for the military draft.

25. Which nation listed below has the smallest earnings gap between men and women:

    a. Iceland   b. Denmark c. Japan   d. United States

CHAPTER 15 SAMPLE QUESTION ANSWERS

TRUE-FALSE ANSWERS:

1. **FALSE**. This would describe equality of result. See page 555.

2. **TRUE**. Only recently have civil rights been extended to groups. See page 556.

3. **TRUE**. After 1875, none were passed until 1957. See Table 15-1

4. **FALSE**. It freed slaves only in the succeeding states; the 13th Amendment was necessary to free slaves in all the states. See page 558.

5. **TRUE**. In return for the support of 3 Southern states, the newly elected national government removed federal troops from the South, and gave up its efforts to rearrange Southern society. Segregation soon returned to the South. See page 558.

6. **FALSE**. Although the Brown ruling struck down segregated schools in 21 states and the District of Columbia, compliance was slow as molasses. See page 564.

7. **TRUE**. Congress has the power to regulate interstate commerce. If discrimination, even private, interferes with this commerce, Congress has the power to pass corrective legislation. This was the basis of the 1964 Civil Rights Act. See page 565.

8. **FALSE**. Although logically it could apply, it was developed to close the gap between male and female earning. See pages 581-582.

9. **FALSE.** Mexican-Americans have this honor. See page 585.

10. **TRUE**. As shameful a situation that can be, Native Americans have fared the least well in American. See page 592.

MULTIPLE-CHOICE ANSWERS:

11. **B** The 14th amendment is one of the most powerful changes to the Constitution. See Table 15-1.

12. **C** Sometimes called the Housing Act of 1968, it was amended in 1988 to cover the handicapped and families with children. See Table 15-1.

13 **A** The Dred Scott decision written by Chief Justice Taney basically considered blacks as property. See page 556.

14. **B** It was in the infamous Plessy v. Ferguson decision, that the lone dissenter Justice John

Marshall Harlan stated that the Constitution is color blind.

15. **A** Washington was content to have a Black America that would improve itself through education. See feature <u>Up Close-African-American Politics in Historical Perspective.</u>

16. **B** DuBois was on the original board of the NAACP when it was founded in 1909 on the 100th anniversary of the birth of Lincoln. See feature <u>Up Close-African-American Politics in Historical Perspective.</u>

17. **D** None of the remedies are allowed if government action did not contribute to the racial unbalance. See page 564.

18. **A** This is a tough question, but you should have some idea about which titles of the CRA impact on education, employment, federal programs and public accommodations. See page 568.

19. **B** More blacks complete college than Hispanics, but in the other categories Hispanics are more favorably placed than blacks. See Table 15-2.

20. **D** The Court voided a 30% set-aside program of the City of Richmond for minority contractors. See page 572.

21. **C** An absolute bar to whites or males is not allowed. See page 573.

22. **B** Quotas were specifically forbidden by the Act. See page 574.

23. **B** The difference in opinion on minority set-aside scholarships is 60%. See <u>Up Close-Black and White Opinion on Affirmative Action.</u>

24. **D** Laws excluding women from the draft were upheld by the Supreme Court.

25. **A** Iceland also has the world's lowest illiteracy rate. See <u>Compared to What-The Earning Gap in Democratic Nations.</u>

I. POLITICS AND ECONOMICS. Politics involves collective decisions and government coercion. A Free Market economic system involves individual decisions and relies on voluntary exchanges. Both politics and markets transform popular demands into goods and services. The proper relationship between politics and economics lies in the field of study called political economy.

II. COMPETING ECONOMIC THEORIES. These competing theories attempt to explain the forces that generate demand-the purchase of goods and services and supply-the willingness and ability of firms to produce the goods and services. Macroeconomic theories also attempt to explain inflation-a general rise of prices; recession-a general decline in economic activity; and growth-an increase in the nation's total economic output, normally measured by the real (inflation adjusted) gross domestic product (GDP).

A. Classical Theory. Adam Smith in the celebrated work The Wealth of Nations was a strong advocate of laissez-faire and free markets. In essence, this theory envisions minimal government intervention in the market which will be self-regulating by an invisible hand of the marketplace. Classical economists say that the normal forces of supply and demand will regulate the economy. **WHAT HAPPENS IN A RECESSION? WHAT CAUSES INFLATION? WHAT CAUSES UNEMPLOYMENT?**

B. Keynesian Theory. The Great Depression of the 1930s shattered faith in classical economic theory. Unemployment averaged 18% for several years, reaching a high of 25% in 1933. John Maynard Keynes believed that economic instability was the fault of lowered demand. Unemployment and lower wages reduced demand for goods and services. Reduced demand led to further layoffs and cuts in production. But these in turn led to further reductions in demand and the spiral continued. Reduction of interest rates would not spur businesses to borrow money if production in demand was falling. Keynes saw that the economy would not turn around unless demand was increased. Therefore, government should spend more money to increase demand and lower taxes to stimulate consumer and business spending, i.e. increased demand. In this situation, the government might have to run up a deficit. During inflationary periods, the government should take the opposite course-cut its spending, raise taxes and run a budget surplus. The net effect of these actions would be to reduce demand and thus check inflation by stabilizing or lowering prices.

C. Employment Act of 1946. Keynes ideas were codified into law in the Employment Act of 1946 which pledged that the federal government would promote maximum employment production and purchasing power through its taxing and spending policies. The act also created the Council of Economic Advisors to develop and recommend to the president national economic policies. The act also required the president to present an annual economic report to the

Congress. While most economists endorse Keynesian theories, politicians have more of a problem with unemployment than inflation. Once in the habit of deficit spending, politicians are reluctant to raise taxes and cut spending to halt inflation and create a budget surplus. The Keynesian theory also had a problem in the 1970s when the U.S. economy experienced both high <u>unemployment and inflation</u> which should not occur simultaneously. This period also saw law economic growth and led to a new word-<u>stagflation</u>-a period of low economic growth and rising prices.

D. <u>Supply Side Economics</u>. **FILL-IN. HOW DO SUPPLY-SIDERS FEEL ABOUT THE ROLE OF GOVERNMENT? WHAT IS THE EFFECT OF ECONOMIC GROWTH ACCORDING TO THIS THEORY? WHY DID THIS THEORY FAIL IN THE 1980S?**

E. <u>Monetarist Economics.</u> While Keynesian theory provided for the expansion of the money supply during a recession and the contraction of the money supply in inflationary periods, monetarist economic theory holds that the expansion of the money supply should be at the same rate as economic growth. They do not agree that manipulation of the money supply effectively influences economic activity. They argue that in the long run real income depends on actual economic output. In short, they feel government manipulation of the money supply is the problem, not the solution to economic inactivity.

F. <u>Clinton's Economic Policies.</u> Clinton's early rhetoric was to grow the economy by investing in education and skill training for workers; and also in the information highway and infrastructure development. All of these would require more government spending and Clinton pushed through a tax increase in his first year in office. But still budget deficits was large and these prevented President Clinton from pursuing a more active government intervention in the economy. And the Republican Congress elected in 1994 further restrained any further growth in spending.

III. ECONOMIC DECISION MAKING. National fiscal policy focuses on taxing, spending, and borrowing by the federal government. The system of checks and balances functions in this area. Within the Executive branch, responsibility for economic policy is divided among the White House, the Office of Management and Budget (OMB), the Treasury Department, the Council of Economic Advisors and the powerful, yet independent, Federal Reserve Board.

A. <u>Congress and the President.</u> The Constitution places all taxing, borrowing and spending powers in the hands of Congress. By terms of the pay all debts and provide for the common defense and general Welfare clause in Article I, the Supreme Court held that any spending that serves the general welfare is allowed. Thus, there is no constitutional barrier to spending or borrowing by Congress. Efforts have been made to pass a balanced budget amendment to the Constitution, but these efforts have not been successful to date. While the President has little formal powers in this area, presidents have acquired leadership over national economic policy by virtue of submitting the Budget of the U.S. Government. In

189

this document, the president lays out his proposals for spending, revenue estimates based on tax levels and the estimates for projected deficits and the need for borrowing if this is necessary.

B.   The President's Economic Team. There are three main players on the team:

    1.   The Office of Management and Budget. This office prepares the Budget of the U.S. and also oversees the budget requests of every federal department and agency.

    2.   The Department of the Treasury. **FILL-IN.**

    3.   The Council of Economic Advisors. A small body of three eminent economists and staff, they prepare forecasts of economic conditions and makes recommendations on economic policies, principally in its Economic Report to the President.

C.   The Federal Reserve Board. Most advanced nations have a central bank to regulate the supply of money and have found it best to remove this bank from direct control of elected politicians. These are tempted to pay for government programs by issuing more money rather than raising taxes. This results in inflation, often hyper-inflation of 500 to 1,000 % per year. The Federal reserve is largely independent of the President and the Congress. It is governed by a 7 member Board of Governors, nominated by the president and confirmed by the Senate for 14 year terms. While members can be removed for cause , none have ever been removed since its creation in 1913. The Chairman of the Board's term is 4 years, but it overlaps the term of the president, so new presidents cannot immediately name their own Chair. The Fed regulates the supply of money to control inflation and recession. It also oversee the operation of the 12 Federal Reserve Banks, which actually issue the nation's currency which is called Federal Reserve Notes. The Federal Reserve banks are banker's banks; they do not serve the general public. They hold the deposits, or reserves of banks, lend money to banks at discount rates, and oversee the operation of the nation's banking system. They also act as a clearing house for checks throughout the banking system. The Fed influences the economy mainly through increasing or decreasing the nation's money supply. When inflation threatens, the Fed:

    1.   Raises the reserve requirement for member banks, thereby decreasing the amount of money in circulation.

    2.   Raises the discount rate for loans to member banks.

    3.   Sells off government bonds and notes in the market to withdraw money in circulation.

IV.   THE PERFORMANCE OF THE AMERICAN ECONOMY. The U.S. economy produces more than $7 trillion in goods and services annually for 265 million people or about $25,000 in output for every citizen.

A.   Economic Growth. Gross Domestic Product (GDP) is a widely used measure of economic performance. It is the nation's total production of goods and services and counts only final purchase of goods and services. For example, it does not count the purchase of steel by an auto manufacturer, but does count the price of the car. This avoids double counting. GDP also excludes financial transactions and income transfers, such as Social Security. Although expressed in current dollars, GDP is also often calculated constant dollars to reflect real values over time, adjusting for inflation. GDP estimates are prepared by the Commerce Department every quarter. Growth in constant dollars measures the overall performance of the economy. Economic recessions and recoveries are measured as fluctuations in GDP. For example, a recession is defined as negative GDP growth in two successive quarters. Economic growth has historically been followed by periods of contraction. In recent decades, the fluctuations have been more moderate suggesting to many economists that countercylical government fiscal and monetary policies have succeeded in greater stability. See Figure 16-1

B. Unemployment. From a political viewpoint, unemployment may be the most important measure of the economy. Unemployment is different than not working. For example, retired persons are not unemployed, nor are those who are sick or attending school. Unemployed is defined as those looking for work or waiting to return to a job. The unemployed include 34% terminated from their last job, 15% temporarily laid off, 15% who voluntarily quit, and 10% who entered for the first time the labor market and 27% who have reentered the labor market. The unemployment rate is calculated monthly by the Labor department by a random sampling of 50,000 households. The unemployment rate fluctuates with the business cycle, but generally lags GDP growth.

C. Inflation. Refers to the general rise of prices for all goods and services. Inflation erodes the value of the dollar, because it takes more money to purchase the same amount of goods. Since money has less value, savings are devalued as well which reduces the incentive to save. Those living on fixed incomes, such as retired persons, are also hurt by inflation. When banks and investors anticipate inflation, they charge more interest for loans to offset the lower value of the inflated dollar. This, in turn, makes it harder to expand businesses, buy homes, or credit purchases. Thus, inflation harms economic growth.

V. UNCONTROLLABLE FEDERAL SPENDING AND BUDGET PRIORITIES. All government spending equaled 35% of GDP. The federal government alone spends $1.6T or 23% of GDP. Much of the growth of the federal budget is attributed to uncontrollables :

A. Entitlement Programs. These are programs which provide legally enforceable rights to beneficiaries and they account for over half of all federal spending. Some notable programs include: Social security, Medicare, federal retirements and veteran benefits. These programs pay benefits regardless of the need of the recipient. Other entitlement programs are based on demonstrated need and these include: welfare, Medicaid, and food stamps. Note that these are not constitutional entitlements, but rather legal ones. Congress could change the law modifying or eliminating a benefit and indeed has passed a welfare reform bill. Note that entitlement payments do not go only to the poor. Social Security, Medicare and federal and veteran retirements amount to 2/3 of entitlements while

191

payments to the poor are only 1/3 of these payments. See <u>Up-Close: Transfers and Entitlements Drive Government Spending</u>.

B. <u>Indexing of Benefits.</u> Congress has indexed some benefits to automatically increase to match inflation. Indexing applies to programs such as Social Security, Supplement Security Income, food stamps, and veteran's pensions. This indexing pushes up the cost of these entitlement programs every year and contributes to inflation. Further, the Consumer Price Index used to calculate the index includes interest on home and purchases of new appliances and cars. Older retirees may have already paid off their mortgages, and do not buy many new appliances and cars as working persons. Thus, the CPI and index may overestimate the needs of these older recipients for cost-of-living increases.

C. <u>Increasing Cost of in-kind Benefits</u>   **FILL-IN. WHAT IS AN IN-KIND BENEFIT?**

D. <u>Interest on the National Debt</u>.   **FILL-IN. WHEN IS THE LAST TIME THE U.S. HAD A BALANCED BUDGET?**

E. <u>Backdoor Spending and Loan Guarantees</u>. Some federal spending does not appear in the budget, e.g. the U.S. Postal Service. Government-guaranteed loans. also do not, yet a default on these loans. creates a fiscal obligation on the part of the federal government.

F. <u>Federal Budget Priorities.</u> Figure 16-3 indicates that federal expenditures for major programs has changed over time. For example, spending for national defense has dropped while spending for Social Security, welfare and Medicare has grown very rapidly. Entitlement programs will grow as medical costs are the fastest growing sector of the federal budget. Interest costs will increase unless Congress balances the federal budget.

VI. THE DEBT BURDEN. The accumulated national debt is over $5 trillion or about $18,000/capita. This debt is owed mostly to banks and financial institutions and individual investors. About 13% is owed to foreign banks or individuals. The current debt equals 68% of GDP. Imagine that your individual debt would equal 68% of your income. The floating of this huge debt depends on continued public confidence that the federal government can continue to pay interest on the debt, and pay off bonds when they become due.

A. <u>Default and Hyperinflation.</u> No one expects the U.S. government to default on its debt-refuse to pay interest when due. But in the past, other nations have done so. Some future administration may be tempted to monetize the debt-that is, print more money to pay off bondholders. Such currency would flood the nation and soon become worthless resulting in hyperinflation-annual inflation between 100-1,000 %. Both would appear to be unlikely in the near future.

B.   <u>Interest for Future Generations</u>.   **FILL-IN. YOU MIGHT CONSIDER THIS AS A NEGATIVE INHERITANCE!**

C.   <u>Slowing Economic Growth.</u>   **FILL-IN. HOW DOES THE HUGE FEDERAL DEBT SLOW ECONOMIC GROWTH?**

D.   <u>Limiting Government Programs.</u> The huge debt limits the ability of the president and Congress to deal with new problems facing the nation.

E.   <u>The Politics of Deficit.</u> The huge debt is the fault of Republicans and Democrats, the Congress and the President. Deficit financing appeals to politicians. They can provide benefits without raising taxes. To be sure this will burden future generations, but these politicians will be long gone. They live to the next election.

F.   <u>Washington's Budget Battles</u>. Since no money can be spent that is not appropriated, if Congress fails to pass or the president fails to sign a spending bill, then the government must shut down for lack of funds. This game was played by the Republican Congress and President Clinton in 1995 and the government was forced to shut down twice. In reality, only non-essential services were closed. Congressional leaders and the president agreed to balance the budget by the year 2002 (again when they will be gone), but this agreement is not binding on them or future leaders.

VII.   THE TAX BURDEN. The U.S. tax burden is modest compared to other countries. See <u>Compared to What: Tax Burdens in Advanced Democracies</u>. Federal revenue is derived from 5 sources:

A.   <u>Individual Income Tax</u>. This is the government's largest source of revenue (See Figure 16-3). Individual income is now taxed at five marginal rates: 15%, 28%, 31%, 36% and 39.6%. That is, up to a certain income level, one pays 15%, the next income level pays 28%, etc. Personal exemptions and refundable earned income tax credit relieve the poorest families from paying any income tax. Tax brackets, personal exemptions and standard deductions are indexed to protect against inflation. Income tax is automatically deducted from the paychecks of employees. This withholding system is the backbone of the individual income tax. Naturally, the government pays no interest on the money they withhold. About half of personal income is not taxed due to exemptions, deductions, etc. These are called tax expenditures which represent revenue lost to the government. Among the major tax expenditures are:

1. Personal exemptions.
2. Home mortgage interest.
3. Property taxes paid on first and second homes.
4. Deferral of capital gains taxes on home sales.
5.
6.
7.
8. Exclusion of Social Security benefits.
9.
10. State and Local income taxes paid.
11.
12. Accelerated depreciation for machinery, equipment and structures.
13. Medical expenses over 7.5% of income.

Much of the political infighting in Washington involves the efforts of interest groups to obtain exemptions, deductions, special treatments, etc.

B.   Corporate Income Taxes.   **FILL-IN. HOW MUCH OF THE FEDERAL GOVERNMENT'S REVENUE IS TAXED FROM BUSINESS INCOME? WHICH ORGANIZATIONS ARE EXEMPT FROM CORPORATE INCOME TAXES? WHO REALLY PAYS FOR CORPORATE INCOME TAXES-THE CONSUMER OR STOCKHOLDER?**

C.   Social Security Taxes. This is the second largest and fastest-growing source of federal revenue. It is also withheld from paychecks as a FICA tax and is currently 15.3% of income, one half paid by the employer and one half by the employee. Since these taxes are largely earmarked for Social Security, those paying FICA feel they have a right to Social Security. After all, they have paid for it. Or have they? Less than 15% of benefits paid today to current Social Security recipients can be attributed to their prior contributions. Current taxpayers pay 85% of the benefits received by current retirees. Today a majority of taxpayers pay more in Social Security taxes than income taxes.

D.   Estate and Gift Taxes. Federal estate taxes begin on estates in excess of $600,000. Any amount over this is taxed at 37%. To avoid the wealthy giving

194

away their estate before death, any gift in excess of $10,000 is taxed.

    E.   <u>Excise Taxes and Custom Duties.</u> Federal taxes on liquor, tobacco, gasoline, telephones, air travel and luxury times plus customs duties amount to about 5% of federal revenue.

VIII.   TAX POLITICS. Who bears the heaviest burden of taxes is at the heart of tax politics. <u>Progressive taxation</u> requires higher-income groups to pay a larger percentage of their income than lower-income groups. <u>Regressive taxation</u> takes a larger share from low income groups. A <u>proportional or Flat Tax</u> requires all income groups to pay the same percent of their income.

    A.   <u>The Argument for Progressivity.</u> This type of taxation is based on the theory that those with the ability to pay more taxes should pay more taxes and the marginal utility theory as it applies to money. That is, each additional amount of income is less valuable to an individual. Thus, for someone earning

    B. $1M a year, an additional $5,000 would hardly be noticed, but for someone earning $25,000/year, an additional $5,000 would mean a great deal.

    C.   <u>The Argument for Proportionality</u>. **FILL-IN. ARE NOT THE ARGUMENTS FOR PROPORTIONALITY REALLY NEGATIVE ARGUMENTS AGAINST PROGRESSIVITY?**

    <u>Reagan's Reductions in Progressivity</u>. The top marginal rate fell from 70% to 28% and the Tax Reform Act of 1986 reduced 14 tax brackets to only two-15% and 28%.

    D.   <u>Read My Lips</u> . At the Republican National Convention in 1988, George Bush promised not to raise taxes in his administration. Yet in a 1990 budget deal with the Democratic Congress he accepted a hike in the top marginal rate from 28% to 31%. Breaking the solemn pledge hurt Bush in the 1992 presidential campaign.

    E.   <u>Soak the Rich</u> . These proposals are always very popular. President Clinton pushed Congress to raise the top marginal rate to 36% for families earning $140,000 and 39.6% for those earning $250,000. These hikes did not bring in that much new revenue since so few families earn these amounts.

    F.   <u>Capital Gains Taxation.</u> All income is not taxed equally. Interest income from municipal bonds is a tax expenditure for the federal government. Capital gains made on income producing property is taxed differently than personal income. The current top rate for capital gains is 28%, while for personal income it is 39.6%. This difference is testimony to the power of the real estate, investment firm and stockbrokers lobby.

    G.   <u>Middle Class Tax Cuts</u> Both Clinton and Dole as presidential candidates championed tax cuts for the middle class. Polls suggest the American people are more interested in balancing the budget than in tax cuts.

CHAPTER 16 SAMPLE QUESTIONS

TRUE-FALSE QUESTIONS:

1. A free market economic system involves collective decisions, while a political system involves individual decisions.

2. The questions of the proper relationship between governments and markets is the subject of political economy.

3. If the price of gasoline goes up, this is a sure sign of inflation.

4. There is a constitutional limit of how much Congress can borrow.

5. The President's budget proposal is prepared by the Treasury Department.

6. The Federal Reserve regulates the supply of money in the market.

7. Since the Federal Reserve control the money supply which affects the economy, voters hold the Fed responsible for bad times.

8. The total national debt works out to about $18,000/individual citizen.

9. The monetarization of the debt would most likely lead to hyperinflation.

10. The Social Security tax is the largest source of revenue in the federal government.

MULTIPLE-CHOICE QUESTIONS:

11. Which of the following would be associated with classical economic theory?
    a. Adam Smith   b. John Smith   c. John Maynard Keynes
    d. Milton Freidman.

12. Which of the following would be associated with monetarist economics?
    a. Adam Smith   b. John Smith   c. John Maynard Keynes
    d. Milton Freidman.

13. Whose ideas were codified in the Employment Act of 1946:
    a. Adam Smith   b. John Smith   c. John Maynard Keynes
    d. Milton Freidman.

14. Which of the following actions by a national government would not be acceptable according to Keynesian theory in a recession?
    a. Cut taxes   b. Increase government spending   c. Raise taxes

d. Spend more than income.

15. To the supply sider, the most important economic factor is:
    a. Inflation   b. Unemployment   c. Economic growth
    d. The supply of money

16. Which one of the following is not a principal player in the executive branch in determining economic policy:
    a. OMB   b. Council of Economic Advisors   c. Treasury Department
    d. Commerce Department.

17. Federal reserve governors are appointed for _____year terms:
    a. 5   b. 10   c. 14   d. 4

18. The Chairman of the Fed serves a _____year term of office.
    a. 5   b. 10   c. 14   d. 4

19. In the face of inflation, the Fed would take all but one of the following actions:
    a. Increase reserve requirement   b. Sell government securities
    c. Buy government securities   d. Raise the discount rate.

20. Gross Domestic Product (GDP) includes all but one of the following:
    a. Annual production of goods and services.
    b. Maid service.
    c. Social security.
    d. Bake goods.

21. A Keynesian is most concerned about:
    a. Inflation   b. Money supply   c. Economic growth
    d. Unemployment

22. When the economy is moribund and prices are increasing, this phenomenon is called:
    a. Inflation   b. stagflation   c. Recession d. depression

23. Which of the following would not be considered unemployed:
    a. A person who quits their job   b. A person laid off from a job
    c. A person looking for a job the first time.
    d. A person who retires from a job

24. Which of the following is not an uncontrolled budget item:
    a. Medicaid   b. Defense spending c. Social security
    d. Federal retirements

25. The U.S. last had a balanced budget in the year:
    a. 1953   b. 1969   c. 1974   d. 1980

CHAPTER 16 SAMPLE QUESTION ANSWERS:

TRUE-FALSE ANSWERS:
1. **FALSE.** It is just the opposite relationship. See page 599.

2. **TRUE.** See page 599.

3. **FALSE.** Inflation is a general rise in prices, not just in a commodity or two. Refer to page 600.

4. **FALSE.** There is no constitutional limit to Congress' spending or borrowing. See page 604.

5. **FALSE.** It is done by OMB. See page 605.

6. **TRUE.** See page 605.

7. **FALSE.** They hold the President responsible. See page 607.

8. **TRUE.** See page 613

9. **TRUE** The value of money would become next to worthless. See page 614.

10. **FALSE** Individual income taxes provide the most, but social security taxes are gaining rapidly. See pages 616, 619.

MULTIPLE-CHOICE ANSWERS:
11. **A** Adam Smith in <u>Wealth of Nations</u> laid out the theory of classical economics. See page 600.

12. **D** Milton Freidman is considered the leading luminary of monetary economics. See <u>People in Politics: Milton Freidman, in Defense of Free Markets</u>

13. **C** Keynes ideas were centered around full employment. See pages 600-601.

14. **C** Raising taxes would only be done in good times, not bad times. See page . 601

15. **C** Economic growth is the key concern of supply siders. See page 602.

16. **D** Only the Commerce Department is odd man out. See page 604.

17. **C** Fourteen years is a long time, but this is what helps to ensure the Fed's independence. See pages 605-606.

18. **D** The Chair's term is four which overlaps the President's. The Chair can be reappointed for a another term. See page 606.

19. **C** Selling government securities pulls money out of circulation which helps to control inflation. Buying government securities puts money into circulation. See page 607.

20. **C** Income transfers are not included, only final purchases. See page 608.

21. **D** Unemployment or full employment is the principal concern of Keynesians.
See page 608.

22. **B** This condition contradicted Keynesian theories. See page 609.

23. **D** Someone retired is not considered unemployed, but rather not working.
See page 609.

24.**B**   While many complain about defense spending, it has actually been coming down while entitlement spending has gone up. See page 611.

25. **B** Sounds like a long time ago-1969 when we last paid our bills without borrowing. See page 613.

CHAPTER 17-POLITICS AND SOCIAL WELFARE

I.   POLITICS AND SOCIAL WELFARE. The federal government redistributes income from one group to another-from the working class to the poor, for example. This social welfare activity of the government is the largest and fastest growing portion of the federal budget and amounts to more than half of government outlays. Many people think of social welfare as a program for the poor, the estimated 35-40 million whose income is below the official poverty line. If the $1 trillion spent on social welfare were directly distributed to the nation's poor, each poor person would receive $25,000/year. But most poor people are not the beneficiaries of social welfare which goes mostly in the form of Social Security and Medicare to the non-poor. Thus, the middle class and not the poor class is the major beneficiary of the nation's social welfare. See <u>Up Close-Who are the Poor?</u>

II.   POVERTY IN THE UNITED STATES. In 1995, the poverty line for a <u>family of four</u> was $16,000. This is the cash income considered necessary to maintain a decent standard of living. This definition of poverty has many critics:

    A.   <u>Liberal Criteria.</u>

        1.   The official definition includes cash income from social welfare and Social Security-without this income the number of poor would be much higher.

        2.   It does not include the near poor, the 45-50 million Americans living below $20,000 of annual income for a family of four.

        3.   It does not account for regional differences, costs of living, climate, and accepted styles of living.

        4.   It does not consider what people think they need to live.

    B.   <u>Conservative Criteria.</u>

        1.   It does not consider the value of family assets. The elderly who own their own homes, furniture, and cars may have incomes below the poverty level, but not suffer hardship.

        2.   **FILL-IN**

        3.   Many underrreport their real income

        4.   In-kind benefits are not included: food stamps, free medicare care, public housing, and free school lunches. If these were included, about 50% of the poor would move above the poverty line.

        5.   <u>Temporary Poverty.</u> Poverty is not necessarily a life time experience. Only 6-8% of the nation's population has lived in poverty more than five

years.

C.   For the temporary poor, welfare is a safety net.

D.   <u>Persistent Poverty.</u> About half of the poor on welfare rolls are persistently poor, or likely to remain on welfare more than 5 years. Welfare becomes a permanent part of their life. This prolonged poverty and welfare dependency b=creates an underclass that suffers from many social ills-teen pregnancy, family instability, drugs, crime, etc. Government education, training and job programs fail to benefit many of these people.

E.   <u>Family Structure.</u> Poverty and welfare dependency are much more common in single-parent families headed by a female. Unwed parenthood has contributed to a rising number of children living in poverty. Traditionally, illegitimacy was held down by powerful religious, and social structures; but these have weakened over time and the availability of welfare cash benefits has grown and removed much of the economic hardship once associated with unwed motherhood. Indeed, it is argued that well-meaning government welfare programs have perpetuated poverty and social dependency.

F.   <u>The Truly Disadvantaged .</u> The nation's largest cities have become the principal location of virtually most of the social problems facing our society. And the location of most of our poor class. Yet this is a recent event. As late as 1970, there were higher rates of poverty in rural areas than cities. The shift in the labor market from manufacturing jobs to professional, financial and technical service have increasingly divided the market into high and low wage sectors. The shift in these better paying jobs to the suburbs has left inner-city dwellers with fewer and lower paying jobs, thus making a major contribution to poverty. This was compounded by the migration of middle class of the inner-city to the suburbs. The loss of these role models has made things worse.

III.   SOCIAL WELFARE POLICY. Public welfare has been recognized as a government responsibility for many centuries. Today, more than 1/3 of the American population receives some form of government benefits. More than 50% of American families have at least one member who receives a government check. Thus, the welfare state covers a large part of our society. Major social welfare programs can be classified as either <u>social insurance</u> or <u>public assistance.</u> If the beneficiary made contributions for the government benefit, it is social insurance. If the program is financed out of general tax revenues and one has to prove poverty to receive the benefit, it is a public assistance program. These later programs are generally labeled welfare.

A.   <u>Entitlements.</u> These are programs for which the government establishes an eligibility criteria-age, income, retirement, disability, unemployment, etc. Everyone who meets the criteria is entitled to the benefits. Almost all of the entitlement programs were established either during the New Deal of Franklin Roosevelt-Social Security, AFDC, Unemployment Compensation, and Aid to Aged, Blind and Disabled (now called Supplemental Security Income) or the Great Society of President Johnson (food stamps, Medicare and Medicaid).

B.   <u>Social Security.</u>   **FILL-IN. HOW MANY PEOPLE RECEIVE**

SOCIAL SECURITY? WHAT PERCENT OF THE WORK FORCE IS COVERED BY SOCIAL SECURITY?

     C.   <u>Unemployment Compensation.</u> Temporarily replaces some of the lost wages of those involuntarily out of a job and helps stabilize the economy during recessions. Overseen by the Department of Labor, but administered by the states and funded by federal and state unemployment taxes on employers.

     D.   <u>Supplemental Security Income.</u> A means tested, federally funded program which provides a cash payment to the needy elderly (over 65), the blind and disabled (which has very loose definition covering alcoholism, drug abuse and attention deficiency among children). This former factor has led to a rapid rise in SSI beneficiaries. Elderly immigrants were also able to collect SSI.

     E.   <u>Aid to Families with Dependent Children (AFDC).</u> Means tested, cash grant program for states to assist needy children. States administer the program and define eligibility (within federal guidelines).

     F.   <u>Medicare</u>.   **FILL-IN. HOW IS PART A FINANCED? HOW IS PART B FINANCED?**

     G.   <u>Medicaid.</u>   **FILL-IN. WHO RECEIVES MEDICAID?**

     H.   <u>Food Stamps.</u> Provides low income households with coupons to purchase food. Overseen by the federal government, but administered by the states.

IV.   SENIOR POWER. Senior citizens are the most politically powerful group. While only 28% of the population, because they have high voter turnout, they equal more than 1/3 of voters. Compare the 65 or older turnout of 68% to the age 18-21 turnout of 36% for presidential elections and 61% compared to 19% for congressional elections. Seniors are also well represented in Washington by the AARP.

     A.   <u>The Aged in the Future.</u> The baby boom following WWII until 1960 produced a large generation. During the boom, women averaged 3.5 births during their lifetime compared to our current 1.8 lifetime births. This boom generation will begin to retire in 2010 and by 2020 will equal 20% of our population. Better lifestyles (less smoking, more exercise and weight control) and advances in medicine may also extend life expectancy.

B. The Generational Compact. The framers of Social Security in 1935 created a trust fund . A reserve would be built from taxes paid by working persons. This reserve would earn interest and the combined reserve and interest would be used in later years to pay benefits. Now Social Security is financed on a pay-as-you-go basis. Income from social security taxes pays the benefits to those retired. This generation is paying for the last generation. This is viewed as a compact between one generation and the other.

C. The Rising Dependency Ratio. **FILL-IN. WHAT WAS THE DEPENDENCY RATIO IN EARLY YEARS OF SOCIAL SECURITY? WHAT IS IT NOW? WHAT WILL IT BE IN 2010?**

D. Burdens on Generation X. Unless changes are made to the social security system, the current generation of young Americans may have to pay 40% of their income for social security taxes and would have to pay many times more than they would ever receive back in benefits.

E. The Trust Fund Myth. It is true that current Social Security income exceeds expenses. But the surplus is used to purchase government bonds and help cover the deficit. Social security taxes are lumped together with general tax revenues. Future retirements will have to be paid from future revenue-the trust fund is an accounting gimmick.

F. Cost-of-Living (COLAs) Increases. **FILL-IN. WHY ARE COLAs TO RETIREES MORE GENEROUS THAN PROBABLY NECESSARY?**

G. Wealthy Retirees. There is no means test for Social Security. Large numbers of affluent Americans receive checks every month. Since the elderly experience less poverty than today's workers and possess more wealth, Social security benefits for some are a negative redistribution of income-from the poorer to the more wealthy.

H. The Third Rail of American Politics. While the most expensive program in the government, Social Security is also the most sacrosanct. For this reason, it is known as the third rail in politics-touch it and you die! Because more beneficiaries live longer and COLAs, spending keeps increasing. Congress could change the law-raise the retirement age for full benefits (already scheduled to increase to age 67), limit or redefine COLAs, means test the benefit, etc.

V. POLITICS AND WELFARE REFORM. Americans face a dilemma in welfare policy.

As a generous people, Americans feel government should aid those in need. On the other hand, many feel welfare fosters dependency, undermines the work ethic, contributes to illegitimate births and the breakup of families. While social insurance programs remain popular, public assistance programs are very controversial.

A.   Work Disincentives.   **FILL-IN. WHY DO PUBLIC ASSISTANCE PROGRAMS DISCOURAGE RECIPIENTS TO WORK?**

B.   The Workfare Experiment. In passing the Family Support Act (FSA) of 1988, both liberals and conservatives agreed that it was necessary to replace welfare with workfare in the AFDC program. The FSA required states to develop a federal job training program (JOBS) for most adults receiving AFDC; provide child care for JOBS participants; and furnish transitional child care and Medicaid after a person left AFDC for a job; and to strengthen child support enforcement programs. The program essentially failed. No state welfare program required all welfare recipients to take jobs or enroll in training. Most states allowed mothers with preschool children to opt out. No state provided enough funds to support child care. As a result, only 10% of AFDC recipients participated in education or job placement programs and even fewer found jobs. Workfare proved to be more costly than welfare!

C.   Time limits on Cash Assistance. Many feel only the threat of a cut-off of cash benefits will inspire welfare recipients to seriously pursue job training and work opportunities. The welfare reform bill passed by Congress and signed into law by the President calls for a five year lifetime limit to cash payments and a two year consecutive limit on benefits. Recipients will be offered job training and placement in private or public sector jobs. The ball is in the state court, i.e., the states have the responsibility for implementing the law.

D.   Limiting Aid to Teenagers. **FILL-IN. WHAT CONDITIONS WOULD NOW APPLY TO UNWED TEENAGE MOTHERS?**

E.   Family (or child) Cap.   **FILL-IN. HOW MANY CHILDREN WILL A WELFARE RECIPIENT BE ALLOWED TO HAVE AND RECEIVE ASSISTANCE?**

F. Obstacles to Reform. There are many major obstacles to reform
    1. Perhaps 25-40% have handicaps-physical, chronic illness, learning disabilities, alcohol or drug abuse which could prevent them from finding or holding a job.
    2. As many as 50% may have no long term work experience.
    3. 2/3s have not graduated from high school.
    4. Almost ½ have 3 or more children.
    5. About 5 million jobs would be necessary. Are there sufficient well-paying jobs available?
    6. Cutting off aid will harm innocent children.

G. Congress and Welfare Reform. Congress passed and President Clinton signed into law on August 22, 1996, legislation that ends 61 years for Federal guarantees of cash assistance for poor children. Major elements of the welfare reform bill are:
    1. Federal cash assistance for poor children would end. Each state will receive a lump sum of Federal money to run its welfare and work programs.
    2. Family heads must work within two years or the family will lose benefits. After receiving welfare for 2 months, adults must preform community service unless they have found a job. States can waive this requirement.
    3. Lifetime welfare benefits are limited to 5 years. States may set stricter limits. 20% of families can be exempt because of hardship.
    4. States may stop payments to unmarried teenage parents and may provide them only if a mother under 18 stays in school and lives with an adult.
    5. States can shift 30% of welfare block grants for child care, social services and child protection.
    6. States must retain their own spending on welfare at 75% of 1994 level or at 80% if they fail to put enough welfare recipients to work.
    7. States may pay benefits to cover additional children born to women on welfare.
    8. States must continue to provide Medicaid to those already covered under current law and for one year when recipients lose their benefits due to increased earnings.
    9. Future legal immigrants, not becoming citizens, would lose most benefits. SSI and food stamps for non-citizens will now end.
    10. Convicted drug felons will no longer be eligible for cash assistance or food stamps.
    11. A woman with a child under 6 cannot be penalized if she cannot find work.
    12. Women on welfare who refuse to identify the child's father will lose at least 25% of benefits.

There was much consternation among liberals when President Clinton signed this legislation. The President indicated it was not prefect and that he would support some later changes or corrections.

VI.   HEALTH CARE IN AMERICA. The U.S. spends more of its resources on health care than any other nation, yet lags behind many other nations in measures of health, such as life expectancy and infant mortality. See Compared to What-Health and Health Care Costs in Advanced Democracies. Most other democracies provide health care for all their citizens, while Americans have no guarantee to medical care. In short, the American medical care system is the most expensive and least universal in its coverage in the world.

A.   The Health of Americans. In historical terms, great advances have been made in sanitation, immunizations, clean water and air, sewage disposal, improved diets and increased standards of living. Many of the causes of death today are linked to heredity, personal habits and lifestyles and the physical environment. See Table 17-2. Better health is likely to be found in altered life styles and personal habits.

B.   Access to Care. **FILL-IN. WHAT % OF THE AMERICAN POPULATION HAVE NO MEDICAL INSURANCE? WHAT RECOURSE DO THEY HAVE?**

C.   Coverage Gaps. Patients frequently have to pay deductibles or co-payments. Most plans do not provide prescription drugs, eyeglasses, hearing aids or routine physical exams. Medicare does not pay for long-term care of catastrophic illness. Medicare covers only 100 days of nursing home care, if the patient is sent there from a hospital. Congress attempted to add catastrophic health care coverage to Medicare, but the surtax charge to Medicare users caused much opposition and the program was scuttled. As the elderly population grows, long term care will be ever more important. Medicaid pays for needy patient nursing-home care, but middle class cannot qualify for Medicaid unless they spend down their savings. Thus, long term care threatens their assets and their children's inheritance. Private insurance to cover this benefit is too expensive. So senior citizens are trying to have long-term nursing care added to Medicare to be paid by all taxpayers.

D.   Health Care Cost Inflation. **FILL-IN. WHAT FACTORS HAVE LED TO THE INFLATION IN HEALTH CARE?**

E.   Coping with Costs. Managed care is the buzzword. Private insurers have negotiated discounts from hospitals and physicians-Preferred Provider

Organizations (PPOs), health maintenance organizations (HMOs) and Medicare no longer pays hospitals what they charge, but pays fixed fees. But these reforms have generated more paperwork which medical professionals feel costs more than the savings.

F. POLITICS AND HEALTH CARE REFORM. Reform centers on two central problems: controlling costs and closing gaps in coverage. Both are interrelated.

1. Achieving Universal Coverage. There are three broad approaches to reform in this area:

a. National health insurance paid by tax revenue. The government would be the single payer. A stipulated set of services would be an entitlement for everyone. Hospital budget costs would be negotiated. Physician fee schedules would be used. Some co-payments could be required. Most costs would be shifted from the private to the public sector.

b. Mandated private insurance for everyone, with vouchers for the poor. Just like auto insurance, citizens would be required to purchase health insurance. Employers could still pay for all or some of the costs.

c. Mandated employer-provided insurance, with expanded government insurance for the nonworkers. Some smaller employers could elect to pay a payroll tax to the government in a play or pay arrangement.

2. Controlling Costs. Again, there are three possible approaches:

a. Market-based Competition. This would depend on insurance companies seeking out more efficient services. Some effort is already taking place in this area as these companies turn to HMOs and PPOs to provide care at discounted prices. Pre-admission screening and prior authorization are other procedures that could be used-but all the above are already in operation and still costs continue to rise.

b. Managed Competition. This envisions the formation of Health Insurance Purchasing Alliances to pool employers and individuals to purchase health insurance. This could promote competition and bargaining power.

c. Health Spending Caps. The federal government would establish caps on health care costs.

3. Health Care Politics. President Clinton in his 1992 campaign promised to reform the health care system and shortly after his inauguration, he assigned this momentous task to his wife, Hillary. As developed, his plan did not include national health insurance, but did shift reliance from the private area to the federal government. It included: Mandated employer-sponsored insurance, managed competition through government health purchasing alliances, and national spending caps. His proposal failed to

gain Congressional support. There are many reasons:

a.   It was too comprehensive, rather than incremental. It would affect 1/6th of the national economy.

b.   The health industry advertising campaign caused a great deal of public confusion. For the eighty-five percent of the population already covered by some type of health insurance, it raised more problems than it solved. Benefits went mostly to the 15% not insured.

c.   Cost containment was ignored.

4.   <u>Interest-Group Battles</u>. Health care reform brings out the most conceivable group of interest groups imaginable! Not all agree with each other, but all are intense:

a.   <u>Employers</u>-big and small-fear added costs.

b.   <u>Physicians</u>-Oppose price controls and treatment guidelines, loss of patient choice in HMOs. Family practice physicians who stand to gain more from reform are more supportive while specialists who may lose more are strongest against reform.

c.   <u>Psychiatrists, psychologists, mental health, drug abuse counselors, chiropractors, optometrists and dentists</u> all want a piece of the pie, i.e. want their services to be included in any comprehensive health care which would greatly increase the cost.

d.   <u>Drug companies</u>-they want to see prescription drugs included, but no price controls.

e.   <u>Hospitals</u>-want patients to be insured, but no government payment schedules.

f.   HMOs and PPOs. They favor reform, but not government health care alliances.

g.   <u>Senior citizens</u>-want more benefits, but fear Medicare folded into a larger system.

h.   <u>Veteran's groups</u>. Want to retain separate medical system.

i.   <u>Opponents of abortion</u> do not want abortion included.

Polls show that the majority of Americans support a reform of health care, and are willing to pay more taxes. But they prefer an increase in sin taxes, but this would not raise much money.

CHAPTER 17 SAMPLE QUESTIONS

TRUE-FALSE QUESTIONS:

1. Direct payments to individuals-Social Security, welfare, pensions, and other transfer payments now amount to more that 50% of all federal government outlays.

2. The middle class, not the poor, are the major beneficiaries of the nation's social welfare system.

3. Only some poverty is persistent: About 50% of the welfare population remains on welfare for more than 5 years.

4. Black Americans experience poverty at roughly three times the rate of white Americans.

5. Today, nearly one-half of the U.S. population receives some form of government benefits.

6. Social Security is the single largest spending program in the federal budget.

7. Most Medicaid spending goes to young, single mothers with children

8. The United States spends more of its resources on health care than any other nation.

9. About 15% of the American population have no medical insurance.

10. Polls show that Americans are not willing to pay more taxes for comprehensive health care.

MULTIPLE-CHOICE QUESTIONS:

11. Approximately, what percent of federal social welfare spending is means tested:
    a. 75%   b. 50%   c. 30%   d. 20%

12. What is the poverty level for a family of four in 1995:
    a. $12,000   b. $14,000   c. $16,000   d. $19,000

13. Liberals criticize the official definition of poverty for all but one of the following reasons:
    a. The definition includes cash from welfare programs. Without this income there would be more poor.
    b. The definition does not include the near poor.
    c. The definition does not consider what people think they need to live.
    d. By using regional differences to calculate the poverty level, a lower poverty level is determined.

14. Conservatives criticize the official definition of poverty for all but one of the following reasons:

    a. Many persons over report income.

    b. Many families and individuals that fall below the poverty line do not consider themselves as poor, e.g. students.

    c. It does not consider the value of family assets.

    d. It does not include in-kind benefits.

15. Which one of the following groups has the largest number of poor?

    a. Blacks   b. Families/female heads   c. Hispanics

    d. Under age 18.

16. Which of the following is the focus of our social problems:

    a. Rural areas   b. Suburbs   c. Indian reservations

    d. Nation's largest cities

17. All but one of the following have had a deleterious impact on the inner city?

    a. Changes in the labor market from industrial goods to professional, financial and technical jobs.

    b. Shift in manufacturing and commercial sales jobs to the suburbs.

    c. Immigration of working-class to the inner city.

    d. Poor schools.

18. Charles Murray argues that government social programs are the root cause of poverty. He supports his thesis with all but one of the following observations/arguments:

    a. With the addition of poverty programs of the Great Society, poverty levels rose.

    b. Discrimination decreased in the 1970s.

    c. Generous welfare programs encourage poor young women to have children before the are ready to support themselves.

    d. People on welfare prefer welfare to work.

19. Which of the following is not a social insurance program?

    a. Social Security   b. Medicare c. Medicaid

    d. Unemployment Compensation

20. The baby boom generation will begin retiring in 2010 and by 2030 they will constitute _____percent of the population.

    A. 10%   b. 20%   c. 30%   d. 40%

21. If no changes are made to the current system of Social Security, persons of the generation X can expect to pay _____of their salary incomes just for social security taxes:

    a. 10%   b. 20%   c. 30%   d. 40%

22. The 1996 Welfare Reform bill included all but one of the following provisions:
    a. The end of federal cash assistance for children.
    b. Lifetime welfare benefits limited to two years.
    c. States may stop payments to unmarried teenage mothers.
    d. States must retain their own spending on welfare at either 75% or 80% of their 1994 level.

23. Which of the following is not a broad approach to achieving universal coverage of health care for all Americans:
    a. National health insurance
    b. Market competition
    c. Mandatory private health insurance with government coverage for those who cannot afford the insurance
    d. Mandatory employer-sponsored health insurance with government coverage for those not covered by employers.

24. Which of the following is not a broad approach for controlling costs of health care for all Americans:
    a. Market Competition
    b. Managed Competition
    c. Health Care Spending caps
    d. National health insurance

25. Which of the following interest groups do not have an interest in health care?
    a. Employees b. Senior citizen's lobby   c. HMOs and PPOs
    d. Drug companies

CHAPTER 17 SAMPLE QUESTION ANSWERS

TRUE-FALSE ANSWERS:

1. **TRUE.** As much as it seems. See page 627.

2. **TRUE.** Although most think that social welfare is for the poor, this is not the case. See page 628.

3. **TRUE.** Only 6-8% of the total population are on welfare more than 5 years, but 50% of those on the welfare rolls are there for some time. See page 630

4. **TRUE.** Compared to whites, black Americans experience far more poverty. See Figure 17-2.

5. **FALSE.** Only 1/3 of Americans receive benefits, but this is still a large number. See page 634.

6. **TRUE.** See page 636.

7. **FALSE.** Most goes to the elderly and non-elderly disabled. See page 638.

8. **TRUE.** See Compared to What: Health Care Costs in Advanced Democracies.

9. **TRUE.** An estimated 35-40 million Americans cannot afford health insurance and are not covered by any employer provided insurance. See page 647.

10. **FALSE.** While polls show Americans would support paying more taxes, they would prefer these be sin taxes which would not raise sufficient revenue.

MULTIPLE-CHOICE ANSWERS:

11. **D** Only about 1/5th is means tested, meaning the rest are treated as entitlements. See page 628.

12. **C** In 1990, the poverty level was $13,359, but rose to $16,000. See page 628.

13. **D** Regional differences are not used and this is what irritates liberals since some regions may be more expensive than others, re: Cost-of-Living, climate, etc. See pages 628-629.

14. **A** If persons over reported income they would not be at the poverty level, but when they under report income, cash payments for example, they may fall below the poverty line. See pages 629-630.

15. **B** Families headed by single females experience the most poverty. See Up Close-Who are

the Poor?.

16. **D** Our nation's largest cities, especially the inner city has become the concentration point of our social ills. See pages 631-632.

17. **C** The out-migration of the working and middle class (those who could afford to move) has depleted the inner city of a stable, role model class. See page 632.

18. **D** Surveys show that welfare recipients prefer to work, but the welfare system acts as a disincentive. See A Conflicting View: Government as the Cause of Poverty.

19. **C** Medicaid is a public assistance program. See Table 17-1.

20. **B** By 2030, this generation will be 1/5th of the total population. See page 638.

21. **D** If income tax were added, one can see that the tax burden would be virtually unsupportable. See page 640.

22. **B** Lifetime benefits are limited to five years; consecutive years on welfare can be limited to two years. See Study Guide.

23. **B** Market competition is used to control costs not access. See page 650.

24. **D** National health insurance is a plan to increase access not control costs. See pages 650-651.

25. **A** Employees generally do not have a special interest group speaking for them on health care unless it is a union. Employers on the other hand are represented by professional and technical interest groups and are extremely interested in reforms of health care that may cost them more money. See page 653.

CHAPTER 18-POLITICS AND NATIONAL SECURITY

I.   **POWER AMONG NATIONS.** International politics is a global struggle for power. This struggle has led to many attempts to bring order to the international system.

   A.   The Balance of Power System. Practiced in the 18th and 19th centuries by European powers, it was a system of alliances designed to balance one group against the other, thereby discouraging war. For almost a century, from the Napoleonic Wars to World War I, it appeared to be effective. But, one defect in the system is that a small conflict between two nations that are members of separate alliances could draw all members into the conflict and quickly turn a small conflict into a major war. This is what essentially happened in WWI, when a minor conflict in the Balkans turned into WWI. This disaster, led to calls for a new system-collective security.

   B.   Collective Security. This is a system where all nations join together to guarantee each other's security against external aggression. This was the central idea of the League of Nations established in 1919. Even though it was the brainchild of our President Woodrow Wilson, the Senate refused to confirm the treaty because of opposition to international involvement. Further, the League failed to deal with acts of aggression by the Axis powers-Germany, Italy and Japan. The result was an even more devastating World War II.

   C.   Formation of the United Nations. Another attempt at collective security, the victorious allies established the UN in 1945. Its essential components are:

   1.   Security Council. Consists of 11 members, five of which are permanent-The U.S., China, Britain, France and the Soviet Union (Russia). Permanent members have an absolute veto-they can stop and defeat any matter before the Council. Has Primary responsibility for maintaining international peace and security.

   2.   General Assembly.   **FILL-IN.**

   3.   Secretariat.   **FILL-IN.**

   4.   Specialized Organizations. Examples include: The Economic & Social Council, Trusteeship Council, and International Court of Justice at the Hague.

   D.   The United Nations in the Cold War. The UN was largely ineffective in the Cold War. While the UN grew from 51 to 185 members, many of these new countries were headed by authoritarian regimes of one sort or another. Western democracies were outgunned in the General Assembly and the Soviet Union used its veto in the Security Council to prevent any action. Anti-U.S. and anti-democratic speeches became the order of the day in the General Assembly. In reality, the UN was overshadowed by the world's two superpowers: the U.S. and Soviet Union.

    E.   <u>Regional Security.</u> **FILL-IN. WHY DID THESE COME INTO EXISTENCE? WHAT WAS THE SOVIET REACTION TO THE FORMATION OF NATO? WHAT HAPPENED TO THE WARSAW PACT?**

    F.   <u>NATO Today.</u> With the demise of the Soviet Union and the Warsaw Pact, what is the role of NATO today? Regional security? Help for the emerging democracies of Eastern Europe? Should it be abolished and a new broader security organization take its place?

    G.   <u>The UN Today.</u> The end of the Cold War has injected new life into the UN. Russia is now cooperating instead of being an obstruction. There is now cooperation on the Security Council to support a new world order. But the help of U.S., as the remaining superpower, is still necessary to help the UN enforce its resolutions.

II.   THE LEGACY OF THE COLD WAR. For more than 40 years, the U.S. and USSR confronted each other in protracted military, political, economic and ideological struggle which became known as the Cold War. By comparison, a hot war would have been an all-out nuclear war. Since this was avoided, by contrast the struggle was cold war.

    A.   <u>Origins.</u> During WWII, the U.S. and the Soviets were allies. Upon conclusion of the war, the U.S. demobilized its armed forces, while the Soviet Union used theirs to install communist governments in the countries of Eastern Europe. Germany and Berlin were divided into occupation zones of the Allied powers. The divided city of Berlin lay 200 miles inside the Eastern German border. In 1948, the East German government with the connivance of the Soviet Union blockaded the rail lines and roads into the Western part of Berlin. The U.S. provided supplies by air for over four months. In 1946, former Prime Minster Churchill of England warned of an iron curtain falling across Europe. The formal start of the Cold War is marked by the establishment of the Truman Doctrine in 1947 under which military and economic aid was provided to Greece and Turkey fighting against Soviet-backed guerillas. The doctrine promised aid to support free peoples fighting armed minorities or outside forces.

    B.   <u>Containment.</u> Russian expert George F. Kennan in a seminal article in <u>Foreign Affairs</u> called for a policy of <u>containment.</u> That is, the U.S. should try to contain communism within its present boundaries. One of the first concrete efforts in this regard was the Marshall Plan to economically build a weakened Europe which, if not aided, might fall to communism.

216

C.   The Korean War. This was the first military test of containment. North Korea with the concurrence of the Soviet Union launched a surprise attack on South Korea. The U.S. brought the matter to the Security Council which the Russians were boycotting because of its refusal to seat the new Communist government of China. The Security Council passed a resolution calling on member nations to send troops or other support to repel the invasion. The U.S. had drastically reduced its armed forces and only had about 30,000 troops in Korea. U.S. and Korean forces were pushed down the peninsula of Korea until their backs were at the sea in the port of Pusan. As U.S. reinforcements moved to hold the line, General Douglas MacArthur launched a surprise amphibious attack at Inchon on the Western side of Korea cutting off the North Korean army. As the trapped North Korean army raced north, the U.N. forces were in hot pursuit. The capital of south Korean, Seoul, was retaken and the UN forces continued to press North,, capturing the North Korean capital of Pyongyang. In spite of warnings by the Chinese government about approaching their border with North Korea, the UN forces kept pressing north. In December, 1950, one million Chinese troops poured across the border and entered the conflict. The sheer mass of this assault forces the UN forces to retreat south. General MacArthur wanted to retaliate against the Chinese mainland, but President Truman did not want to expand the war. MacArthur took his plans and complaints public and Truman showing great courage, fired the hero of WWII. The Korean War became a stalemate in which the UN forces suffered more casualties than locked in conflict. Eisenhower was elected president in 1952 and promised to end the conflict using nuclear weapons if necessary. Eventually, an armistice was signed which reestablished the boundary between South and North Korea along the 38th parallel. While communist expansion was contained, the cost was high-38,000 U.S. killed.

D.   The Cuban Invasion. During the Cold War, the Soviets sought to expand its influence in the Third World. Many new countries were former colonies that had become independent. Fidel Castro fought a guerilla war in Cuba against the repressive regime of Batista. In 1959, Castro was successful and soon thereafter allied his government with Moscow. The U.S. sought his ouster and in 1961, the CIA planned a covert operation involving a brigade of Cuban exiles. The plan developed when Eisenhower was president called for the U.S. to provide air cover, but the new president Kennedy refused to provide the air cover. Without it, the invasion failed. Kennedy was also tested in the same year by the erection of the Berlin wall. Despite heated words, the U.S. did nothing concrete and the wall became of symbol a of Soviet repression.

E.   The Cuban Missile Crisis. Taking advantage of the perceived weakness of the young American president, in 1962, the Soviets sought to secretly install nuclear weapons in Cuba which would threaten U.S. cities. U.S. intelligence photos showed the installation of the missiles which led to a direct confrontation with the Soviets. Rejecting military advice to bomb the installations, Kennedy instead opted for a blockade of Cuba, threatening to halt Soviet missile-carrying ships by force, if necessary. This confrontation was the most serious threat of nuclear holocaust during the entire Cold War-U.S. nuclear forces were on alert. If the U.S. had to use force against Soviet ships, we were not sure what would be the reaction of the Soviets. Secret diplomacy was used-the U.S. agreed in writing never to invade Cuba and to remove missiles from Turkey which threatened the Soviet Union. The Soviets agreed to remove their missiles from Cuba. Since most Americans did not know of the deal, Kennedy was hailed as a hero. Khrushchev was soon removed from power because of adventurism.

F.   The Vietnam War. Vietnam was another test of Asian containment. Remember the first test was Korea. The domino theory was prevalent at this time and arguments were made that if the U.S. did not stop in Vietnam, it would spread to Laos and Cambodia. Vietnam was part of what was known as French Indochina. The French were defeated by the Japanese Army and had to abandon French Indochina during WWII. As opposed to other colonial powers, the French after WWII reentered Indochina and attempted to reestablish their colonial control. During WWII, Ho Chi Minh was in France and a member of the Communist party. He tried to interest the Western powers in supporting Vietnam's independence, but his pleas fell on deaf ears. Consequently, he returned to Vietnam and began the guerilla movement which harassed the French and finally in a classical positional maneuver which involved taking the high ground, his forces defeated the French army at Dien Bien Phu in 1954. The Geneva Accords of 1956 divided Vietnam into two parts-North and South and also called for elections in 1958 to reunify Vietnam. The North was dominated by Ho Chi Minh and in the South-a U.S. backed government. In 1958, the South government, fearing that Ho Chi Minh might win the election, refused to participate in elections. Shortly thereafter, the Viet Cong, Southern based communist guerillas, began operations in South Vietnam. With the South Vietnamese government threatened, President Kennedy sent a force of 12,000 advisors and counter-insurgency forces to assist the South Vietnamese. By 1964, elements of the regular North Vietnamese army were assisting the Viet Cong. An alleged attack by North Korean gunboats in the Tonkin Gulf led Congress to pass the Tonkin Gulf Resolution which basically opened the door to U.S. involvement in the war. President Johnson ordered U.S. combat troops to Vietnam and authorized limited air strikes against North Vietnam. This precipitous action was not undertaken with specific Congressional approval, nor was any attempt made to mobilize American public opinion. Eventually over 500,000 troops were sent to Vietnam in what became a war of attrition. U.S. superior firepower and the use of air power, including helicopters was expected to tip the balance in our favor. Instead of a decisive victory, the war dragged on and popular support started to slip away. President Johnson claimed we were winning and General Westmoreland, the military commander claimed there was light at the end of the tunnel. It was quickly extinguished by the surprise, deceitful attack by Viet Cong and North Vietnamese forces during the Tet holiday. They struck on January 31, 1968 and a

218

Viet Cong unit actually captured the U.S. Embassy in Saigon for 6 hours. Attacks were made throughout Vietnam and were especially severe at Hue and Ky San. All attacks were eventually repulsed and Communist losses were severe. The communists were hoping for popular uprisings and support which never materialized. However, the Communist defeat on the battlefield, became a victory in the field of American public opinion. The American media turned vicious and portrayed the action a defeat for the U.S. and South Vietnamese and began a campaign to force U.S. withdrawal. In early 1968, President Johnson halted the bombing on North Vietnam and announced he would not seek another term in office. Formal peace talks opened in Paris on May 13th. In late 1968, Richard Nixon was elected as president. Nixon and Henry Kissinger, his national security advisor wanted to end the war, but honorably. They also wanted a peace settlement that would give South Vietnam a fighting chance for survival. The North Vietnam stonewalled the peace negotiations, and in 1972, President Nixon in December ordered a resumption of air attacks on North Vietnam which this time included Hanoi, the capital. Critics of the war labeled this action, the Christmas bombings, but in January, 1973, the Vietnamese returned to the negotiating table and quickly agreed to peace terms. This agreement called for the return of POWs and allowed the Thieu government to remain in South Vietnam. The agreement also called for the U.S. government to provide economic assistance to North Vietnam. The U.S. did not fulfill any promise either to North or South that it made in the agreement. Congress refused to appropriate any further funds. This and the forced resignation of Nixon in August, 1974 convinced the North Vietnamese that the U.S. would not interfere any further in South Vietnam. In early 1975, the North Vietnamese army launched an attack and the rout was on. The U.S. did not intervene and the U.S. ambassador had to flee from the roof of the embassy by helicopter. By April, 1975 Vietnam was unified. For the U.S., it was a period of national humiliation. We lost our first military engagement on the battlefield in our entire history. We suffered over 47,000 battle deaths for what? Probably over 1 million Vietnamese (North and South) lost their lives. Communist forces in Cambodia killed more than 2 million in a genocide not seen since WWII. Yet most of the world was silent again. More than 1.5 million South Vietnamese were forcibly reeducated in harsh circumstances. U.S. invincibility had been shattered and a national catharsis was the result.

G. The Vietnam Syndrome. A new period of isolationism permeated U.S. foreign policy. No more Vietnams became the rally cry. The Soviet Union took advantage of our isolationist mentality by expanding its military and political influence in Asia, Africa, the Middle East, the Caribbean and Central and South America. The U.S. did little to halt this expansion. The Soviet invasion of Afghanistan finally galvanized the U.S. to have the CIA back in a covert way the Afghan guerillas which forced the Soviet Union's armed forces into a stalemate which some dubbed Russia's Vietnam.

H.   Rebuilding America's Defenses. **FILL-IN. IN WHOSE ADMINISTRATION DID THE BUILD-UP BEGIN? HOW MUCH OF ITS GNP DID THE SOVIET UNION SPEND ON ITS MILITARY?**

I.   <u>Gorbachev, Perestroika and Glasnost.</u> Gorby was committed to a policy of perestroika (restructuring of the Soviet command economy by decentralization of state planning) and also called for glasnost (openness) in soviet life and politics. Real opposition parties were allowed (the Soviet had allowed docile other fringe parties to exist), the police state apparatus was reined in and more freedoms were allowed-religion, press and speech. The aim of Gorbachev was to save communism. But once the genie was out of the bottle, the forces of change swept timidity aside. Gorbachev also began a reduction of the Soviet armed forces, and indicated that these armed forces would no longer be used to keep communist governments in power in Eastern Europe. This announcement encouraged democratic forces in all of Eastern Europe and one after the other, communist governments fell from power, culminating in the destruction of the Berlin Wall.

J.   <u>The Collapse of Communism</u>. **FILL-IN. WHAT FORCES OPPOSED GORBACHEV'S REFORMS? WHO LED THE ATTEMPTED COUP? WHAT EFFECT DID THE ATTEMPTED COUP HAVE ON THE COMMUNIST PARTY?**

K.   <u>The Disintegration of the Soviet Union.</u> Strong independence movements began life as the power of the Soviet Communist Party waned. The Baltic countries of Lithuania, Estonia, and Latvia led the charge. Soon all 15 republics of the Soviet Union had declared their independence and the USSR ceased to exist at the end of 1991. The hammer and sickle communist flag that had flown over the Kremlin since 1917 had been replaced by the flag of the Russian Republic.

III.   THE NUCLEAR THREAT. While nuclear weapons raised the threshold of a nuclear holocaust, they also acted to retrain the superpowers. While there were scores of clashes in the Cold War, there were never any directed between the forces of the Soviet Union and the U.S.

A. Deterrence. This doctrine is predicted on the notion that one nation could absorb a first nuclear strike and still have enough residual nuclear forces to retaliate against the attacking country in a devastating counter-attack. Rationally, this assured counter-attack should prevent the first attack. To ensure the survivability of its nuclear forces, the U.S. developed a triad of deterrent platforms-land-based missiles in silos (ICBMs), undersea launched nuclear missiles (SLBMs) and air delivered weapons. The dispersion of these forces made it virtually impossible that a nuclear surprise attack could succeed. Therefore, a second retaliatory attack would be certain.

B. MAD Balance of Terror. By the 1970s, each side had enough missiles and delivery systems to destroy the other side. This mutual balance of terror. In essence, each country's populations were held hostage against a nuclear attack. The MAD balance began to become unstable in 1975 when the Soviets deployed a highly accurate, multi-warhead missile, the SS-18, that would be more effective in a first strike against U.S. land based missiles in silos. The value of the traid was confirmed, because SLBMs were not compromised by the SS-18 and could still deliver a potent sting. The U.S. responded by also building a hard-kill, land based missile the MX. President Reagan had wanted to build 100, but disputes about where and how they would be based led Congress to approve only 50. The Navy's Trident SLBMs were also hard-kill and multi-headed. To upgrade the air delivery system, the B-1 bomber was developed and a follow-on, high tech B-2 was developed. Only 20 of these later planes were constructed as the Cold War ended.

C. Limiting Nuclear Arms: SALT. The development of space-based satellite intelligence enabled both sides to see what the other was doing in regards to strategic weapons. Verification was always one of the principal hangups with arms reduction talks. Now with space intelligence, verification of arms reductions was easier. First talks about nuclear arms reductions were initiated during the Nixon administration. In 1972, the Strategic Arms Limitation Treaty (SALT) I was concluded which froze existing nuclear weapons at their current levels and included an Anti-ballistic Missile (ABM) agreement. The ABM treaty essentially ratified the idea the each country's citizens were nuclear hostages as it severely limited the construction of defensive anti-ballistic missile batteries. The U.S. never did construct an ABM site. While each side could upgrade and develop new nuclear weapons, they would have to dismantle older weapons to stay within the ceiling limits. Both sides also agreed not to interfere with the space intelligence-gathering activities of the other. In 1979, after 7 years of hard negotiations, the SALT II Treaty was concluded. It set an overall limit on strategic nuclear launch vehicles to 2,250 for each side. This included: ICBMs, SLBMs, bombers and cruise missiles. When the Soviet Union invaded Afghanistan, President Carter withdrew the treaty from further Senate consideration and to this date the treaty has never been ratified by the U.S. Senate; although the U.S. has continued to abide with its provisions.

D.   <u>Reducing Nuclear Arms: Strategic Arms Reduction Talks (START).</u> The Reagan administration wanted to achieve three things in further negotiations: reductions of nuclear inventories, equality between the U.S. and USSR and on-site verification. The START I treaty was signed by Presidents Bush and Gorbachev in 1991. An earlier treaty, the Intermediate-Range Nuclear Forces (INF) treaty signed in 1987 called for the destruction of Soviet SS-20 missiles and U.S. Pershing II and Ground Launched Cruise Missiles (GLCM). This set the precedence for the reduction and destruction of nuclear weapons. The START I treaty called for a ceiling of 1,600 delivery systems from 2,250, a total ceiling of 6,000 warheads, and Soviet reduction of the SS-18 missiles by 50%. In addition, verification included on-site inspections as well as other surveillance. In 1993, the START II treaty was signed. All MIRV warheads are to be eliminated by the year 2003, all Russian SS-18 missiles will be eliminated, the U.S. will eliminate all MX missiles, and convert all MIRV Minuteman missiles into single warheads. The overall level of nuclear warheads is to be reduced to 3.500.

E.   <u>Continued Minimal Deterrence.</u> With the demise of the USSR, over 27,000 nuclear weapons are still stockpiled in the former republics-Russia, Ukraine, Belarus and Kazakhstan. While we assume that responsible leaders in these republics will maintain control over these weapons, the U.S. must continue to maintain some level of nuclear forces to deter attack or intimidation from any leader that may come into control of these awesome weapons. The U.S. will retain some 500 single shot Minuteman and its Trident SLBM force.

F.   <u>Nuclear Terrorism.</u> The possibility of an attack by a terrorist nation or group is a real threat as nuclear proliferation and theft of fissionable materials may enable some group to use a nuclear weapon as a form of terrorism. To guard against this or some accidental launch, some feel a Ballistic Missile Defense (BMD) system should be developed and deployed. Some research has been done , but there are no current plans to proceed any further. See <u>Feature-What Do You Think? How Should We Defend against a Ballistic Missile Attack?</u>

IV.   POST-COLD WAR THREATS. The end of the Cold War does not mean that the world is at peace. It simply means that the bi-polar conflict between the U.S. and USSR has ended.

    A.   <u>Guarding against Reversal of Democratic Trends.</u> If former communist countries made a full transition to democracy and a market economy, the world should be more peaceful. But dangers lurk on the horizon:

        1.   Continuing economic deterioration in Russia may undermine the weak conditions of democracy.

        2.   **FILL-IN**

        3.   Continued differences among the former Soviet republics may rekindle

ancient hatreds among ethnic groups and result in armed conflict.
4.   **FILL-IN**

    B.   <u>Western Europe and the Future of NATO.</u> A Russian threat to Western Europe is relatively nil. The Russian armed forces have been reduced from 4 million to under 2 million and morale is low and their equipment is in a poor state. This raises the question of why we still maintain troops in Europe? The complete withdrawal of troops would most likely wreck NATO. Which raises a further question: What is the future role of NATO? Should former Communist nations be admitted to full membership? Should Russia be allowed to join? Should NATO forces be deployed outside of Europe?

    C.   <u>European Ethnic Conflicts.</u>   These are as old as the continent. Do such conflicts, such as Bosnia, threaten the security of Western Europe?

    D.   <u>Regional Threats.</u> These appear to be the most likely threats in the future.
        1.   <u>Iraq</u>. Saddam Hussein's military forces were considerably reduced in the Gulf War, but he remains a threat in the area.
        2.   <u>Iran.</u>   **FILL-IN.**

        3.   <u>Syria</u>. Still has a powerful military force, but since the former Soviet Union was its main supplier, it now has to look for other support. It still is technically at war with Israel and its troops still occupy large parts of Lebanon.
        4.   <u>Libya.</u> Still remains a major base for worldwide terrorism.
        5.   <u>North Korea.</u> It remains the world's most authoritarian and militarist regime. It spends a great deal on its military forces and has a well-developed nuclear weapons program. It still poses a threat to South Korea and U.S. support of South Korea would be necessary in the event of hostilities.
        6.   <u>China.</u> Currently has the world's largest armed forces and has nuclear weapons. Taiwan is still a contentious issue and China will assume control of Hong Kong in 1997. While China has made some market reforms, it still maintains tight political control.
    E.   <u>Terrorism.</u> This threat creates two military requirements: Punish any aggressor and deter other nations from supporting terrorism.
    F.   <u>Unanticipated Threats.</u> The record of forecasting future threats is very poor. Which simply means, the U.S. must always be ready to respond to unanticipated threats on a global scale.
V.   MILITARY FORCES LEVELS. In theory, the overall level of military forces of any nation should be determined by the size and nature of a perceived threat to its national

security. Political influences often distort this determination-the buying of certain weapons systems is often dictated by powerful political leaders as is the construction of military bases. For over 40 years the Soviet threat drove our defense policy-force planning, training, strategy and tactics, weapons research and procurement, force deployments, and budgets. With the new world order, a complete reexamination was in order.

A. The Base Force. Post-Cold War reductions began in 1990 under the Bush administration and called for a reduction of U.S. military forces from 2.1 to 1.6 million. While still maintaining a presence in Europe, U.S. force levels in Europe were cut by more than half.

B. The Bottom-Up Review. The Clinton administration began a bottom-up review which called for further reductions. See Table 18-1.

C. Iraqi-Equivalent Regional Threats. Current force planning envisions having sufficient forces to fight and win two nearly simultaneous major regional conflicts. Nearly simultaneous is very ambiguous and recognizes the U.S. may not have sufficient airlift and sealift to move the necessary forces. Under these restrictions, it is planned that we will fight to win one regional conflict while holding the aggressor in the other-once victory is obtained in the first- forces can be repositioned to defeat the second aggressor.

D. Future Force Levels. The Army will have 10 divisions (15,000-18,000 personnel), the Air Force 13 fighter wings (72 combat aircraft), the Navy will have 11 carrier battle groups (one in a training status). The Marine Corps will retain its three expeditionary forces.

E. Criticism. **FILL-IN. WHAT ARE THE MAIN POINTS OF CRITICISM?**

VI. THE USE OF MILITARY FORCE. One of the most agonizing decisions faced by a president-the end must justify the means.

A. To Protect Vital Interests.
  1. Use only to protect vital national interests.
  2. Must have clearly defined military objectives.
  3. Sufficient forces to ensure overwhelming and decisive victory.
  4. Support of the American people.
  5. Use force as last resort.

These guidelines were followed in the Desert Storm operation and are strongly supported by military leaders. Contrary to some popular opinion, military leaders are not warmongers; they have to pay the ultimate price-death or serious injury. See Up Close-Use of Force: Operation Desert Storm.

B. In Support of Important Political Objectives. Some objectives may be important but not vital. In addition to carrying out conventional war, U.S. military forces must:

1.   Demonstrate U.S. resolve in a crisis situation.
2.   Demonstrate U.S. support for democratic governments.
3.   **FILL-IN**
4.   **FILL-IN**
5.   Peacekeeping Hostile Missions.
6.   Peacekeeping missions to support a peace agreement.
7.   Provision of humanitarian aid under hostile conditions.

In pursuit of these objectives, U.S. forces have been sent to Lebanon, Grenada, Panama, Somalia, Haiti, and Bosnia. Opponents of some of these actions claim we are acting as the world's policeman. Proponents argue that each case is evaluated on cost-benefit basis.

VII.   THE PRICE OF PEACE. The United States has invested much money in national defense, but this investment deterred nuclear war and maintained the peace and security of Western Europe.

    A.   <u>Historical Trends.</u> In 1955, defense spending consumed 58% of the federal budget and equaled 10.5% of GDP. Ten years later, it was 40.1% of the federal budget and 7.5% of GDP. By 1978, the defense sector cost 23% of federal spending and 4.5 % of GDP. This was the low point and it began to creep up during the last budget of President Carter. During Reagan, defense spending rose to 29% of budget and 6.5% of GDP.

    B.   <u>The Military-Industrial Complex and Other Myths.</u> President Eisenhower warned of the Military-Industrial Complex and there is no question that defense contractors lobby for defense contracts with friendly Congresspersons, but there is no evidence that this results in higher levels of defense spending.

    C.   <u>Post-Cold War Defense Spending.</u> Current projections are down and defense spending is projected to equal less than 15% of the federal budget and less than 3% of GDP-or roughly defense spending levels before the attack on Pearl Harbor in 1941.

CHAPTER 18 SAMPLE QUESTIONS

TRUE-FALSE QUESTIONS:

1. International politics is a struggle for power.

2. Because of its size and contribution to the UN budget, the U.S. has three votes in the General Assembly.

3. Disappointment with the concept of collective security led to the concept of regional security.

4. The Korean War was the first military test of the containment policy.

5. The U.S. initially welcomed the overthrow of the Batista regime by Fidel Castro.

6. The Vietnam War Tet offensive was a decisive military victory for the Viet Cong.

7. The U.S. humiliation in Vietnam did not have long-lasting national consequences.

8. Nuclear weapons caused the superpowers to be more cautious with each other.

9. One effect of the MAD policy was to hold hostage the civilian populations of the USSR and US.

10. The use of military force can only be justified if vital U.S. interests are involved.

MULTIPLE-CHOICE QUESTIONS:

11. In the 18th and 19th centuries, European countries employed the _____ to stabilize international relations.

      a. Containment   b. Balance of Power
      c. Collective Security   d. Balance of Terror

12. All but one of the following are examples of collective security:

      a. NATO   b. UN c. League of Nations
      d. U.S.-Korean Mutual Defense Treaty.

13. The UN Security Council has how many permanent members?

      a. 5   b. 11   c. 13   d. 15

14. Approximately how many nations belong to the UN General Assembly?

      a   51 b. 130 c. 185 d. More than 200.

15. Which of the following countries were known as the superpowers?
    A. The USSR and China   b. The US and USSR
    b. China and India   d. The US and NATO members

16. What marked the beginnings of the cold war:
    a. the Yalta conference.
    B. Churchill's "iron curtain" speech in Fulton, Missouri.
    C. the initiation of the "Truman doctrine"
    d. U.S. development of the atomic bomb.
    F. The East German blockade of Berlin.

17. The architect of the "containment" policy was:
    a. President Truman.
    b. Secretary of State Acheson.
    c. George Kennan
    d. John McCoy
    e. Jimmy Carter

18. There was always some confusion about the level of Soviet defense spending. Recent
revelations indicate it was about _____ of Russia's GNP.
    a. 15%   b. 18%   c. 20%   d. More than 25%

19. Which of the following Soviet words means restructuring?
    A. Gorbachev   b. Perestroika c. Glasnost   d. Apparatchniks

20. The attempted coup against Gorbachev involved all but one of the following groups:
    a. Soviet military leaders   b. KGB   c. Hard-line Communists
    d. Retired Russians

21. Which of the following is not a reason for America's triad delivery system?
    A. ensure survivability in case of a surprise attack
    b. not put all eggs in one basket
    c. ability to absorb an attack and retaliate.
    D. ability to destroy and defeat the USSR in one attack

22. Which arms control treaty banned MIRV warheads from missiles after 2003:
    a. SALT I   b. SALT II   c. START I   d. START II

23. Which of the following nations is the most authoritarian and militarist in the world?
    a. North Korea   b. South Korea   c. Libya   d. Iraq

227

24. Which of the following nations has the largest armed forces?
    a. North Korea   b. China   c. Russia   d. Iraq

25. All but one of the following are force levels in the Bottoms-Up review:
    a. 10 active Army divisions   b. 11 carrier battle groups
    c. 15 Air Force fighter wings   d. 3 Marine expeditionary groups

CHAPTER 18 SAMPLE QUESTION ANSWERS

TRUE-FALSE ANSWERS:

1. **TRUE.** All types of politics involves a struggle for power. See page 657.

2. **FALSE.** And this is a major bone of contention on the part of the U.S. See page 660.

3. **TRUE.** This was the major reason for the creation of NATO. See page 660.

4. **TRUE.** But it was not to be the last! See pages 652-663.

5. **TRUE.** But when Castro showed his true communist colors, U.S. support evaporated. See page 663.

6. **FALSE.** But it was a great political and psychological victory. See page 664.

7. **FALSE.** It lead to the Vietnam Syndrome which paralyzed U.S. foreign policy for year. Desert Storm finally put the syndrome to rest. See Page 666.

8. **TRUE.** This was somewhat paradoxical considering their destructive power. Refer to page 668.

9. **TRUE.** As bizarre as this may seem. See page 669.

10. **FALSE** They can also be used to support important political objectives., See page 679

MULTIPLE-CHOICE ANSWERS:

11. **B** It lasted from the Congress of Vienna in 1815 until the outbreak of WWI. Refer to pages 658-659.

12. **D** A bi-lateral defense treaty cannot be an example of collective security which involves many nations, not just two. See Page 659

13. **A** While the Council has 11 members, only 5 are permanent. See page 659.

14. **C** As more nations have achieved their independence, the membership has grown from 51 to 185 members. Refer to page 659.

15. **B** The U.S. and USSR were the world's superpowers. See page 660.

16. **C** The initiation of the Truman Doctrine marks the formal beginning of the Cold War. See page 662.

17. **C** George Kennan first called for the policy of containment. See page 662.

18. **D** This heavy expenditure was, in effect, robbing the civilian sector of the economy. See page 667.

19. **B** Perestroika was supposed to restructure and strengthen the communist nation. See page 667.

20. **D** Retired Russians now would most likely participate in a coup since they have been decimated by the falling value of the ruble. But they were not involved in the coup against Gorbachev. See page 668.

21. **D** The purpose of the Triad was to survive a Soviet surprise attack and still have a punch left. See page 669.

22. **D** The last major treaty was the START II and this was a major accomplishment of this treaty. See page 671.

23. **A** North Korea has this dubious distinction. See page 676.

24. **B** China also has the world's largest population. See page 676.

25. **B** The Air Force will be limited to 13 fighter wings. See Table 18-1.